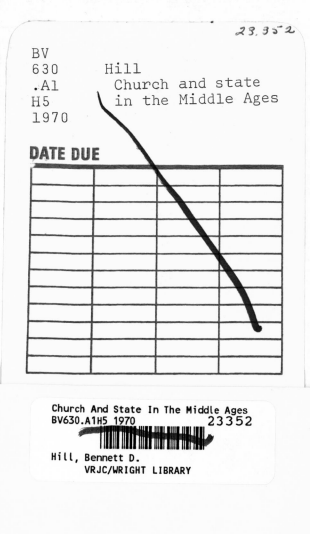

MAJOR ISSUES IN HISTORY

Editor

C. WARREN HOLLISTER

University of California, Santa Barbara

William F. Church: *The Impact of Absolutism in France: National Experience under Richelieu, Mazarin, and Louis XIV*

Robert O. Collins: *The Partition of Africa: Illusion or Necessity*

J. B. Conacher: *The Emergence of Parliamentary Democracy in Britain in the Nineteenth Century*

Gerald D. Feldman: *German War Aims, 1914-1918: The Development of an Historical Debate*

Frank J. Frost: *Democracy and the Athenians*

Paul Hauben: *The Spanish Inquisition*

Bennett D. Hill: *Church and State in the Middle Ages*

Boyd H. Hill: *The Rise of the First Reich: Germany in the Tenth Century*

C. Warren Hollister: *The Impact of the Norman Conquest*

C. Warren Hollister: *The Twelfth-Century Renaissance*

Thomas M. Jones: *The Becket Controversy*

Tom B. Jones: *The Sumerian Problem*

Jeffry Kaplow: *France on the Eve of Revolution*

Archibald Lewis: *Islamic World and the West*

Anthony Molho: *Social and Economic Foundations of the Italian Renaissance*

E. W. Monter: *European Witchcraft*

Donald Queller: *The Latin Conquest of Constantinople*

Joachim Remak: *The First World War: Causes, Conduct, Consequences*

Jeffrey Russell: *Medieval Religious Dissent*

Max Salvadori: *European Liberalism*

Arthur J. Slavin: *Humanism, Reform, and Reformation*

W. Warren Wagar: *The Idea of Progress Since the Renaissance*

Bertie Wilkinson: *The Creation of the Medieval Parliament*

L. Pearce Williams: *Relativity Theory: Its Origins and Impact on Modern Thought*

Roger L. Williams: *The Commune of Paris, 1871*

CHURCH AND STATE
IN THE MIDDLE AGES

EDITED BY

Bennett D. Hill

University of Illinois

John Wiley & Sons, Inc.
New York · London · Sydney · Toronto

For
Laura, Thomas, Charles, Mary Claire,
and
Sarah

Library of Congress Catalogue Card Number: 75-126226

Cloth: ISBN 0-471-39650-8   Paper: ISBN 0-471-39651-6

Printed in the United States of America

10 9 8 7 6 5 4 3 2 1

SERIES PREFACE

The reading program in a history survey course traditionally has consisted of a large two-volume textbook and, perhaps, a book of readings. This simple reading program requires few decisions and little imagination on the instructor's part, and tends to encourage in the student the virtue of careful memorization. Such programs are by no means things of the past, but they certainly do not represent the wave of the future.

The reading program in survey courses at many colleges and universities today is far more complex. At the risk of over-simplification, and allowing for many exceptions and overlaps, it can be divided into four categories: (1) textbook, (2) original source readings, (3) specialized historical essays and interpretive studies, and (4) historical problems.

After obtaining an overview of the course subject matter (textbook), sampling the original sources, and being exposed to selective examples of excellent modern historical writing (historical essays), the student can turn to the crucial task of weighing various possible interpretations of major historical issues. It is at this point that memory gives way to creative critical thought. The "problems approach," in other words, is the intellectual climax of a thoughtfully conceived reading program and is, indeed, the most characteristic of all approaches to historical pedagogy among the newer generation of college and university teachers.

The historical problems books currently available are many and varied. Why add to this information explosion? Because the Wiley Major Issues Series constitutes an endeavor to produce something new that will respond to pedagogical needs thus far unmet. First, it is a series of individual volumes—one per problem. Many good teachers would much prefer to select their own historical issues rather than be tied to an inflexible sequence of issues imposed by a publisher and bound together between two covers. Second, the Wiley Major Issues Series is based on the idea of approaching the significant problems of history through a deft interweaving of primary sources and secondary analysis, fused together by the skill of a scholar-editor. It is felt that the essence of a historical issue cannot be satisfactorily probed either by placing a body of undigested source materials into the hands of inexperienced students or by limiting these students to the controversial literature of modern scholars who debate the meaning of sources the student never sees. This series approaches historical problems by exposing students to both the finest historical thinking on the issue and some of the evidence on which this thinking is based. This synthetic approach should prove far more fruitful than either the raw-source approach or the exclusively second-hand approach, for it combines the advantages—and avoids the serious disadvantages—of both.

Finally, the editors of the individual volumes in the Major Issues Series have been chosen from among the ablest scholars in their fields. Rather than faceless referees, they are historians who know their issues from the inside and, in most instances, have themselves contributed significantly to the relevant scholarly literature. It has been the editorial policy of this series to permit the editor-scholars of the individual volumes the widest possible latitude both in formulating their topics and in organizing their materials. Their scholarly competence has been unquestioningly respected; they have been encouraged to approach the problems as they see fit. The titles and themes of the series volumes have been suggested in nearly every case by the scholar-editors themselves. The criteria have been (1) that the issue be of relevance to undergraduate lecture courses in history, and (2) that it be an issue which the scholar-editor knows thoroughly and in which he has done creative work. And, in general, the second criterion has been given precedence over the first. In short, the question "What are the significant historical issues today?" has been answered not by general editors or sales departments but by the scholar-teachers who are responsible for these volumes.

University of California,　　　　　　　　*C. Warren Hollister*
Santa Barbara

ACKNOWLEDGMENTS

I wish to acknowledge the assistance of colleagues at the University of Illinois in Urbana-Champaign who suffered interruptions and gave their valuable time to help me. I am grateful to Professor Luitpold Wallach of the Department of the Classics who directed me to some important materials and who is ever vigilant in reminding younger scholars of their limitations; to Professor Paul Schroeder of the Department of History who helped me with a difficult German translation; to Professor Benjamin Uroff, also of the History Department, who read portions of this book and gave me the benefit of his literary expertise; and to Edward Ratcliffe, Head of Reference at the University of Illinois Library, for his more than generous assistance.

INTRODUCTION: ASPECTS OF THE PROBLEM

Students of history have long been aware that one of the central issues in the development of Western civilization is the problem of the relations of Church and State. This subject was especially popular with nineteenth-century historians who believed that if one could understand the origins of an institution, he could better learn its nature and development. Students of German history have often seen in the various conflicts between ecclesiastical authorities and secular rulers in the Middle Ages one of the basic causes of Germany's "retarded" development toward a united and constitutional national State. The peculiar circumstances of the early history of England, France, and Italy, which made those countries a part of the conflict, have certainly influenced their later evolution. In colonial America and the United States, because of Puritan hostility to Rome and "popery," and because of the customary but dangerous identification of Protestantism with democratic institutions, the subject of the relations of Church and State has been a fundamental political issue.

Strictly speaking, the term "relations of Church and State" is an inappropriate one when used with reference to the period before the fully developed national State. For a thousand years after the disintegration of the Roman Empire in the West, the State, in the modern sense, simply did not exist. The modern State is an organized institution, with bureaucratic organs of government, with definite geographical boundaries, and especially with a clearly defined legal jurisdiction over all citizens and subjects. The medieval polity had none of these. The modern State has sovereignty which, for want of a better definition, means that the State possesses a monopoly over the instruments of justice and the use of force within its boundaries; equally basic, it has the power to make law. So long as private individuals raised and deployed armies, and so long as an international corporation maintained courts of law with jurisdiction over many types of persons and issues, then the State did not exist. Medieval society represented what the great Cambridge historian Frederic W. Maitland called "the standing denial of sovereignty, the rivalry of *regnum and sacerdotium.*"[1] The word "state," then, when applied to political and social conditions in Western Europe before 1300 is a modern convenience for want of a more precise term. The word "church" is, also, often used promiscuously, meaning both the whole community of the Christian faithful and, in a narrower sense, the ecclesiastical hierarchy of which the Bishop of Rome was the head.

Moreover, the phrase, "the relations of Church and State," would have no meaning or reality for medieval man. The world in which he lived was characterized by conflicting, confusing, and often contradictory jurisdictions. He was usually a baptized member of the institutional Church and an inhabitant[2] of some relatively small territory which may or may not have had some form of stable government. The bishop who administered to him the sacrament of Confirmation may well have been the same lord under whom he fought in battle, the judge who held a court and settled his property dispute with his neighbor, and the ecclesiastical officer from whom he sought a dispensation to marry his second cousin. Medieval man, if one may speak of such an abstraction, did not think in terms of such a separation.

Once this fundamental fact of the confusion of powers is perceived, it is possible to paint a picture of the medieval problem that suggests the ideologies and theories which divided popes and princes, bishops and barons. Much of the picture will always remain in shadowy outline. As E. H. Carr has recently reminded us, the historian cannot, or can only with difficulty, escape the patterns of thought of his education and upbringing. Modern man, imbued with the belief in "progress" and eighteenth century notions of the perfectibility of man, cannot understand the great politico-theological issues that raged in the Middle Ages without some consciousness of the medieval *weltanschauung* (world view), based as so much of it was on St. Augustine's belief in the essentially corrupt nature of man.

What is the significance of the church–state problem in the Middle Ages? The story of the conflict between ecclesiastical authorities and secular princes is, in part, the history of a tension. Perhaps this tension was inevitable because of the overlapping claims and rights of the two forces involved—

[1] Freely translated, kingship and priesthood, secular and sacred.

[2] He could not call himself a "citizen" because, with the disintegration of the Greco-Roman city-state, the ancient concept of citizenship with all its legal, social, and religious connotations no longer had any significance. On this point, see Fustel de Coulanges, *The Ancient City*, Doubleday Anchor Books (New York, 1955). The modern historian, then, uses the term "citizen" at his peril.

over land, over jurisdiction, over conflicting concepts of the nature of the Church and civil society, and, ultimately, over the loyalties of Christian peoples in the West. Both laymen and clergy made claims on the allegiance of their peoples. The clergy's claims rested on the argument that the kingdom of God was not of this world, that they must answer to the Highest Authority, God, for the actions of all men. The opposition the clergy faced was caused by the ubiquitous spirit of anticlericalism, which represented the resistance of weak human nature to the simple but absolute claims of Christ, as well as an awareness of the contrast between the life of Christ and the lives of His ministers. Secular resistance to ecclesiastical demands was also the result of the exorbitant nature of those demands, some of which could be justified in Scripture or ancient tradition only with great difficulty. Lay princes sought ultimate and final authority over all their subjects. They justified this power drive on the grounds that it was their sacred duty to provide justice and order. Man may live according to all the words that flow from the mouth of God, kings allowed, but he still required his daily bread, meaning peace and security here on earth. Yet temporal rulers believed themselves appointed by God and ruling with the "grace of God," and so long as they depended on the sacred coronation of the Church for the support of their governments, they could achieve neither independence from ecclesiastical support nor an effective principle for the intrinsic and autonomous dignity of the temporal power. In the thousand-year history of this rivalry, neither side won a decisive victory.

Yet, for the development of political thought and institutions in the West, the medieval conflict had one profound result. Constitutionalism consists of the limitation of government by law, in the very apt phrase of Charles Howard McIlwain.[3] Constitutionalism also involves a balance between the authority and powers of the government, on the one hand, and the rights and liberties of the individual on the other. As Brian Tierney has so succinctly put it, "The very existence of two power structures competing for men's allegiance instead of one compelling obedience greatly enhanced the possibilities for human freedom. In practical life over and over again in the Middle Ages men found themselves having to make genuine choices according to conscience or self-interest between conflicting appeals to their loyalty."[4] This concept of constitutionalism, which is the product of and unique to Western civilization, is in large part the child of that medieval tension between the Church and the State over the loyalties of the individual.

---

[3] *Constitutionalism: Ancient and Modern*, rev. ed., Great Seal Books (Ithaca, N.Y., 1958), p. 22.

[4] Brian Tierney, *Crisis of Church and State 1050–1300* (Englewood Cliffs, N.J., 1964), p. 2.

CONTENTS

PART IV
The Age of the Gregorian Reform Movement

PART V
Henry II and Archbishop Thomas Becket

PART VI

The Culmination of the Gregorian Reform Movement: The Pontificate of Innocent III

PART VII

Philip the Fair and Boniface VIII: Origins of the National State

PART ONE

The Biblical Foundation

The starting point for any study of the relations of Church and State, as well as for any other aspect of the history of Christianity or of the Christian Church, is the collection of texts which Christians have always accepted as the Word of God. This consists of the body of writings on the life and teachings of Christ, together with several letters from the apostles to early Christian communities. Throughout the Middle Ages, scholars, students, polemicists, and popes defended their positions largely with interpretations of the relatively few Scriptural passages that dealt with political authority. The first commentary on Biblical selections that follow offers a very lucid interpretation by John L. McKenzie, a leading student of the problem of church–state relations. The discussion of the same passages by O. Cullmann provides a significant and relevant discussion of the claims of the totalitarian state by a distinguished and learned authority.

1 FROM *The New Testament*

FROM THE GOSPEL ACCORDING TO ST. MATTHEW

When Jesus came to the region of Caesarea Philippi he put this question to his disciples, 'Who do people say the Son of Man is?' And they said, 'Some say he is John the Baptist, some Elijah, and others Jeremiah or one of the prophets'. .'But you', he said 'who do you say I am?' .Then Simon Peter spoke up, 'You are the Christ', he said 'the Son of the living God'. .Jesus replied, 'Simon son of Jonah, you are a happy man! Because it was not flesh and blood that revealed this to you but my Father in heaven. .So I now say to you: You are Peter and on this rock I will build my Church. And the gates of the underworld can never hold out against it. .I will give you the keys of the kingdom of heaven; whatever you bind on earth shall be considered bound in heaven; whatever you loose on earth shall be considered loosed in heaven'.[1]

On Tribute to Caesar

Then the Pharisees went away to work out between them how to trap him in what he said. .And they sent their disciples to him, together with the Herodians to say, 'Master, we know that you are an honest man and teach the way of God in an honest way, and that

[1]Chapter 16, verses 13–20, *The Jerusalem Bible*, New Testament, pp. 41–42.

SOURCE. Alexander Jones, ed., *The Jerusalem Bible* (London: Darton, Longman & Todd Ltd., copyright, 1966; New York: Doubleday & Co., Inc.), pp. 41–42, 50, 186, 286–287, 402–403. Reprinted by permission of the publishers.

you are not afraid of anyone, because a man's rank means nothing
to you. .Tell us your opinion, then. Is it permissible to pay taxes to
Caesar or not?' .But Jesus was aware of their malice and replied,
'You hypocrites! Why do you set this trap for me? .Let me see the
money you pay the tax with.' They handed him a denarius, .and he
said, 'Whose head is this? Whose name?' .'Caesar's' they replied.
He then said to them, 'Very well, give back to Caesar what belongs
to Caesar—and to God what belongs to God'. This reply took
them by surprise, and they left him alone and went away.[2]

FROM THE GOSPEL ACCORDING TO ST. JOHN

So Pilate went back into the Praetorium and called Jesus to him,
'Are you the king of the Jews?' he asked. .Jesus replied, 'Do you
ask this of your own accord, or have others spoken to you about
me?' .Pilate answered, 'Am I a Jew? It is your own people and the
chief priests who have handed you over to me: what have you
done?' .Jesus replied, 'Mine is not a kingdom of this world; if my
kingdom were of this world, my men would have fought to prevent
my being surrendered to the Jews. But my kingdom is not of this
kind.' .'So you are a king then?' said Pilate. 'It is you who say it'
answered Jesus. 'Yes I am a king. I was born for this, I came into the
world for this: to bear witness to the truth; and all who are on the
side of truth listen to my voice.' .'Truth?' said Pilate. 'What is
that?'; and with that he went out again to the Jews and said, 'I find
no case against him. .But according to a custom of yours I should
release one prisoner at the Passover; would you like me, then, to
release the king of the Jews?' .At this they shouted: 'Not this man,'
they said 'but Barabbas'. Barabbas was a brigand.[3]

FROM THE LETTER OF PAUL TO THE CHURCH IN ROME

Submission to Civil Authority

You must all obey the governing authorities. Since all government
comes from God, the civil authorities were appointed by God, .and
so anyone who resists authority is rebelling against God's decision,

[2]Chapter 22, verses 15–22, *The Jerusalem Bible*, New Testament, p. 50.
[3]Chapter 18, verses 33–40, *The Jerusalem Bible*, New Testament, p. 186.

and such an act is bound to be punished. .Good behaviour is not afraid of magistrates; only criminals have anything to fear. If you want to live without being afraid of authority, you must live honestly and authority may even honour you. .The state is there to serve God for your benefit. If you break the law, however, you may well have fear: the bearing of the sword has its significance. The authorities are there to serve God: they carry out God's revenge by punishing wrongdoers. .You must obey, therefore, not only because you are afraid of being punished, but also for conscience' sake. .This is also the reason why you must pay taxes, since all government officials are God's officers. They serve God by collecting taxes. .Pay every government official what he has the right to ask—whether it be direct tax or indirect, fear or honour.

Love and Law

Avoid getting into debt, except the debt of mutual love. If you love your fellow man you have carried out your obligations. .All the commandments: *You shall not commit adultery, you shall not kill, you shall not steal, you shall not covet,* and so on, are summed up in this single command: *You must love your neighbour as yourself.* .Love is the one thing that cannot hurt your neighbour; that is why it is the answer to every one of the commandments.[4]

THE FIRST LETTER OF PETER (ADDRESSED TO ALL CHRISTIANS)

The Obligations of Christians : Towards Pagans

I urge you, my dear people, while you are *visitors and pilgrims*, to keep yourselves free from the selfish passions that attack the soul. .Always behave honourably among pagans so that they can see your good works for themselves and, when the day of reckoning comes, give thanks to God for the things which now make them denounce you as criminals.

Toward Civil Authority

For the sake of the Lord, accept the authority of every social institution: the emperor, as the supreme authority, .and the governors

[4]Chapter 13, verses 1–10, *The Jerusalem Bible*, The New Testament, pp. 286–287.

as commissioned by him to punish criminals and praise good citizenship. .God wants you to be good citizens, so as to silence what fools are saying in their ignorance. .You are slaves of no one except God, so behave like free men, and never use your freedom as an excuse for wickedness. .Have respect for everyone and love for our community; fear God and honour the emperor.

Towards Masters

Slaves must be respectful and obedient to their masters, not only when they are kind and gentle but also when they are unfair. .You see, there is some merit in putting up with the pains of unearned punishment if it is done for the sake of God .but there is nothing meritorious in taking a beating patiently if you have done something wrong to deserve it. The merit, in the sight of God, is in bearing it patiently when you are punished after doing your duty.

This, in fact, is what you were called to do, because Christ suffered for you and left an example for you to follow the way he took. .He had not done anything wrong, and *there had been no perjury in his mouth*. .He was insulted and did not retaliate with insults; when he was tortured he made no threats but he put his trust in the righteous judge. .He was *bearing our faults* in his own body on the cross, so that we might die to our faults and live for holiness; *through his wounds you have been healed*. You had *gone astroy like sheep* but now you have come back to the shepherd and guardian of your souls.[5]

[5]Chapter 2, verses 11–24, *The Jerusalem Bible,* The New Testament, pp. 402–403.

2 FROM John L. McKenzie
The Power and the Wisdom

THE CHRISTIAN AND THE STATE

The Church in Society

The Church is a society. As such, it has relations with other societies. Its members are members of other societies. From the

SOURCE. John L. McKenzie, S.J., *The Power and the Wisdom* (Milwaukee, Wisconsin: Bruce Publishing Company, copyright 1965), pp. 233–242. Reprinted by permission of the publisher and the author.

very beginnings of the Church these relationships, which can be the occasions of divided loyalties, created problems. The individual man has very little activity which is strictly private; and whenever he acts within a social framework, the framework is a condition and a determinant of his action. Other persons limit the area of his activity and turn it in certain directions; his Christian freedom and his personal freedom, when analyzed, are under numerous and constant restraints. Most of these social relationships have no direct reference to the Church and the Christian life; of themselves they are neither friendly nor hostile, but they can turn into one or the other. The Christian does not live in isolation from other social relations; he must be a Christian within a framework which he is unable to control.

The State

That other society which has bulked largest in the history of the Church is the State. The Church has always existed within a state; and she has never arrived at a final and definitive statement of her relations with the State. The history of her relations with the State shows a bewildering variation of arrangements. . . . The Church has dealt with all kinds of states, and in each instance she has been concerned with what is vital, the preservation of her own identity. To this end she has been willing to make any adjustment with any state which leaves her what she is. Some of these adjustments in particular cases may have been more yielding than they ought to have been; one should be careful in showing hindsight, but at the same time we can be sure that the Church will not again follow some precedents from her past.

The Gospel and the State

In a matter of such profound importance we should look for guidance to the gospel as a theological source. It happens that the gospel does not afford much explicit guidance in the sense that a large number of passages can be assembled from which a doctrinal synthesis can be synthesized. This itself, as I hope to show, is significant. Furthermore, when we generalize from the Bible we must be careful to notice the differences between the concrete situation of the gospel and our own situation. The State in which the gospel arose has no parallel in the modern world; this could be significant, and one must advert to the fact before making any judgments. Nor is the historical situation of the Church today the same as the situation of the apostolic Church. The identity of the Church has not changed; but her concrete reality has, and her actions occur in concrete reality, not in abstraction. With these reservations, we should be deeply interested in whatever the New Testament has to say about the relations of the apostolic Church with the State.

The Roman Empire

The State in which the apostolic Church arose was the Roman Empire. . . . We saw that it was a cosmic rather than a political phenomenon, the first and so far the last world state, a political power without competition and seriously questioned by very few of its subjects. We saw that it governed better than any of its predecessors; the fact that this is not much of a tribute to Rome has nothing to do with the attitude of the subjects of Rome. It is, I think, safe to say that no state has ever governed with such a complete consent of the governed; in our own Declaration of Independence this is one of the conditions of a just government. There are other conditions which Rome did not meet quite as well; it was far from the ideal society, but neither in this chapter nor elsewhere in theological literature does the question arise of how the Church is to deal with an ideal political society which meets all conditions perfectly. This question is simply not practical. The practical question is how a Church whose leadership and membership in particular times and places is imperfectly Christian is to deal with a state which may be a polite gang of brigands. In historical situations discussions of the ideal Church and the ideal state have little reference to the realities. Neither the Church nor the State loses its rights when its leadership is corrupt; but they make it much more difficult to present a convincing case for their rights.

The Church in the Empire

Within the Roman Empire the Church in its earliest phase was . . . a Jewish sect as far as the Empire was concerned. The Church was therefore no particular concern of the government, which tolerated Judaism as a lawful religion. When it became evident that the Church was a community distinct from Judaism, the toleration of Judaism was extended to the Christians. This toleration endured throughout the New Testament period in the sense that Christianity remained a legal religion; the Empire made no deliberate general effort to destroy the Church, and the persecutions which occurred were brief and irregular. The persecutions are responsible for the sharp change in the attitude of Christians themselves which can be seen in the Apocalypse. There Rome has become the Beast and the Great Whore who sheds the blood of martyrs. But in the Gospels and the epistles Rome is still accepted as the world government, as much a part of the cosmic structure as the atmosphere.

Jesus and the Government

In John 18 Jesus expressly denies any relationship with the secular government. His explanation was accepted by Pilate, who certainly did not take his claims seriously but recognized that he was not a rebel. All four Gospels are rather insistent on the fact that Jesus was not executed for any political offense; this insistence certainly reflects the image which the apostolic Church wished to project. The Church had nothing to contribute to the government and nothing to receive from the government. The activities of the Church and of the government were simply unrelated; there was neither friendship nor hostility. Christians were subjects of Rome and they could be expected to fulfill their duties as citizens—which in the Empire consisted principally in the payment of taxes. They were not lawbreakers and they had no complaint against the government; the government should have no complaint against them. Like the Jews, they could not take part in the Caesar cult; and in the apostolic period this was understood and tolerated by Rome. The kingship of Jesus was not of this world, and it took away nothing from the kings of this world. Nor did it demand anything from the kings of this world.

Tribute to Caesar

Besides John 18:36–37 there are only two New Testament passages from which a doctrine of the relations of Church and state can be deduced. The first of these is in the Gospels; it is the saying of Jesus in which he tells a questioner to render to Caesar what belongs to Caesar and to God what belongs to God (Mt 22:15–22; Mk 12:13–17; Lk 20:20–26). This is not the easiest of the sayings of Jesus; and its background must be looked at closely. The question asked was whether it was lawful to pay tribute to Caesar. This was a theological question in Judaism. For a Jew, to acknowledge an overlord by paying tribute could be a denial of the supremacy of God; and it was so understood by the fanatic groups in Judaism. In rigorous Pharisaic Judaism the use of a coin with a human image was a violation of the Second Commandment. The question was also a highly explosive political issue; as it was phrased, it seemed to leave Jesus no avenue of escape. He must either offend Jewish sensibilities or declare that Rome had no right to demand tribute.

In this situation the words of Jesus may be an evasion rather than an answer. When I speak of an evasion, I do not imply that Jesus withheld an answer from human respect; I mean that his answer tells us that his gospel has no simple answer to this question. Luke has preserved a saying in which Jesus refused to act as judge or arbiter in a question of inheritance (Lk 12:13–14). As far as the gospel is concerned, Jesus has nothing in particular to say about how inheritance should be divided. Similarly it is possible that he implied that his gospel has no answer to the question about tribute, which was actually a question whether the Roman government of Palestine was legitimate. It was a political question which he did not intend to settle. It should not be hard to understand why Jesus should refuse to become involved in a political issue.

The answer certainly seems to allow the payment of the tribute; but the permission is based on the practice of the Jews and not on anything in the teaching of Jesus. It amounts to this: as long as you use Caesar's money you accept his claim to it. You cannot answer the question about tribute by itself; and you have already answered it by your practice. Your answer raises other questions to which I have only one answer: Give Caesar what is his and give God what is his. We can hardly think that Jesus meant by this answer to divide the universe between God and Caesar. Caesar has nothing that is not God's. But God does not demand tribute; Caesar does, and he has the power to exact it. As long as you submit yourselves to his power, which you cannot resist anyway, you have no choice but to pay him tribute. Should Caesar demand something which God prohibits, or should Caesar prohibit something which God demands, you know what you must do.

What is Political Power?

A political philosophy based on this statement would be rather
skimpy. Jesus says nothing about the roots of political power, its
legitimacy, its competence. He takes political power as a fact of life
and offers nothing except submission to the fact. He places no
limitation on the exercise of political power except the sovereignty
of God; this is a vital limitation, but he does not define it. One may
say at least that if the Roman Empire usurped the sovereignty of
God in any notable degree, we should expect Jesus to say something
about it. The apostolic and postapostolic Church saw clear usurpa-
tions and refused submission. We may notice in passing that their
only weapon against the usurpation was passive resistance; we shall
have to return to this. But as long as Caesar is there he can ask and
get his tribute. Jesus offers no reason for paying it and no reason
for withholding it.

The saying of Jesus thus interpreted shows a certain indifference
to the Empire, to say the least; and we shall have to see whether
this impression is correct in the course of our discussion. If it is so
interpreted, it is in harmony with the saying preserved in John about
his kingship. The denial of any mutual concern between Jesus and
the government is maintained consistently in both passages. Here
we must remind ourselves that we may not extend the application
of the New Testament beyond due limits. The Roman Empire is not
the abstract state as such; and the attitude of the Christian toward
the State is not necessarily the same if the character of the State
changes. But it is important to get the attitude of the New Testament
as clearly in our minds as we can; for it should not be assumed that
the New Testament is irrelevant to the more recent state.

The Power in St. Paul

The second saying is found in Romans 13:1–7. I take this as the
typical passage; the State is mentioned in a few other epistles, but
no passage adds anything to what is found in Romans. Here Paul
commands submission to authority, for all power is from God. To
resist authority is to resist God, for authority is God's minister for
good. Therefore, submission is a duty of conscience. This passage
seems to offer a much broader base for a political philosophy; and
much Christian political ethics appeals to Paul for support. The
problem is that the easiest political philosophy to erect from this

passage is the divine right of kings. No one in modern times thinks this is what Paul means; and when the passage is interpreted in some other way, there is a vague suspicion that the interpreters are not catching the mind of Paul.

Here, as so often, the mind of Paul is more surely apprehended if we look at the Old Testament background of his thought. In the Old Testament there are only two political societies: Israel and the nations. Israel is the people of God. It existed in a political society which God destroyed because of the sins of Israel. It was destroyed by the nations who were agents of God's wrath. The nations, like Israel, are under judgment for sin, and they too will inevitably fall. The Old Testament recognizes no durable political society; it passes from the nations of the world to the Reign of God.

Power from God

Where does Paul put Rome in this scheme? It is not Israel, certainly; and it is even more certainly not the Reign of God. Has Paul without warning given the Roman Empire a dignity and a permanence which no other state possesses in biblical thought? Such a departure from biblical thought demands more and clearer evidence than this passage. If it is taken to mean the divine right of government, it says so much more than Jesus said about tribute that a genuine problem arises. The key may perhaps lie in the idea of power. In the Old Testament all power is from God; but power as such is morally neutral. No nation and no person can have any power which is not committed to it by God; but the exercise of the power is not thereby authenticated. Assyria was the rod of God's anger for Israel (Is 10:5); Assyria was still Assyria, an object of judgment no less because it was an instrument of judgment. God brought down the kingdom of Judah and the city of Jerusalem through Nebuchadnezzar of Babylon; and Jeremiah preached submission to Nebuchadnezzar because God had given him the rule of the earth (Jer 25:8–11; 27:1–15) and counseled the Jews who had been transported to Babylon to seek the welfare of the city (Jer 29:5–7). I think one recognizes in these passages the ideas in which Paul moves; and they permit one to say that Paul does not clearly give the Roman Empire any value which the Old Testament does not give to Assyria and Babylonia. If Rome has power, it must be because God has given it power. God gives it power as he gave power to the nations of the East, for the purpose of punishing evildoers; to resist this power is to resist God, and this is true both of Babylon and of Rome. No positive value is attributed to either state as such.

Cosmic Power

Paul like Jesus says that Caesar should receive what is his—taxes, respect, and honor. He should receive it because he has the power to exact it. Paul adds what Jesus did not, that the power is committed by God as a punishment of evildoers. And here an idea begins to emerge which it is difficult to translate into more modern language without the risk of going beyond the ideas of the New Testament. The effort, nevertheless, must be made; for it suggests an insight into the gospel. There is only one power in the universe and that is the power of God. This is a power to judge and to save. God exercises his power through agents. Nature is such an agent; the stories of the exodus from Egypt show God saving and judging through the phenomena of nature. Men and nations are likewise such agents; unlike nature, they are moral agents. But when they act as agents of God's power to save or to judge, they are morally neutral in so far as they are agents; it makes no difference whether they are good or bad, for God can use either. Samson as savior and the Assyrians as agents of judgment are not men of morally elevated stature. When God commits his power to them, they are on the moral level of the phenomena of nature. They will be judged on other factors than the commission of power.

Hence the power through which God executes his saving acts and his judgments can be considered a part of the cosmic structure; and it is not by mere coincidence that I return here to the phrase which I used earlier to describe the world state of Rome. It belongs to the cosmos as nature belongs to the cosmos; it is indeed created precisely for the evildoers. Man suffers the state because he is under judgment, and the state is a part of the curse which lies upon him for his sins. The Roman Empire is a component of the universe of Sin and Death; man must accept it as he accepts concupiscence and disease. It belongs to the fourfold plague which Jeremiah mentions several times: the sword, famine, pestilence, and captivity.

This view of the state, I believe, sets the state much more neatly in biblical thought than the view of it as a divine institution. It suits both the sayings of Jesus, who said that the power which

Pilate had over him came from above (Jn 19:11), and the prophetic view of the state. No one has thought of using John 19:11 as evidence of the divine right of the state; yet Jesus is not saying anything different from Paul. The power is given from above in the sense described; the power can be used to punish evildoers and it can be used to crucify Jesus. It is the same power in either case, and it is not diminished by its misuse. If one nation falls, God establishes another as the agent of his judgment. Nothing suggests that Paul thought that Rome would endure forever; there is nothing likewise to suggest that he thought it would be succeeded by anything but another Rome. The New Testament, like the. Old, puts nothing between the kingdoms of the nations and the Reign of God.

Legitimacy of Power

I have observed that the New Testament introduces no consideration of the legitimacy of government or of the just use of the powers of government. Tribute is to be rendered to Caesar; I think it is legitimate to extend this to all the Caesars, whether it be Tiberius, in whose reign the saying is uttered, Caligula, Claudius, Nero, Vespasian, Titus, or Domitian; and where shall we end the line?

The New Testament knew Caligula, a madman, Nero, a psychopath, and Domitian, probably a paranoiac. Even the Apocalypse does not suggest that Caesar is no longer Caesar when he is a paranoiac. The legitimacy of Rome's claim to rule was in almost every instance based on conquest, which is not the most ethical of claims. The administration of the Empire was, as we have seen, generally superior to the administration of the kingdoms which Rome conquered; when we have said this, we have not said much. The American colonists rebelled over a tax on tea, and they have become national heroes. Had the subjects of Rome ever thought of rebelling over taxes, they would have had a much more urgent case than the merchants of Boston. When we mention these things we know they are unimportant. The New Testament examines neither the credentials of Rome nor its use of its power; it would make no more sense than the examination of the credentials of an earthquake. There is no concern with whether the government is just or not; it is to be obeyed because it exists. Would the answer of Jesus have been different in any other state? Would he have altered the saying if Nero had been Caesar? Would he have altered it if he had lived under George III or Abraham Lincoln? And if we alter it, we should be sure we have the right to do so. The impact of the New Testament sayings is that Caesar has no more claim to power because he is just and no less claim because he is unjust.

3 FROM   *Oscar Cullmann*
          The State in the New Testament

THE CHRISTIAN AS CRITIC OF THE STATE

The fact that the problem of Church and State is of such central importance is a corollary of the eschatological attitude of Christianity. Because the Gospel presents itself as the "politeuma," the community of the coming age, it must accordingly see as its most intrinsic concern its disposition toward the present "polis," the secular State. Where the expectation of the end is taken seriously in Christianity, it becomes necessary to assume toward the earthly State an attitude based on principle—and yet not in such a way that the State as such would be renounced a priori.

The relationship of the Christian to the State is accordingly expressed first of all in temporal categories: the State appears as something "provisional." For this reason we do not find anywhere in the New Testament a renunciation of the State as such as a matter of principle; but neither do we find an uncritical acceptance—as if the State itself were something final, definitive.

It is all the more important to gain precise knowledge of the New Testament attitude toward the State. This is especially true of the Apostle Paul's interpretation of the State. Here things have come to such a pass that men are willing to classify Paul as an almost servile, uncritical servant of any State, as if he would say Yea and Amen to every claim of the State, be it never so totalitarian. They base their

SOURCE. Oscar Cullman, *The State in the New Testament* (London: SCM Press, Ltd.; New York: Charles Scribner's Sons, copyright 1956 by the Trustees under the Will of Waterman T. Hewett), pp. 3–5, 55–58, 58–60, 61–62, 64–65. Reprinted by permission of the publishers and the author.

case on the single Pauline statement in the Epistle to the Romans, 13:1: "Let every man be subject to the powers prevailing over us." Few sayings in the New Testament have suffered as much misuse as this one. As soon as Christians, out of loyalty to the Gospel of Jesus, offer resistance to a State's totalitarian claim, the representatives of that State, or their collaborationist theological advisers, are accustomed to appeal to this saying of Paul, as if Christians are here commanded to endorse and thus to abet all the crimes of a totalitarian State.

If this were really Paul's opinion, it would stand in flagrant contradiction to that of Jesus. But it would also contradict the opinion of other New Testament authors as well, chiefly that of the author of the Johannine Apocalypse. Above all, moreover, Paul would contradict himself. For we find in Paul exactly the same thing we find in Jesus: side by side stand two sorts of assertions, which *seem* to be contradictory, but actually proceed from one and the same fundamental attitude. Thus we find in the Pauline epistles not only this most famous passage, Romans 13:1ff, but also quite different passages, chiefly I Cor 6:1ff and I Cor 2:8. With Paul also, just as with Jesus, both classes of texts must be borne in mind and considered together. The fountainhead of all false biblical interpretation and of all heresy is invariably the isolation and the absolutizing of one single passage. This applies most especially to the interpretation of Romans 13:1ff.

But it is necessary not only to confront this passage with the other Pauline passages which contain, directly or indirectly, Paul's opinion of the State: it is also necessary above all to consider the context of the passage at hand. Even this connection is all too often disregarded. But this context teaches us two things: First, the matter under discussion at this point is the Christian commandment of love—evil is not to be rewarded with evil, rather one is to do good to his enemy. This stands in Romans 12 immediately before the section about the State in Romans 13:1ff; and directly afterwards, in verse 8, the same theme is resumed. Second, the expectation of the End is also under discussion: the night is far spent, the day draws near (Rom 13:11ff).

This background to the section is important, and shows in itself that there can be no question here of an unconditional and uncritical subjection to any and every demand of the State. It arises immediately out of the context that the State does properly exactly the opposite of what the Christian is to do: it takes vengeance on him

who does evil (verse 4). Immediately before this (ch. 12:17) it is
stated that the Christian on the contrary is by no means to repay
evil with evil. *Nevertheless* we are to accept the State; thus in spite
of the fact that it does exactly the opposite of what the Christian
is to do, we are to submit ourselves to the State as such. For if it
takes vengeance, it does so as "the servant of God"; v. 4: "It is
God's servant for vengeance upon the evil-doer." Even if it does
not know this itself, it stands nevertheless unconsciously in the
service of God. How this is possible, is not explicitly explained. We
shall ask at the end of this work if there is not an implicit answer
to this question.

Therefore we are not to oppose the State because it represents
other than Christian principles. The State is concerned with the
judicial principle of the retribution of evil. Indeed it even bears the
sword, we hear in v. 4, while the Christian is not to kill. Only God
may take vengeance, and he avails himself of the service of the State
for this purpose. For even the heathen State, insofar as it really is a
state, knows how to distinguish between good and evil. This is
explicitly stated in this section: vv. 3 4. Only he who does evil has to
fear the State (which really is a State); not he who does good. The
State, therefore, has sound judgment over good and evil. Only its
bearing toward evil is not the same as that which is appropriate to
the Christian; and yet the Christian is to subordinate himself to the
State in its proper sphere. Therefore a "nevertheless" is to be fixed
above this command of Paul. Paul does not consider it self-evident
in and of itself that the Christian is to recognize the existence of the
State. Just for this reason it is necessary for him to give an explicit
commandment about this to the Romans to whom he is writing
here. It is not self-evident, for the State proceeds according to the
principle, not of love, but of retribution.

The context in which this section about the State stands and in
which Christian love is discussed, shows plainly that here just as in
the teaching of Jesus the only thing repudiated is the renunciation
of the validity of the State as a matter of principle. Basically, the
paragraph states no more and no less than the saying of Jesus:
"Render unto Caesar the things that are Caesar's; and to God the
things that are God's." It is probable that the Apostle even alludes
to this saying in v. 7, when he speaks of the tribute which is to be
given to whom it is due. "Pay all of them, what is due them," he
writes at the beginning of the verse. In the background, then, the

tacit negative amplification stands here as well: "Do not give them
what is not their due." Let us not forget that it is Nero's State which
is under discussion here—the same State which will demand of the
Christians things which do not belong to it. Paul does not speak
of these things here. His own condemnation however proves that he
does not recommend subjection in these things. But where it is a
question of the existence of the State, the commandment stands
none the less: "Give even to this State its due." For the fact that
there still is a State is willed by God. The present age still endures.

And this brings us to the second of the declarations mentioned
previously as important in connection with our paragraph: the
expectation of the End, about which Paul speaks in equally close
connection, in v. 11. This connection reminds us that the State is a
temporary institution. As for Jesus, this has two implications: 1.
The State is nothing final, nothing absolute. It will pass away.
2. For the duration of this present age it is not, indeed, a divine
entity, but it is nevertheless willed by God as a temporary institution. God makes use of the State as long as this age endures, and
therefore *we* as Christians do not have to oppose the institution of
the State as such, but rather have to acknowledge its existence.

For the settlement of their quarrels Christians are not to make
use of the State's legitimate institution of justice. Here we see
clearly that for Paul there exists a limit to the recognition of any
State. Even to the extent that it remains within its legitimate limits
(and the administration of justice in the Roman State is a legitimate
function) the State is nothing absolute, nothing final. Everywhere
the Christian can dispense with the State without threatening its
existence, he should do so. The existence of the State will not be
threatened if the Christians avoid bringing their litigation before
the State and use ecclesiastical justice in their congregations. This
does not mean that they will also take over the other affairs of the
State. But admittedly this chapter shows us in an especially clear
manner that it is false to ascribe to Paul in Romans 13:1ff the
opinion that the State is by nature a divine form and that its principles are equally valid as those Jesus deduced from the expectation
of the Kingdom of God.

What consequences can we draw from them for the problem
"Paul and the State?" The State in itself is nothing divine. But it
maintains a certain dignity in that it stands in an order which is

still willed by God. Hence it is true for Paul also: the Christian is
commanded on the basis of the Gospel to maintain a critical
attitude toward the State; but he has to give the State all that is
necessary to its existence. He has to affirm the State as an institution.
Of the totalitarian claim of the State which demands for itself what
is God's, Paul does not speak directly. But there can be no doubt
that he too would not have allowed the Christians to obey the
State just at the point where it demands what is God's. What we
know about his *life*, proves this. He would not have permitted them
to say "Caesar is Lord" and "anathema Jesus" (let Jesus be
accursed), and this was demanded by the same Roman State to
which the Christian is to pay taxes and whose institution he is to
acknowledge as willed by God.

PART TWO

The State in the City of God: The Thought of St. Augustine

The greatest thinker in the early Christian Church, and probably the most influential thinker in all of Western Christianity, was a Roman citizen of African origin, Augustine (354–430), Bishop of Hippo Regius, a small city of ancient Numidia, whose ruins lie one mile south of the modern Bône in Algeria. His abiding importance still rests in his profound understanding of Christianity, his remarkable psychological insight into the nature of man, and his fundamental exposition of the Christian philosophy of history.

St. Augustine's interpretation of the conflicting interests of the City of God and the City of Man was the basic influence on political thought in the West down to the end of the thirteenth century. His argument that the state was the necessary result of Adam's fall and of man's consequent propensity toward sin was used by medieval churchmen to defend their belief in the natural superiority of the spiritual power over the temporal. At the same time, the universal acceptance of Augustine's theocentric political thought prevented civil authorities from developing a rationale for the state, one that would justify its existence independent of the support of religion.

1 FROM

Gerald G. Walsh
City of God

Chapter 1

I have already said, in previous Books, that God had two purposes in deriving all men from one man. His first purpose was to give unity to the human race by the likeness of nature. His second purpose was to bind mankind by the bond of peace, through blood relationship, into one harmonious whole. I have said further that no member of this race would ever have died had not the first two—one created from nothing and the second from the first—merited this death by disobedience. The sin which they committed was so great that it impaired all human nature—in this sense, that the nature has been transmitted to posterity with a propensity to sin and a necessity to die. Moreover, the kingdom of death so dominated men that all would have been hurled, by a just punishment, into a second and endless death had not some been saved from this by the gratuitous grace of God. This is the reason why, for all the difference of the many and very great nations throughout the world in religion and morals, language, weapons, and dress, there exist no more than the two kinds of society, which, according to our Scriptures, we have rightly called the two cities. One city is that of men who live according to the spirit. Each of them chooses its own kind of peace and, when they attain what they desire, each lives in the peace of its own choosing.

SOURCE. Gerald G. Walsh et al., trans., *City of God, Book XIV* (New York: Doubleday & Co., Inc., 1958), pp. 295, 300–301. Reprinted by permission of The Catholic University of America Press.

Chapter 4

When man lives according to himself, that is to say, according to human ways and not according to God's will, then surely he lives according to falsehood. Man himself, of course, is not a lie, since God who is his Author and Creator could not be the Author and Creator of a lie. Rather, man has been so constituted in truth that he was meant to live not according to himself but to Him who made him—that is, he was meant to do the will of God rather than his own. It is a lie not to live as a man was created to live.

. . . . .

Why this paradox, except that the happiness of man can come not from himself but only from God, and that to live according to one-self is to sin, and to sin is to lose God? When, therefore, we said that two contrary and opposing cities arose because some men live according to the flesh and others live according to the spirit, we could equally well have said that they arose because some live according to man and others according to God. St. Paul says frankly to the Corinthians: "Since there are jealousy and strife among you, are you not carnal, and walking as mere men?" Thus, to walk as a mere man is the same as to be carnal, for by "flesh," taking a part for the whole, a man is meant.

Chapter 13

Hence it is that just because humility is the virtue especially esteemed in the City of God and so recommended to its citizens in their present pilgrimage on earth and because it is one that was particularly outstanding in Christ, its King, so it is that pride, the vice contrary to this virtue, is, as Holy Scripture tells us, especially dominant in Christ's adversary, the Devil. In fact, this is the main difference which distinguishes the two cities of which we are speaking. The humble City is the society of holy men and good angels; the proud city is the society of wicked men and evil angels. The one City began with the love of God; the other had its beginnings in the love of self.

Chapter 15

This family arrangement is what nature prescribes, and what God intended in creating man: "let them have dominion over the fish of the sea, the birds of the air, the cattle, over all the wild animals and every creature that crawls on the earth." God wanted rational man, made to His image, to have no dominion except over irrational nature. He meant no man, therefore, to have dominion over man, but only man over beast. So it fell out that those who were holy in primitive times became shepherds over sheep rather than monarchs over men, because God wishes in this way to teach us that the normal hierarchy of creatures is different from that which punishment for sin has made imperative. For, when subjection came, it was merely a condition deservedly imposed on sinful man. So, in Scripture, there is no mention of the word "servant" until holy Noe used it in connection with the curse on his son's wrongdoing. It is a designation that is not natural, but one that was deserved because of sin.

The Latin word for "slave" is *servus* and it is said that this word is derived from the fact that those who, by right of conquest, could have been killed were sometimes kept and guarded, *servabantur*, by their captors and so became slaves and were called *servi*. Now, such a condition of servitude could only have arisen as a result of sin, since whenever a just war is waged the opposing side must be in the wrong, and every victory, even when won by wicked men, is a divine judgment to humble the conquered and to reform or punish their sin. To this truth Daniel, the great man of God, bore witness. When he was languishing in the Babylonian captivity he confessed to God his sins and those of his people and avowed, with pious repentance, that these sins were the cause of the captivity. It is clear, then, that sin is the primary cause of servitude, in the sense of a social status in which one man is compelled to be subjected to another man. Nor does this befall a man, save by the decree of God, who is never unjust and who knows how to impose appropriate punishments on different sinners.

Our heavenly Master says: "everyone who commits sin is a slave of sin." So it happens that holy people are sometimes enslaved to wicked masters who are, in turn, themselves slaves. For, "by what-

SOURCE. Gerald G. Walsh et al., trans., *City of God, Book XIX* (New York: Doubleday & Co., Inc., 1958), pp. 460–471. Reprinted by permission of The Catholic University of America Press.

ever a man is overcome, of this also he is a slave." Surely it is better
to be the slave of a man than the slave of passion as when, to take
but one example, the lust for lordship raises such havoc in the
hearts of men. Such, then, as men now are, is the order of peace.
Some are in subjection to others, and, while humility helps those
who serve, pride harms those in power. But, as men once were,
when their nature was as God created it, no man was a slave either
to man or to sin. However, slavery is now penal in character and
planned by that law which commands the preservation of the
natural order and forbids its disturbance. If no crime had ever been
perpetrated against this law, there would be no crime to repress with
the penalty of enslavement.

It is with this in mind that St. Paul goes so far as to admonish
slaves to obey their masters and to serve them so sincerely and
with such good will that, if there is no chance of manumission, they
may make their slavery a kind of freedom by serving with love and
loyalty, free from fear and feigning, until injustice becomes a thing
of the past and every human sovereignty and power is done away
with, so that God may be all in all.

Chapter 16

Our holy Fathers in the faith, to be sure, had slaves, but in the
regulation of domestic peace it was only in matters of temporal
importance that they distinguished the position of their children
from the status of their servants. So far as concerns the worship of
God—from whom all must hope for eternal blessings—they had
like loving care for all the household without exception. This was
what nature demanded, and it was from this kind of behavior that
there grew the designation "father of the family," which is so
widely accepted that even wicked and domineering men love to be
so called.

Those who are true fathers are as solicitous for everyone in
their households as for their own children to worship and to be
worthy of God. They hope and yearn for all to arrive in that
heavenly home where there will be no further need of giving orders
to other human beings, because there will be no longer any duty
to help those who are happy in immortal life. In the meantime,
fathers ought to look upon their duty to command as harder than
the duty of slaves to obey.

Meanwhile, in case anyone in the home behaves contrary to its peace, he is disciplined by words or whipping or other kind of punishment lawful and licit in human society, and for his own good, to readjust him to the peace he has abandoned. For, there is no more benevolence and helpfulness in bringing about the loss of a greater good than there is innocence and compassion in allowing a culprit to go from bad to worse. It is the duty of a blameless person not just to do no wrong, but to keep others from wrong-doing and to punish it when done, so that the one punished may be improved by the experience and others be warned by the example.

Now, since every home should be a beginning or fragmentary constituent of a civil community, and every beginning related to some specific end, and every part to the whole of which it is a part, it ought to follow that domestic peace has a relation to political peace. In other words, the ordered harmony of authority and obedience between those who live together has a relation to the ordered harmony of authority and obedience between those who live in a city. This explains why a father must apply certain regulations of civil law to the governance of his home, so as to make it accord with the peace of the whole community.

Chapter 17

While the homes of unbelieving men are intent upon acquiring temporal peace out of the possessions and comforts of this temporal life, the families which live according to faith look ahead to the good things of heaven promised as imperishable, and use material and temporal goods in the spirit of pilgrims, not as snares or obstructions to block their way to God, but simply as helps to ease and never to increase the burdens of this corruptible body which weighs down the soul. Both types of homes and their masters have this in common, that they must use things essential to this mortal life. But the respective purposes to which they put them are characteristic and very different.

So, too, the earthly city which does not live by faith seeks only an earthly peace, and limits the goal of its peace, of its harmony of authority and obedience among its citizens, to the voluntary and collective attainment of objectives necessary to mortal existence. The heavenly City, meanwhile—or, rather, that part that is on pilgrimage in mortal life and lives by faith—must use this earthly peace until such time as our mortality which needs such peace has passed away. As a consequence, so long as her life in the earthly city is that of a captive and an alien (although she has the promise of ultimate delivery and the gift of the Spirit as a pledge), she has no hesitation about keeping in step with the civil law which governs matters pertaining to our existence here below. For, as mortal life is the same for all, there ought to be common cause between the two cities in what concerns our purely human living.

Now comes the difficulty. The city of this world, to begin with, has had certain "wise men" of its own mold, whom true religion must reject, because either out of their own day-dreaming or out of demonic deception these wise men came to believe that a multiplicity of divinities was allied with human life, with different duties, in some strange arrangement, and different assignments: this one over the body, that one over the mind; in the body itself, one over the head, another over the neck, still others, one for each bodily part; in the mind, one over the intelligence, another over learning, another over temper, another over desire; in the realities, related to life, that lie about us, one over flocks and one over wheat, one over wine, one over oil, and another over forest, one over currency, another over navigation, and still another over warfare and victory, one over marriage, a different one over fecundity and childbirth, so on and so on.

The heavenly City, on the contrary, knows and, by religious faith, believes that it must adore one God alone and serve Him with that complete dedication which the Greeks call *latreía* and which belongs to Him alone. As a result, she has been unable to share with the earthly city a common religious legislation, and has had no choice but to dissent on this score and so to become a nuisance to those who think otherwise. Hence, she has had to feel the weight of their anger, hatred, and violence, save in those instances when, by sheer numbers and God's help, which never fails, she has been able to scare off her opponents.

So long, then, as the heavenly City is wayfaring on earth, she invites citizens from all nations and all tongues, and unites them into a single pilgrim band. She takes no issue with that diversity of customs, laws, and traditions whereby human peace is sought and maintained. Instead of nullifying or tearing down, she preserves and appropriates whatever in the diversities of divers races is aimed at one and the same objective of human peace, provided only that they do not stand in the way of the faith and worship of the one supreme and true God.

Thus, the heavenly City, so long as it is wayfaring on earth, not only makes use of earthly peace but fosters and actively pursues along with other human beings a common platform in regard to all that concerns our purely human life and does not interfere with faith and worship. Of course, though, the City of God subordinates this earthly peace to that of heaven. For this is not merely true peace, but, strictly speaking, for any rational creature, the only real peace, since it is, as I said, "the perfectly ordered and harmonious communion of those who find their joy in God and in one another in God."

When this peace is reached, man will be no longer haunted by death, but plainly and perpetually endowed with life, nor will his body, which now wastes away and weighs down the soul, be any longer animal, but spiritual, in need of nothing, and completely under the control of our will.

This peace the pilgrim City already possesses by faith and it lives holily and according to this faith so long as, to attain its heavenly completion, it refers every good act done for God or for his fellow man. I say "fellow man" because, of course, any community life must emphasize social relationships.

Chapter 18

Turning now to that distinctive characteristic which Varro ascribes to the followers of the New Academy, namely, universal skepticism, the City of God shuns it as a form of insanity. Its knowledge of truth, gleaned by intelligence and reasoning, is indeed slender because of the corruptible body weighing down the soul. As St. Paul says, "We know in part." Still, this knowledge is certain. Believers, moreover, trust the report of their bodily senses which subserve the intelligence. If they are at times deceived, they are at least better off than those who maintain that the senses can never be trusted.

The City of God believes the Old and New Testaments accepted as canonical. Out of these she·formulates that faith according to which the just man lives. And in the light of this faith we walk forward without fear of stumbling so long as "we are exiled from the Lord." This perfectly certain faith apart, other things which have not been sensibly or intellectually experienced nor clearly revealed in canonical Scripture, nor vouched for by witnesses whom it is reasonable to believe—these we can doubt and nobody in justice can take us to task for this.

Chapter 19

The City of God does not care in the least what kind of dress or social manners a man of faith affects, so long as these involve no offense against the divine law. For it is faith and not fashions that brings us to God. Hence, when philosophers become Christians, the Church does not force them to give up their distinctive attire or mode of life which are no obstacle to religion, but only their erroneous teachings. She is entirely indifferent to that special mark which, in Varro's reckoning, distinguishes the Cynics, so long as it connotes nothing shameful or unbalanced.

Or take the three modes of life: the contemplative, the active, the contemplative-active. A man can live the life of faith in any of these three and get to heaven. What is not indifferent is that he love truth and do what charity demands. No man must be so committed to contemplation as, in his contemplation, to give no thought to his neighbor's needs, nor so absorbed in action as to dispense with the contemplation of God.

The attraction of leisure ought not to be empty-headed inactivity, but in the quest or discovery of truth, both for his own progress and for the purpose of sharing ungrudgingly with others. Nor should the man of action love worldly position or power (for all is vanity under the sun), but only what can be properly and usefully accomplished by means of such position and power, in the sense which I have already explained of contributing to the eternal salvation of those committed to one's care. Thus, as St. Paul wrote: "If anyone is eager for the office of bishop, he desires a good work." He wanted to make clear that the office of bishop, *episcopatus*, implies work rather than dignity. The word is derived from *epískopos*, which is Greek for "superintendent." Thus, a bishop is supposed to superintend those over whom he is set in the sense that he is to "oversee" or "look out for" those under him. The word, *skopein*, like the Latin *intendere*, means to look; and so *episkopein*, like *super-intendere*, means "to oversee" or "to look out for those who are under one." Thus, no man can be a good bishop if he loves his title but not his task.

In the same way, no man is forbidden to pursue knowledge of the truth, for that is the purpose of legitimate leisure. But it is the ambition for the position of dignity which is necessary for government that is unbecoming, although, of course, the dignity itself and its use are not wrong in themselves. Thus, it is the love of study that seeks a holy leisure; and only the compulsion of charity that shoulders necessary activity. If no such burden is placed on one's shoulders, time should be passed in study and contemplation. But, once the burden is on the back, it should be carried, since charity so demands. Even so, however, no one should give up entirely his delight in learning, for the sweetness he once knew may be lost and the burden he bears overwhelm him.

Chapter 21

I have arrived at the point where I must keep my promise to prove, as briefly and clearly as I can, that if we accept the definitions of Scipio, cited by Cicero in his book *On the Republic*, there never existed any such thing as a Roman Republic.

Scipio gives a short definition of a commonwealth as the weal of the people. Now, if this is a true definition, there never was any Roman Republic, because there never was in Rome any true "weal of the people." Scipio defines the people as "a multitude bound together by a mutual recognition of rights and a mutual co-operation for the common good." As the discussion progresses, he explains what he means by "mutual recognition of rights," going on to show that a republic cannot be managed without justice, for, where there is not true justice, there is no recognition of rights.

For, what is rightly done is justly done; what is done unjustly cannot be done by right. We are not to reckon as right such human laws as are iniquitous, since even unjust law-givers themselves call a right [*ius*] only what derives from the fountainhead of justice [*iustitia*] and brand as false the wrong-headed opinion of those who keep saying that a right [*ius*] is whatever is advantageous [*utile*] to the one in power.

It follows that, wherever true justice is lacking, there cannot be a multitude of men bound together by a mutual recognition of rights; consequently, neither can there be a "people" in the sense of Scipio's definition. Further, if there is no "people," there is no weal of the "people," or commonwealth, but only the weal of a nondescript mob undeserving of the designation "the people." To resume the argument: If a commonwealth is the weal of the people, and if there is no people save one bound together by mutual recognition of rights, and if there are no rights where there is no justice, it follows beyond question that where there is no justice, there is no commonwealth.

Let us see. Justice is the virtue which accords to each and every
man what is his due. What, then, shall we say of a man's "justice"
when he takes himself away from the true God and hands himself
over to dirty demons? Is this a giving to each what is his due? If a
man who takes away a farm from its purchaser and delivers it to
another man who has no claim upon it is unjust, how can a man
who removes himself from the overlordship of the God who made
him and goes into the service of wicked spirits be just?

To be sure, in *On the Republic* there is a hard-fought and powerful
debate in favor of justice as against injustice. First, the side of injustice was taken. At that point it was claimed that only by injustice
could the republic stand firm and be efficiently managed. And this
was put down as the most telling proof: that it is unjust that some
men should have to serve others as masters; that, nevertheless, the
capital of the Empire to which the commonwealth belongs must
practice such injustice or surrender her provinces. Then the side of
justice made the following rebuttal: that such procedure is, in fact,
just because such submission is advantageous to the men in question,
that it is for their good, when such sovereignty is properly managed,
that is, when the lawless marauding of criminals is repressed and
order established. For, the conquered peoples thereafter are better
off than they were in liberty.

Next, to bolster this reasoning, a new argument was brought
forward in the form of an admirable example taken, so they said,
from nature herself: "Why, otherwise, does God have mastery over
man, the mind over the body, reason over lust and the other wrongful movements of the soul?"

Surely, now, this example teaches plainly enough for anyone that
it is for the good of some to be in an inferior position, and that it is
good for all without exception to be subject to God. The soul that is
submissive to God justly lords it over the body; in the soul itself,
reason bowing down before its Lord and God justly lords it over lust
and every other evil tendency.

Because this is so, what fragment of justice can there be in a man
who is not subject to God, if, indeed, it is a fact that such a one
cannot rightfully exercise dominion—soul over body, human reason
over sinful propensities? And if there is no justice in a man of this
kind, then there is certainly no justice, either, in an assembly made
up of such men. As a result, there is lacking that mutual recognition
of rights which makes a mere mob into a "people," a people whose
common weal is a commonwealth.

What shall I say of the common good whose common pursuit knits men together into a "people," as our definition teaches? Careful scrutiny will show that there is no such good for those who live irreligiously, as all do who serve not God but demons and, particularly, those filthy spirits that are so defiant of God that they look to receive sacrifices as if they were gods. Anyway, what I have said with regard to mutual recognition of rights I consider sufficient to show that, on the basis of the definition itself, a people devoid of justice is not such a people as can constitute a commonwealth.

I am supposing that no one will raise the objection that the Roman Republic served good and holy gods, and not unclean spirits. Surely, I do not have to repeat the same old arguments which I have so often and so more than sufficiently stated. No one but a thickhead or an irrepressible wrangler can have read all the earlier Books of this work and still doubt that the Romans worshiped evil and dirty demons. In any case, what does it matter to what kind of demons they offered sacrifices? In the law of the true God it is written: "He that sacrificeth to gods shall be put to death, save only to the Lord." The dreadful sanction of this command makes it clear that God wanted no sacrifices offered to such gods, good or bad.

2 FROM *Charles Norris Cochrane*
Christianity and Classical Culture

THE EARTHLY CITY VERSUS THE HEAVENLY CITY— A CONFLICT OF VALUES

In human history the new principle of unity and division finds expression in two societies, which may be described mystically (*mystice*) as two cities. These societies are at every point in sharp contrast: "The one is the city of Christ, the other of the devil; the one of the good, the other of the evil; both composed of angels as well as men." This vast generalization serves to comprehend the whole human race, "all the numerous peoples scattered throughout

SOURCE. Charles Norris Cochrane, *Christianity and Classical Culture* (New York: Oxford University Press, 1944), pp. 488–496. Reprinted by permission of the publisher.

the earth, living by diverse rites and customs, distinguished by the utmost variety of languages, arms, and clothing." It comprehends also the whole of human history: the life of these two societies extends "from the beginning of the race to the end of the *saeculum*, during which they are mixed physically but separated morally (*voluntate*), on the day of judgement to be separated physically as well." They are secular society and the society of God.

The point of divergence between these two forms of association is to be found in their respective desires.

"That which animates secular society (*civitas terrena*) is the love of self to the point of contempt for God; that which animates divine society (*civitas caelestis*) is the love of God to the point of contempt for self. The one prides itself on itself; the pride of the other is in the Lord; the one seeks for glory from men, the other counts its consciousness of God as its greatest glory."

These desires may therefore be described respectively as greed (*avaritia*) and love (*caritas*). "The one is holy, the other foul; the one social, the other selfish; the one thinks of the common advantage for the sake of the higher association, the other reduces even the common good to a possession of its own for the sake of selfish ascendancy; the one is subject to, the other a rival to God; the one is peaceful, the other turbulent; the one pacific, the other factious; the one prefers truth to the praises of the foolish, the other is greedy of praise on any terms; the one is friendly, the other envious; the one desires the same for his neighbour as for himself; the other to subject his neighbour to himself; the one governs his neighbour in his neighbour's interest, the other in his own."

From this standpoint the *civitas terrena* presents itself as a reflection of values which have their roots in self-assertive egotism (*amor sui*). As such, its genesis depends upon the fact that sheer antagonism is suicidal; as within the individual life, so also for the relations between men, some degree of order is indispensable. Accordingly, *amor sui*, accepted as a principle of order, begins with an assertion of the animal right to live which resolves itself basically into a satisfaction of the demands of belly and loins. In this sense it gives rise to the kind of concord exhibited, e.g. by a gang of pirates, which may thus be taken to represent the lowest limit of co-operative endeavour. But this by no means exhausts its possibilities as a basis for cohesion; since indeed it serves to embrace the whole vast array of secular values. These include, to begin with, "the body and its goods, i.e. sound health, keen senses, physical strength and beauty, part of them essential to a good life and therefore more eligible, part of less account. In the second place, freedom, in the sense in which one imagines he is free when he is his own master, i.e. the sense in which it is coveted by slaves. Thirdly, parents, mothers, a wife and children, neighbours, relatives, friends and, for those who in any way share our (Graeco-Roman) outlook, membership in a state which is venerated as a parent, together with honours, rewards, and what is called popular esteem. Finally, money, the term being taken to comprehend everything which we legally possess and are empowered to sell or otherwise dispose of."

The values of secularism find expression in characteristic mechanisms wherein form and function are more or less perfectly reconciled, and these mechanisms constitute the secular order. This order, the *pax terrena*, manifests itself in at least three phases. The first is that of the *pax domestica*, the order which determines life in the household. This order depends ultimately upon the union of male and female (*copulatio maris et feminae*). But this union, as the source of offspring "according to the flesh," may at the same time be regarded as the seed-bed of the city (*seminarium civitatis*). Accordingly, the order of the household gives rise to a second and more comprehensive order, the *pax civica*. A third phase of human association emerges as household and city expand on a world-wide scale (*a domo et ab urbe ad orbem*) to blossom forth as the imperial state. Differing as they do both in constitution and objectives, these three forms of secular society have this much at least in common, that their existence depends upon will. The will in question, however, is not that of an "oversoul," nor may it be described as "general" except in so far as it marks "a composition or fitting together of individual human wills with respect to such objects as pertain to mortal life." This being so, such order as is evolved within secular society can hardly be more than imperfect.

"Associations of mortals, scattered as they are throughout the earth and confronted by the greatest possible diversity of local conditions, are nevertheless impelled by the bond of a common nature to pursue their respective advantages and interests. So long therefore as the object of appetition is insufficient for any or for all, since it does not possess that character (or, 'since its character lacks permanence'—*quia non est id ipsum*)—the association is normally divided against itself and the stronger element oppresses the weaker ('adversus se ipsam plerumque dividitur et pars partem, quae praevalet, obprimit'). The vanquished submits to the victor, because he prefers peace and safety on whatever terms to mastery or even to freedom, so that those who have chosen to die rather than be slaves have always excited the greatest wonder.

By thus rewriting Thucydides in a no less realistic spirit, Augustine denies the pretensions of philosophic idealism as enunciated by the Ciceronian Scipio who, in the *De re publica*, had defined the commonwealth "as the interest of the people, the people being a group (*coetus multitudinis*) associated together by the tie of common advantage (*utilitatis communione*) and by a common sense of right (*iuris consensu*)." "For how," he asks, "can there be right where there is no justice?" As he elsewhere puts it, "in the absence of justice, what are realms except great robber-bands? And what are robber-bands except little realms?" From this standpoint there is no essential difference between the empire of Alexander and that of the pirate whom he had arrested. "The one infests the sea, the other the whole earth." Accordingly, he rejects the idealist contention in order to redefine the state as "a group of rational beings, associated on the basis of a common tie in respect of those things which they love." From this standpoint the quality of any community may be measured in terms of the objects of its desire.

We may here pause to insist that according to Augustine the objects in question are not to be classified as either material or ideal; that is to say, the line of demarcation is not between ponderables and imponderables. They are accurately described as temporal; and the *pax terrena* represents a consolidation of temporal goods. Divine providence, says Augustine, has furnished mankind with the physical basis for an adequate human order by providing him with goods which are congruous to mortal life. These goods comprehend certain "ideal" values such as "safety and the society of his kind, whatever indeed is necessary for maintaining and repairing this order—light, a voice, air to breathe, water to drink, and all that goes to nourish, cover, care for, and adorn the body."

To Augustine the point of real significance is not so much the goods of secular life as the attitude which secularism adopts towards them. This attitude he designates as one of "possessiveness;" and, from this standpoint, the distinctive mark of the *civitas terrena* is greed or the lust for possession (*libido dominandi*). That is to say it treats those goods as "private" (*privatum*), claiming a right to make them "its own" for distribution within the group (*sua cuique distribuere*); a claim which presumes at the same time the right of exploitation (*uti abutique*, in the phraseology of Roman law). In the secular order, the claim thus indicated finds expression in "property" which thus, whatever form it may assume, becomes the "immovable foundation of human relationships," destined as such to warp and pervert conceptions like that of personality, marriage, and the family. But to "appropriate" in this sense is also to "divide"; its ideal of independence is at the same time an ideal of isolation, the isolation of economic and moral self-sufficiency. Furthermore, the greed for property in temporal goods is inevitably exclusive and monopolistic. "For he who desires the glory of possession would feel that his power was diminished, if he were obliged to share it with any living associate." Secular society may thus discover its prototype in Babylon, "the city of confusion," hopelessly rent by schism and dissension which, by reason of self-imposed limitations, it cannot overcome. And, since "Cain signifies possession," it may look to the fratricide as its founder and first citizen.

Such limitations are those of a society whose ideal of concord never rises above that of composing individual interests in relation to the demands of temporal life. Accordingly, the dominant passion must find a vicarious fulfilment "in the persons of its leading members or in those of the nations which it subdues. . . . Accordingly, it cherishes its own manhood in its own powerful men (*in suis potentibus diligit virtutem suam*)." The result is that it becomes the theatre of a struggle for survival, the law of which is "fish eat fish." "This world," says Augustine, "is a sea wherein men devour one another in turn like fish." By thus reducing secular life to purely biological terms he does ample justice to the Herodotean concept of conflict in society. Such conflict is an inherent and ineradicable feature of secularism from which, on its own principles, there is no conceivable escape. "For if the household, the common refuge from the evils of human life, affords but imperfect security, how much more so the state which, the larger it is, is the more full of civil suits and crime, even when for the moment it earns a respite from turbulent, often bloody, seditions and civil wars, from the occurrence of which states are rarely free, from the apprehension of them never." From this standpoint the maintenance of the *pax civica* depends in the last analysis upon fear, i.e. upon the power to coerce the recalcitrant (*metus quo coerceat*). Or, in the words of a modern: "l'armée est la manifestation la plus claire, la plus tangible, et la plus solidement attachée aux origines que l'on puisse avoir de l'état."

Thus envisaged, the *polis*, so far from being a cure for heresy, is itself the greatest and most shameless of heresies; and this is equally true whether it assumes the form of kingdom or commonwealth, realm or republic (*regnum vel civitas, res publica*). This truth applies in the first instance to Assyria, the prototype of Oriental achievement in statecrafts, exemplar of brutal conquest and exploitation, "to be described only as brigandage on a colossal scale." But it is no less evident in the case of European than of Asiatic political experiment; of Athens, "mother and nurse of liberal learning, home of so many great philosophers, the glory and distinction of Hellas"; of Rome which, by reconciling the civic claim to "a good life" with the demands of imperial security, had epitomized and completed the political endeavour of the West, triumphantly realizing the secular ideals of stability, prosperity, military glory and untroubled peace.

The advice of Augustine is therefore not to put your trust either in princes or in peoples, in kingdoms or in commonwealths. Of kingdoms and kings he observes that they estimate their achievement in terms, not of the righteousness but of the servility, of their subjects. The vice of the commonwealth, on the other hand, lies in its ideal of merely economic and political (utilitarian) justice with which is bound up the equally vicious ideal of conformity or, as we should say, social adjustment. "Like the Athenian woman," he says, "you can by a series of small doses accustom yourself to poison." Yet such is the pressure to conform that recusancy means nothing less than social ostracism and "he is a public enemy to whom this ideal of happiness does not appeal." But it is an illusion to suppose that there can be any escape from the evils of organized society through a return to primitivism, since this involves the fallacy that "nature" is intrinsically virtuous and "law" the mark of degeneracy. This, however, is a heresy, for it presumes that corruption is somehow inherent in the political fabric, independently of the wills which create and sustain it. In primitive Rome this notion led to a revolution against the kings; but "republican liberty" was no sooner achieved than it gave rise to oppression, by exposing the weak to the "injuries of the strong," whose excesses presently resulted in a secession of the plebs. To those excesses there was but one effective check, the fear of danger from abroad; the sense of the Romans that, if they did not hang together, they would hang separately. This fear induced a kind of cohesion, but one merely of a negative character. It thus fell short of a sound basis for creative peace.

Subsequent events of Roman history served merely to emphasize the original deficiencies of the secular ideal. The economic motive being dominant, it found expression in "the exploitation of plebeians by patricians as though they were slaves," through the greedy monopolization of land and a barbarous administration of the law relating to interest and debts. Yet, so far from attempting to correct their shortcomings, the Romans proceeded to aggravate them by embarking upon an extensive programme of conquest and acquisition, in which "they pleaded the necessity of defending security and freedom, as an excuse for satisfying their greed for human glory." Yet the national passion for prestige was not without its value; as "the one vice for the sake of which they suppressed all other vices," it served to bring them an unprecedented measure of material prosperity (res prosperae). But material prosperity was to carry with it no real prospect of relief from the maladies which afflict the competitive state; and the successes of Rome in Italy and abroad simply provided increased opportunity "for making and spending money." In this way they promoted the growth of economic dynasties "as the more powerful employed their wealth to subject the weaker to their sway." At the same time they gave rise to a veritable flood of social evils, a scramble for wealth which threatened the principle of private property itself, "as a generation grew up which could neither keep its own estates nor suffer others to do so." Coupled with this was a novel form of parasitism in which, while the poor battened on the rich in order to enjoy an "inert quiet," the rich preyed upon the poor as a means of ministering to their sense of pride. The upshot was that "concord was disrupted and destroyed, at first by savage and murderous seditions, subsequently by a long series of iniquitous civil wars." Accordingly, "the lust for possession, thus exhibited in its purer form among the Romans, triumphed in the persons of a few men of exceptional power, only to reduce and exhaust the remainder and, ultimately, to impose upon them the yoke of servitude." Yet, in attempting to fix responsibility for these developments, it should be remembered that "ambition would have had no chance whatever, except among a people corrupted by avarice and luxury." In these circumstances, how feeble the argument of Scipio that Rome was or ever had been a true commonwealth.

Finally, the acquisition of empire serves merely to increase the perils to which competitive politics are exposed, by producing "a happiness dazzling as crystal but equally fragile, and a still more terrible fear lest it should suddenly be shattered." For the dangers of a body of water are proportionate to its size. Conscious of these dangers the imperial state

"seeks to neutralize them by imposing upon its subjects not merely its yoke but its culture (*linguam*). But at what cost in the effusion of human blood! Nevertheless there still remain foreign nations to subdue! And, with the increase of dominion, there increases also the possibility of intestinal strife, more pernicious even than foreign war. And yet, they declare, the wise man will be ready to wage just wars! As though, if he remembered his humanity, he should not rather deplore the necessity of wars which, if they were not just, he would not have to wage. Accordingly, for the wise man there would be no wars."

It thus appears that, for Augustine, conflict is an inevitable function of organized secular society. To this fact he attributes the illusory character of secular achievement. For, in the conflicts to which secularism is committed, even "its victories are deadly or at any rate deathly"; so that the doom with which it is ultimately confronted is that of Assyria and of Rome. In these terms Augustine does justice to facts of social history to which Classicism had vainly endeavoured to give intelligibility, whether through the Herodotean "principle of decline" or through the humanist myth of corruption, the corruption of *virtù*. At the same time he gives to secular history a moral such as none but the Hebrew prophets had as yet perceived, when he declares that, "by devoting themselves to the things of this world, the Romans did not go without their reward."

"God the author and giver of felicity, because He is the one true God, Himself grants earthly kingdoms both to the good and to the evil, yet not at haphazard and, so to speak, fortuitously, inasmuch as He is God; nor yet by fortune, but in accordance with the order of times and seasons, an order which, though hidden from us, is fully known to Him. This order He observes though Himself in no sense subject to it, but governing and disposing of it as lord and master. Felicity, however, He does not grant except to the good.

"The greatness of the Roman empire is not therefore to be ascribed either to chance or fate. Human empires are constituted by the providence of God."

God thus "disposes the times and issues of battles," permitting those to win whose martial qualities enable them to do so. To suppose, however, that the martial qualities are, on that account, necessarily exalted is a fallacy; since there is no way of consecrating egotism, and power, whether material or moral, if taken in abstraction from charity, is a "vice," the exercise of which cannot but have deleterious consequences. In this law Augustine perceives, not the operation of an Herodotean *nemesis*, but the hand of God working in history to visit the sins of the fathers upon their children from generation to generation. Those visitations they may indeed escape, but upon one condition only; viz. that they cease to dope themselves with illusion and make up their minds to face the facts. This, however, was precisely what Classicism stubbornly and persistently refused to do.

PART THREE

Charles the Great and the Papacy

After almost twelve hundred years of scholarly controversy, there is still no consensus about the significance of the imperial coronation of the Frankish ruler, Charles the Great (768–814). Did Charles himself instigate the celebrated event in St. Peter's Basilica on Christmas Day, 800? Did he actually stand to gain from the coronation? Did a coronation actually occur, in fact, or are our accounts of the incident later interpolations? Did Pope Leo III (795–816) plan the coronation in order to associate the Frankish monarchy with Rome and papal policy? If so, did the Pope intend to place the royal power of the Franks in a position subordinate to papal authority and then to use it as a bulwark against the claims of the imperial Byzantine Court? However these problems are finally resolved, the coronation of Charlemagne had profound consequences for the course of German history, and later ecclesiastical apologists repeatedly cited the event as proof that the dignity of the emperor could be bestowed only by the Bishop of Rome.

The documentary evidence is inevitably cryptic because of its almost fragmentary nature. The best collection of original sources on the imperial coronation of Charlemagne is probably that of Heinz Dannenbauer, which contains all extant evidence from biographies, chronicles, *laudes regiae*, letters, and litanies. All sources and page references below are to this volume; the translations are by the editor.

An important, if not entirely persuasive, interpretation of papal policy in the eighth century and of Charles' response to it, together with a wide appreciation of contemporary international conditions, is that of Walter Ullmann, whose views have been severely challenged by Friedrich Kempf. Selections from the work of the two men follow.

1 FROM *Heinz Dannenbauer*
Die Quellen zur Geschichte der KaiserKrönung Karls des Grossen

(801) On the very day of the most holy nativity of the Lord, when the king at Mass had risen from prayer before the tomb of Blessed Peter the Apostle, Pope Leo placed the crown on his head, and by all the people of Rome he was acclaimed: Long Life and Victory to the August Charles, the Great and Peace-Giving Emperor, crowned by God. And after the ovations, the pope did obeisance to him according to the custom observed before the ancient emperors, and the title of Patricius being dropped, he was called Emperor and Augustus.[1]

After these things, the day of the birth of Our Lord Jesus Christ having arrived, all gathered once again in the aforesaid Basilica of Blessed Peter the Apostle. And then the venerable and generous pope, with his own hands, crowned him with the most precious crown. Then all the faithful Christians of Rome, understanding the defense that he (Charles) had provided and the love that he bore the Holy Roman Church and her Vicar, by the will of God and Blessed Peter, keeper of the keys of the kingdom of heaven, unanimously shouted with a loud voice: "Life and Victory to Charles, the most pious Augustus, crowned by God, the great and peace-giving

[1]Frankish Royal Annals (*Annales Laurissenses Mairores et Einhardi*), p. 10.

SOURCE. Heinz Dannenbauer, *Die Quellen zur Geschichte der KaiserKrönung Karls des Grossen* (Berlin: Walter de Gruyter & Co., 1931), pp. 10, 17–18, 23, 27–28. Translated for this volume by Bennett D. Hill by permission of the publisher.

Emperor." As he was praying to many saints before the sacred tomb of Blessed Peter the Apostle, it was established by all that he is Emperor of the Romans. Then the most holy priest and pope anointed Charles with holy oil, and then his most excellent son, on the same day, that of the birth of Our Lord Jesus Christ.

And after the celebration of the Mass, the most serene Emperor himself brought gifts of silver to the altar.[2]

(801) And because at that time the name of emperor had ceased to exist in the empire of the Greeks and the empire itself was held by a woman, accordingly, it appeared to the Apostolic Leo himself and to all the holy fathers gathered for the council[3] as well as to the remaining Christian people that they ought to name Charles, King of the Franks, as emperor, because he held the city of Rome where the Caesars were always accustomed to reside, as well as the cities in Italy, Gaul and Germany. Since Almighty God had granted all these cities into his power, therefore, it seemed to them to be just, with the help of God and at the prayer of all the Christian people that the title (of emperor) should not be denied to him. King Charles did not wish to refuse their request, but with all humility, submitting himself to God and to the petition of the priests and of all the Christian people, on the very day of the birth of the Lord Jesus Christ he received the name of emperor with the consecration of the Lord Pope Leo. And the first thing he did there (at Rome) was to put down the disorder which had disrupted it and to restore the Holy Roman Church to peace and harmony. And at Rome he celebrated the paschal season.[4]

His last journey there (to Rome) was due to another factor, namely that the Romans, having inflicted many injuries on Pope Leo—plucking out his eyes and tearing out his tongue, he had been compelled to beg the assistance of the king. Accordingly, coming to Rome in order that he might set in order those things which had exceedingly disturbed the condition of the Church, he remained there the whole winter. It was at that time that he accepted the

---

[2]Life of Pope Leo III (*Vita Leonis III*), p. 23.

[3]On the significance of this synod which investigated the charges against Pope Leo, see Luitpold Wallach, "The Roman Synod of December 800 and The Alleged Trial of Leo III," in *Harvard Theological Review*, XLIX, No. 2 (April 1956), pp. 123–142.

[4]*Annales Laureshamenses*, p. 17.

name of Emperor and Augustus. At first he was so much opposed to this that he insisted that although that day was a great (Christian) feast, he would not have entered the Church if he had known beforehand the pope's intention. But he bore very patiently the jealousy of the Roman Emperors (i.e. the Byzantine rulers) who were indignant when he received these titles. He overcame their arrogant haughtiness with magnanimity, a virtue in which he was considerably superior to them, by sending frequent ambassadors to them, and in his letters addressing them as brothers.[5]

Just as I entered into an agreement with the most blessed father your predecessor, so also I desire to conclude with Your Beatitude a permanent treaty of the same faith and charity; in order that with Divine grace being called down by the prayers of your Apostolic Holiness, the Apostolic benediction may follow me everywhere, and the most holy See of the Roman Church may always be defended by the piety which God gives to us. We, on our part, with the assistance of divine holiness, will defend with armed might the holy Church of Christ everywhere from the outward onslaught of the pagans and the devastation of the infidels, and within the Church we will support the knowledge of the catholic faith. It is your obligation, Most Holy Father, to help our armies with hands lifted up to God like Moses, so that by your intercession and by the leadership of God the Christian people may everywhere and always have victory over the enemies of His Holy Name, and that the name of Our Lord Jesus Christ may be glorified throughout the entire world.[6]

[5] Einhard's Life of Charlemagne (*Einhardi vita Karoli Magne*), pp. 17–18.
[6] This letter of Charlemagne's, written to Pope Leo III in 796, presents the Frankish ruler's views of the relations of Church and State (pp. 27–28).

2 FROM   *Walter Ullmann*
The Growth of Papal Government in the Middle Ages

Charlemagne "a Deo coronatus"—the Pope creates a Universal Christian Protector

There is no gainsaying the lesson which the papacy had learnt in the preceding two centuries [i.e., the seventh and eighth]. Perhaps the chief lesson which they taught was that the papacy as an institution was powerless, if it did not have at its disposal a protector and defender, when protection and defence were called for. The papacy had, so to speak, grown into the texture of the already existing Roman empire, precisely because the papal church was the Church of Rome, when Rome was still the capital of the empire. Considered from this historical point of view, there was indeed no possibility for the Roman Church as a Roman institution to create a defender and protector in the shape of the Roman empire which had turned out to be its oppressor. But there was no secular power which could have been made a protector and defender of the Roman Church. In short, then, by virtue of the papacy's being part and parcel of the Roman empire, it could not only not offer effective resistance to the Roman emperor, but there was also no possibility of obtaining an effective protector and defender. In order to attain these two objectives emancipation from the imperial framework was essential. The pontificate of Gregory[1] II began this process of emancipation. . . .

Although it had emancipated itself from the constitutional framework of the Eastern empire, the papacy had little cause to rejoice in its newly won "freedom." The position of the pope as the lord of the Duchy of Rome drew the Roman nobility conspicuously to the fore: it now demanded a share in the making of the pope and the "election" of Constantine (II),[2] himself a soldier, and the subsequent tumultuous scenes brought forth a vigorous opposition

[1]Pope, 715–731.
[2]Anti-pope, 767–768.

SOURCE. Walter Ullmann, *The Growth of Papal Government in the Middle Ages* (London: Methuen & Co., Ltd., 1962), pp. 45, 87–102. Reprinted by permission of the publisher and the author.

party under the able leadership of Christophorus. The Council held at Rome in April 769 in which many Frankish bishops as well as of course still more Italian bishops participated, proceeded to the condemnation of Constantine (II) and, what is more important for us, to the promulgation of an election decree. This election decree was later to serve as the model on which a better known papal election decree was built. The synodists of 769 laid down that no layman must partake in the election of a pope—only clerics were allowed to vote, whilst all the laymen were permitted to do was to salute the thus elected pope as the "lord of all."

This election decree, however, lacked proper backing. And the subsequent history of papal elections and consecrations and the ever-increasing military influence of the Roman nobility made it imperative for the papacy to appoint an effective protector, a protector who was to guarantee the "freedom" of papal elections and thereby also to guarantee the authority of the newly elected pope. In course of time this need for protection was to lead to a number of special arrangements made in the ninth century which were to enshrine in documentary form the defence and protection of the Roman Church and herewith of the pope himself.

None was better qualified for this office than the Frankish "patricius Romanorum." Whilst the father had refused to bear the title, the son adopted it, certainly from 774 onwards. The intimate connexion between the Roman Church and the Frankish Church, no less than the strengthening of the bonds between it and the Frankish monarchy in the two decades since Ponthion, were not without effects upon the mind of Charlemagne. The acceptance of the title and office of "patricius Romanorum" by Charlemagne is, we think, the effect, not of any political consideration on his part, but of his purely religious views. To him "Romanitas" and "Christianitas" were tautological expressions. Romanism for Charlemagne was not a historical-political term, but had an exclusively religious connotation: it signified the contrast to "Grecism," to that kind of faith which was not Roman-directed. Romanism simply meant Latin Christianity—that Christian faith which was directed and orientated by the Roman Church. The Bonifacian work, its concomitant close association with Roman-papal organization, the spreading of the characteristically Roman liturgies and their prayers, the religious orientation of the Frankish domains towards Rome, led to a complete amalgamation of Christian and Roman elements. This Roman ferment in that eighth-century Christianity of the Franks was of decisive importance, because "Christianitas" and "Romanitas" became virtually indistinguishable. It is assuredly no coincidence that Charlemagne requested Adrian I[3] for an "authentic" copy of the sacramentary which the great Gregory had created. It is furthermore significant that at this time also the Benedictine Rule with its typically Roman features spread so rapidly through Frankish and newly conquered lands. Not less significant is it that a copy of the canonical collection of Dionysius Exiguus in the expanded and modified form given by Adrian I was personally handed to Charlemagne by the pope in 774.

All these vehicles of Romanist transmission effected the imperceptible, though significant orientation towards Rome in all things that mattered most, namely, in those of religion and its cult. The old Roman formulae were repeated, the old Roman liturgical prayers were said and spoken by the Franks who might not always have fully grasped the intrinsic meaning of these prayers. The prayer that was originally in the Leonine Sacramentary went in its original form and with the entreaty for the *Roman* security into the Frankish sacramentaries. In other prayers the amalgamation of "Christianitas" and "Romanitas" went so far that the original term "Romanus" was exchanged for "Christianus." Thus, for example, in the Gelasian sacramentary the reference to the "Romani" was altered in the Frankish sacramentaries to "Christiani." In yet another of the prayer texts, contained in the Gelasian Sacramentary of the eighth century for a copy of which Pippin had already asked the pope, we find the amalgamation still more pronounced. The original prayer for security of the "Romani fines" was changed into one for security of the "Christianorum Romani fines."

> Deus . . . pax a tua pietate concessa Romanos fines—Christianorum Romanos fines—ab omni hoste faciat esse securos.

In short, the Romanization of the Western mind by virtue of these diverse channels led to the ideological conflation of Romans and Christians.

Set against this background it is perhaps understandable that Charlemagne should have had no hesitation in adopting the title and in playing the role of the "patricius Romanorum." When "Romanus" equalled "Christianus," there was indeed no obstacle to prevent his assuming that role which virtually meant no more than that of a military defender of the "Romans." that is the

[3]Pope, 772–795.

"Christians," a role which in fact he was accustomed to play in any case. What the title meant to him was that his protective function natually embraced also those Romans who were the epitome of all the Romans in the world, that is, the geographical Romans: they were merely the Christians, as it were, in a condensed and crystallized form. And it was in his function as "patricius Romanorum," in his function as a protector of the Church of Rome, that he not only confirmed the "donation" of his father, but also added a considerable part of Italy to the territories which his father had "restored" to their rightful owner, the Church of Rome.

The biography of Adrian I informs us of the details of this "donation" as well as of the solemn reception given by the pope: Charlemagne was received with all the honours due to the former exarch, now transformed into the "patricius Romanorum." According to Adrian's biographer, on the Wednesday following Easter, 6 April 774, Charlemagne ordered his chaplain and notary Etherius to draw up two copies of the "donation," the one to be handed to the pope, the other to be deposited at the Confession of St. Peter. This instrument was drawn up and modelled on that made twenty years earlier. Charlemagne conceded to St. Peter, and vowed that he would hand over to the pontiff, the territories enumerated, that is Luna (near Specia), Parma, Reggio, Mantua, Monteselice, the "exarchate of Ravenna," the whole of Venetia and Istria; Corsica, the duchies of Spoleto and Benevento. Although the biographer does not speak of a restitution but of a concession of territory, Einhard, on the other hand, considered the transaction as a "restitution" of stolen territory. This witness tells us that Charlemagne would not rest before he had subdued Desiderius and expelled him, nor before all the robbed territories were restored to the Romans.

It seems clear that the Easter transaction of 774 had the same character as its precursor of twenty years earlier: in each case the transaction concerned "restoration" of property, stolen by the Lombards from its legitimate owner, the Roman Church. The test here as there lies in the transfer of property that was not in the hands of the Lombards—in our case, Venetia and Istria, to mention only the two most conspicuous examples. For both Venetia and Istria were still Byzantine and therefore belonged to the empire. The insistent demands of the pope put to Charlemagne for the implementation of the "donation" of 6 April 774 show us the rift between the pope's intentions and the king's actions, a rift that seems to have become particularly clear after Charlemagne's assumption of the title "Rex Langobardorum" on 5 June 774. What is, moreover, very characteristic of these many letters sent by the pope as the emphasis on the function of the Roman Church as the "spiritualis mater" of the king and the emphasis on his duty of protecting his spiritual mother—for this reason, if for no other, he ought to be a fighter "pro justitiis beati Petri exigendis." The prospect of appropriate reward is not omitted in these papal letters: if he fulfilled his promises the king would exalt the Roman Church and herewith the universal Church, and thereby the ortho- dox Christian faith would be preserved.

The exaltation by Charlemagne of the Roman Church is in fact the dominant theme in all these numerous papal appeals to the Frankish king. In one of his communications the pope goes even so far as to remind Charlemagne of the exaltation of the Roman Church by the Emperor Constantine: he is held up to the Frank as the model, for he had exalted the Church through his grant and had bestowed upon the pope these parts of the West, so that the "sancta Dei ecclesia" might flourish and blossom forth. "Et pro hoc petimus eximiam precellentiam vestram, ut in integro ipsa patrimonia beato Petro et nobis *restituere* jubeatis." Divers emperors, Adrian I claims, patricians and other God-fearing men had conceded to St. Peter and the apostolic Roman Church terri- tories, such as Tuscany, Spoleto, Corsica. and so forth, and "of these transactions we have the documents in our Lateran archives." Hence Charlemagne should imitate the great emperor Constantine who had exalted the Church under Silvester so enormously and who had given the Roman Church the "potestas" over these Western parts of the world.

Even though the pope's territorial ambitions remained largely unfulfilled, the papal creations of Pippin, Charles's son, as "King of Italy," and of Louis as "King of Aquitaine," when there was no precedent for these offices and for papal conferments of royal dignity and function, should be appraised adequately as regards their symbolic significance. Taken in conjunction with the creation of the Carolingian "patricius Romanorum" by Stephen II, these actions throw into clear relief the steady continuity of papal doctrine and plainly herald the much more significant act on Christmas Day 800. Ponthion, Kierzy, Pavia, the creation of the "patricius Romanorum," Charlemagne's donation, the creation of the Italian and Aquitanian kings—these are powerful preparatory steps cul-

minating in the creation of Charlemagne as "Imperator Romanorum." It is as if the papal theme gained momentum towards the
closing years of the eighth century.

For we must bear in mind that during the pontificate of Leo III
there were some very specific signs pointing to great changes. It will
be recalled that, according to the *Liber Diurnus*, the newly elected
pope was to announce his election to the emperor or, in order to
save time, to the exarch at Ravenna, so as to obtain imperial confirmation of the election. But when Leo III became pope, there was
no longer an exarch nor did the papacy consider itself as part of the
Roman empire. Yet Leo III sent a "decretalis cartula" to
Charlemagne immediately after his election. We hold that the
reason why the deed of the election was despatched, was not indeed
to adhere to an obnoxious system—the requirement of imperial
confirmation was of course fundamentally inimical to the papal
point of view—but in order to utilize this old rule for quite a different purpose: the papacy thereby implied clearly the role for
which the Frankish king was destined—that of an emperor, for it
was the emperor (or on his behalf the exarch) who had to give
imperial confirmation to the papal election. But whilst the purpose
of notification was previously to obtain imperial confirmation, the
purpose now was, we consider, to implement the duty of the protector of the Roman Church and of the pope. The notification was
to serve as the signal to the "patricius Romanorum" that a new
pope had assumed his office, who is now to be protected by the
patrician.

Furthermore, Adrian I had disregarded the rule laid down by
Justinian that all documents, including therefore papal ones, must
be dated according to imperial years. Leo III definitely abandoned
this prescription of Justinian, but substituted, in a document issued
on 20 April 798, the regnal years of Charlemagne's rule in Italy for
the imperial years (of the Eastern emperor). The idea behind this
innovation was the same as in the case of notification: it was to
indicate the role for which the Frankish king was destined.

The plan of Charlemagne to erect a Second Rome at Aix-la-
Chapelle was an additional motive for Leo III to expedite matters
in the direction in which they had already been moving. This plan
of Charlemagne was revealed to him on the occasion of his visit to
Paderborn in the summer of 799. Expelled by the Romans Leo
sought to implore the help of the protector, the "patricius
Romanorum." We shall have an opportunity to make some

observations on what may be called Charlemagne's imitative rivalry
with the Eastern emperor, who lived in "New Rome" and, moreover, had at hand his chief priest, the patriarch. According to
Charlemagne, the "Old Rome" was to be transplanted to Aix: next
to the minster and the "*sacrum* palatium" which was the residence of
the Frankish king, there was a third building, the "Lateran." Like
Constantinople, Aix was to be the Second Rome: the Lateran is in
fact the "house of the pontiff" in Einhard's description. And the
court poet tells us of the "coming Rome"—"ventura Roma"—
which Charlemagne is about to erect at Aix. It was the *secunda
Roma*.

When Leo III implored the help of Charlemagne, the latter's
intentions cannot have remained hidden from the pope. Did not in
fact everything point to a most uncomfortable exchange of
Byzantium for Aix? Was this exchange not a repetition of the set-up
which the papacy had hoped to relegate to the past? Did not
Charlemagne's exhortation to the pope have an ominous ring: he
should lead an honest life, respect the canons, guide the Church
religiously and diligently and fight simony—when this is compared
with Justinian's view on the functions of the priesthood? What other
role but that of an archpriest was the pope to play in the scheme
of things devised by the Frank? For the king's task was the effective
strengthening, consolidating, propagating and preserving the faith
—the pope's task was to support the king in this duty by praying
for him like Moses did with elevated hands.

The Carolingian idea of a Second Rome at Aix, we hold, was one
of the most severe challenges which the papal programme had to
meet. For if this scheme of things had gone through, the foundations of the papal theme would have been sapped. European
Christianity, drawing its life blood from Romanism and nurtured
by the Church of Rome, would have been deprived of its strongest
and most attractive foundations. To have acquiesced in this plan of
Charlemagne would have been a betrayal of all the Church of
Rome stood for. And had not the instrument been carefully prepared,
though primarily as a weapon against the East? The Donation of
Constantine was precisely the handle by which the emancipation of
the papacy from the clutches of the Eastern emperor could be
effected: and the threatening clutches of the Frankish king were a
sufficient justification for employing the same weapon against him.
The "vacancy" in the empire provided the pretext; Leo's trial by
Charlemagne two days before Christmas provided the additional

stimulus for the momentous action on Christmas Day—for the transfer of the empire from the Bosphorus to the Tiber, by making the Frank the *Imperator Romanorum*. The historic significance of the act is only heightened when this twofold objective is appraised: the coronation was aimed against the empire as well as against the Frankish king. The seat of the empire was where the pope wished it to be—the seat of the *Roman* empire was *Rome*, not Constantinople, not Aix-la-Chapelle.

It was a magnificent political and symbolic device which Leo adopted. There can be no doubt that the initiative lay in papal hands: the act was well prepared—the Romans knew exactly what they had to shout, although no pope had ever crowned an emperor in Rome. The accounts in the official papal book and in the Frankish annals are substantially the same: because the pope had put the crown on Charlemagne's head, the Romans acclaimed him, in accordance with the previous arrangements, "imperator Romanorum." This acclamation by the Romans was to announce publicly the meaning of the papal act. Charlemagne became, by virtue of the pope's action, "imperator Romanorum"; but he also had to be designated and named as such in a public manner by the Romans present. That all this must have been carefully arranged goes without saying: these previous arrangements, however, appear in the official papal accounts as the spontaneous inspiration of the Romans. Because the Romans—we follow the account—saw how much Charlemagne defended and loved the Roman Church and its vicar, they unanimously in a raised voice exclaimed, at the bidding of God and of St. Peter: "To Charles, the most pious Augustus crowned by God, the great and peace loving emperor, life and victory." It is plain that the "spontaneous inspiration" was well planned and need not detain us.

It is not, however, without significance that the Romans witnessing the act with their own eyes acclaim Charlemagne as "a Deo coronatus." And it is as a result of divine and Petrine inspiration that they shout thus. The significance of this lies in that the whole ceremony is presented as the working of the divine will—it is not the pope who crowned the Frank, but God Himself: "a Deo coronatus."

If we wish to understand this, we must keep in mind that, according to the papal standpoint, there was no difference at all between the function of the newly created emperor and that of the patrician of the Romans: he was the protector and defender of the Roman

Church. In both of our sources this vital point breaks through. The *Liber Pontificalis* declares that out of recognition for Charlemagne's *defence* of the Roman Church the Romans had acclaimed him emperor; according to the Frankish annals the patrician became absorbed in the emperor. And this is exactly what the papal book also says: "et ab omnibus constitutus est imperator Romanorum." This means that the patrician was now acclaimed or called —as the Frankish annals have it—or was "set up" as "emperor of the Romans" because the pope had crowned him: papal action preceded the acclamation—the Romans acclaimed the thus crowned Frank an "imperator" who had as a consequence of the papal coronation been raised from the office of patrician of the Romans to the dignity of the emperor of the Romans. The constitutive act was that of the pope: the acclamation derives its meaning from the papal act: the papal act is announced to the world. The patrician wears no crown; the emperor does, and he wears it because the pope has imposed it: the crowned emperor is acclaimed.

The "vacancy" on the imperial throne—and we take note that the increase of the indications pointing to fundamental changes coincides with Irene's rule as empress[4]—provided the pretext for transforming an office into a dignity: the office of the patrician was transformed into the dignity of Roman emperorship. Functionally, however, nothing changed, as far as papal intentions went: whether patrician or emperor his function was defence and protection of the Roman Church. Constitutionally, however, there was a radical change for there was now an emperor of the Romans where previously there had been none—the consequence was the emergence of the "problem of the two (Roman) emperors." Charlemagne's coronation was, so to speak, the final and solemn and public act by which the papacy emancipated itself from the constitutional framework of the Eastern empire. There remains to be answered the question, By what authority did the pope proceed in the manner in which he did?

If we keep in mind that according to the accepted doctrine all power comes from God; if we recall that ideologically there was no difference between the famous Gelasian statement and the Donation of Constantine; if we consider the function which, in the papal view, the (secular) Ruler was to play—if we duly appraise all this, it will not be too difficult to realize that the pope acted not

[4]The reference is to the unprecedented rule of a woman, the Empress Irene, 797–802.

only as the mediator between God and man in imposing the crown—hence Charlemagne is "a Deo coronatus"—but also as the dispenser of the highest available dignity and power (*potestas*), of Roman emperorship. In fact, the dignity and power conferred by the pope could be no other but a conceptually universal one: the Roman Church, being the epitome of universal Christianity, can confer through the pope only a universal Christian power: and the only universal power that was available at the time was that designated by the title "emperor of the Romans." Moreover, although the imperial crown was in Constantinople, it was there on sufferance by the pope (Silvester): not only was there no emperor now, but those emperors who had been there before were not worthy being called *Roman-Christian* emperors. For—we try to follow papal reasonings—these emperors had in fact constantly infringed the—for the papacy—most vital principle, that of the *principatus* of the Roman Church. With particular reference to this point Gelasius had declared that the emperor held his empire as a trust, as a *beneficium*, from God: but by demonstrably setting aside the divinely instituted papacy, the Eastern emperors had misused their trust—hence the pope considered himself entitled to withdraw his consent which by implication he had given to Constantine's taking his crown to Constantinople.

The emperors in the East, although ostentatiously styling themselves *Roman* emperors, had, by virtue of their opposition to the *Roman* Church, forfeited their claim to be *Christian* emperors. They were considered—as later terminology will have it—unsuitable emperors, and the papacy therefore was, always provided that the Donation was efficacious, entitled to transfer Roman emperorship from Constantinople to Rome: the Donation was the basis upon which Leo could proceed. This is nothing extraordinary, for, as we pointed out, the Donation was originally intended to be employed as a weapon against the East, so as to effect the emancipation of the papacy from the Eastern constitutional framework. And the possibility of a withdrawal of Roman emperorship from the East was as much inherent in the document as the papal consent to Constantine's taking the crown thither.

Gelasius had maintained that Christ was "Rex" and "Sacerdos" the "potestas regalis"—signifying the "Rex"—and the "auctoritas sacrata pontificum"—signifying the "Sacerdos"—were united in Him, but "by a marvellous dispensation" He had distinguished between the function of the priest and that of the king. It was

Christ's own act: Christian imperial power therefore originated in Christ. There was no possibility of asserting that the pope conferred imperial power: until his position as vicar of Christ was fully developed there was indeed no possibility for him to combine —like Christ—"potestas regalis" and "auctoritas sacrata"; therefore, there was also no possibility of conferring imperial power or of withdrawing it. This defect was made good by the Donation: as a consequence of Constantine's grant, the pope disposed of the crown, the external symbol of imperial power. And in this capacity Leo III acted on Christmas Day 800. Had not his predecessor, Adrian I, declared that the Roman Church was the "caput totius mundi," an obvious allusion to Gelasius's "mundus"—and was it not the same Adrian who quoted the Donation? The "mundus" could be nothing else but Christendom, of which the Roman Church was the epitome and head: Charlemagne should conquer the barbaric nations; he in fact was already hailed as *the* Christian Ruler, Christian, because the spiritual son of the *Roman* Church. The empire in the East, though so ostentatiously calling itself Roman and Christian, could not justify these appellations—Leo took the step which was, from the point of view of papal doctrine, wholly understandable. The Roman Church being the "caput" of the (Christian) universe ("Mundus") creates through the pope a universal (Christian) protector who alone deserves the dignity of an "emperor of the Romans." This is his dignity—his function is that of a protector and defender, in the Roman-papal sense: the *principatus* of the Roman Church over the ideational universal entity, the *corpus Christi* (the universal Church), can be exercised through the agency of an ideational universal *potestas*, the emperor of the Romans.

Friedrich Kempf
Miscellanea Historiae Pontificiae

Friedrich Kempf replies to Ullmann

For the place in the *Constitutum*[1] where Constantine attested that he had offered (Pope) Sylvester the imperial diadem and that he had refused the diadem . . . is, according to Ullmann, to be interpreted in the following manner: Constantine had taken back the diadem which he had offered to the Pope with the silent acquiescence of Sylvester and brought it to Byzantium. The Greek emperors therefore bore the symbols of world domination solely because the Pope allowed it. They were dependent on the Pope, for he could take away their claim to the crown by the same right as he formerly had granted it. If, however, the Empire itself, the highest pinnacle of worldly rule, was a gift of papal grace, a papal *beneficium*, then there was no such thing as secular government in its own right at all. What Gelasius had hinted at, in representing the empire as a God-given *beneficium*, now makes its appearance [in the eighth century] as so clearly developed a thesis that the very separation of powers which appears in Gelasius[2] is rendered obsolete. By virtue of the Donation of Constantine, the Pope disposes of the imperial crown, he alone is the true monarch; he alone can confer dominion over the world; and, in fact he creates in the Emperor merely a helper, merely a *defensor, advocatus ecclesiae Romanae,* not a monarch.

[1]The reference is to the "Donation of Constantine," a document written ca. 750–850 probably in the papal chancery, according to which the papacy was conceded, because Pope Sylvester I (314–335) had cured the Emperor Constantine of leprosy, temporal jurisdiction over Italy and most of Western Europe. This "Donation," which was widely used by papal apologists from the ninth century onwards as proof of the pope's temporal jurisdiction, was proved a palpable forgery by Lorenzo Valla in the fifteenth century. Ullmann often refers to it as the *Constitutum.*

[2]Pope from 492–496. He advanced the theory that within the Christian Commonwealth there were two spheres of authority, the spiritual and the secular, each entirely separate from the other, but should there be any conflict the spiritual authority must be superior, because the priest must answer to God for the souls of all, even those of kings.

SOURCE. Friedrich Kempf, "Die Päpstliche Gewalt in der mittelalterlichen Welt," in *Miscellanea Historiae Pontificiae,* XXI (1959), pp. 123–125, 162–165. Translated for this volume by Bennett D. Hill by permission of the publisher and the author.

The raison d'être for the Emperor is simply this protective function. Through the *Constitutum* the universality of Rome as Church and Rome as Empire are once and for all united. From this time on the political conception of imperial rule was an integral part of the papal theory of supremacy.

What the forgery had paved the way for spiritually became reality through Leo III—for Ullmann one of the most outstanding popes— who had indeed intended the role of Emperor for Charlemagne from the beginning; but he first really felt spurred to act in the matter when Charlemagne began to build a second Rome at Aachen. The weapon had long been ready in the *Constitutum,* which conferred the right of *Translatio Imperii* [the transference of the imperial power]. As executed in 800 this was directed both against the Byzantine Emperor and against Charlemagne; neither Byzantium nor Aachen was to be the seat of the Empire. Leo III succeeded, in this solemn act, in keeping the initiative completely in his own hands; since the coronation by the Pope was the truly constitutive act, which raised Charlemagne from Patricius to Emperor. The acclamation by the Roman people had only a declaratory significance.

Leo III regarded the Empire in the historical-political sense as a universal, world-controlling institution, but yet always under the true supposition that the raison d'être of the Empire consisted in the *defensio ecclesiae Romanae.* Considered functionally, there was for Leo no difference between *patricius Romanorum* and *imperator*: the Emperorship had merely a more universal character, the Emperor was a universal protector. What was involved was not independent monarchy, but simply a dependent office which, because of its universal character, only the Pope could confer. The fundamental idea of the *Constitutum* had triumphed: the only monarch in the Christian world was the Pope. . . .

It is certainly unnecessary to say much about Ullmann's inter- pretation of the *Constitutum* of Constantine, which makes the Pope the true world-monarch, and imperial rule into the papally con- ferred protective function of a mere *defensor, advocatus ecclesiae*; what is constructive in this train of thought, as well as its particular flaws, can be easily recognized. Rather, let us refer to two new works, which deriving from the true historical situation of the eighth century, throw new light on the *Constitutum.* Both arrive at a conclusion essentially in agreement with Caspar: that the forgery was a timely expression of the (papal) striving at that time to pre- serve an autonomous position between the great empires of the east and west; that the question at issue for the forger was the imperial position of the popes and the spiritual underpinning of the period in Roman history that elapsed from 754 to 800; and also that there is no direct link connecting the *Constitutum* to the imperial coronation, but rather that it was only the breakdown of the papal policy of autonomy under Leo III, which became final in 799 and which consequentially raised the idea of an imperial coronation.

The imperial coronation of Charlemagne is explained by the great majority of scholars quite otherwise than Ullmann, without producing new evidence or important new points of view, explains it. It is scarcely conceivable that prior to Christmas no discussions had been held with Charlemagne about the acceptance of the emperorship and [it is scarcely conceivable] that nothing had been positively concluded. The element of surprise may well have consisted for Charlemagne in the matter of the time and the mode and method of the conveyance of the crown.

Moreover, the parallels to be observed in the coronation proceedings [at Rome] with the customary ceremonial for an imperial coronation at Byzantium certainly do not allow one to make the coronation by Leo the constitutive act, and [the customary ceremonial does not allow one] to attribute only a declaratory significance to the acclamation of the Romans. For in Byzantium the constitutive act was *not* the coronation by the Patriarch, but rather the election by the people. Why, again, does Ullmann ignore the proskynesis [a bowing down, an act of deepest obeisance] carried out by the pope after the completed coronation, [an act] by which Leo III acknowledges himself to be the vassal of the Emperor?

Then, since the founding day of the Western Empire, certainly a Roman-papal and a Frankish interpretation [of this event] had stood in opposition to one another, and a quiet struggle arose in which the papacy occasionally relied on the *Constitutum* of Constantine. So perhaps Leo III did in 804, and almost certainly Stephen IV,[3] who in 816 put a "Constantine's Crown," which he had himself brought along, on the head of Louis the Pious. Thus through reference to [the events of Christmas Day] 800 the *Constitutum* acquired a new meaning, however we do not know what concrete inference the Papacy drew from this. That these inferences could reach all the way to the idea of a "Supreme Emperor" can indeed be admitted as a logical possibility; but the question

[3] Pope, 816–17.

remains whether at that time [of Leo III] this logical possibility was comprehended, or indeed could have been. . . .

The imperial coronation of Charlemagne created the supposition for the formation of the church's transposition-idea. . . . If Leo III and his successors had really held the view that in the year 800 the rule of the world, by virtue of the papal supremacy, had been transferred from the Greeks to the Franks, i.e. if the church's transposition-idea had already inspired the papacy at that time, then certainly this thought would have to be able to be found in the sources of the ninth century. In reality they hardly got beyond the first beginnings and they were still at this stage in the second half of the century. The transferral-idea is first clearly developed in the twelfth century, and even then it played only a subordinate role. Against these facts Ullmann's argument does not hold up, especially since his interpretation of the *Constitutum* is more than problematical and his reference to Stephen IV proves nothing. But here again certainly the backward looking element of his method is evident: a teaching which achieved the true hierocratic interpretation in the Roman Curia only in the time of Innocent IV[4] has been projected back into the time of Stephen IV.

[4]Pope, 1243–1254.

PART FOUR

The Age of the Gregorian Reform Movement

The Gregorian Reform takes its name from Pope Gregory VII (1073–1085), but it actually started about a quarter of a century before his pontificate. It was a movement beginning within the Church which had as its goal not only the centralization of the Church under the authority of the pope and the moral and intellectual regeneration of the clergy, but also the *libertas ecclesiae*—the freedom of the Church—by which was meant the freedom to obey the newly codified canon law, freedom from royal control and from interference by laymen. This last objective, in which the issue of lay investiture was a most important aspect, has frequently been considered the central part of the entire movement. While the basic ideas of the papal polemicists may not have been new in the eleventh century, historians no longer deny that the efforts of Gregory VII and his successors to put those ideas into practice constituted a serious departure from accepted tradition.

Consequently, in the history of the relations of Church and State in the Middle Ages, the century from roughly 1050 to 1150 was a revolutionary period. It was revolutionary, first, because papal theory sought to subordinate the temporal power of lay rulers to the sacerdotal authority of the papacy by depriving kings of their previously acknowledged spiritual character. Second, papal protagonists struck at the foundations of royal power when they attempted to abolish lay investiture, the practice of laymen investing bishops and abbots with the religious symbols of their offices—the ring (a sign of the bishop's union with his diocese) and the crozier or staff (the symbol of his pastoral authority). Investiture implied selection and appointment, and since many high ecclesiastical officials held offices in the government of feudal monarchies, the inability of secular

63

rulers to choose their public officials would have been disastrous for stable government. As is the case in most times of radical change, the age of the Gregorian Reform was a highly seminal period. The achievements and failures of the movement with regard to the "freedom of the Church" laid the ideological foundations for the mutual relations of Church and State for the next two centuries.

A rich body of documentary material on the controversy survives. The first section below sets forth the ideological basis of the papal reform, revealing the broad problem of the "freedom of the Church" and the related issue of lay investiture. In the second section, the Imperial or German phase of the conflict may be traced in the correspondence of King Henry IV (1056–1106) and Pope Gregory VII. Gregory's attempts to exercise jurisdiction over the Church in France, to reform it, and the general state of his relations with King Philip I (1060–1108) are clearly shown in the third section.

A protracted propoganda campaign over the juridical limits of papal and royal theocracy followed the initial dispute between the pope and the German emperor. For the Empire, the conflict over investitures was ultimately settled in 1122 by Pope Calixtus II (1119–1124) and the German Emperor Henry V (1106–1125), on the same terms as those by which agreement had already been reached between the papacy and the King of England in 1107. The Concordat of Worms (1122) comprised two separate declarations, with each party announcing concessions to the other. The emperor agreed to renounce the right to invest bishops with the ring and crozier, and bishops were to be selected according to canon law. But, since the lay rulers were permitted to be present at episcopal elections, or to nominate a candidate, or to receive or refuse the homage of new prelates for their fiefs, they still possessed an effective veto power over ecclesiastical appointments. The other issues of the Gregorian Reform Movement remained very much alive for at least another century.

Two significant discussions of the problem follow. In a model of careful, methodical scholarship, Karl F. Morrison examines the development of Gregory VII's thought. Z.N. Brooke, in his now classic monograph, "Lay Investiture and Its Relation to the Conflict of Empire and Papacy," emphasizes the relative unimportance of the issue of lay investiture in the entire struggle.

1 FROM H. Bettenson
Documents of the Christian Church

Decree on Papal Elections, 1059

. . . We (Pope Nicholas II)[1] decree and establish that, on the death of the pontiff of this Roman universal church, the cardinal bishops shall first confer with most diligent consideration and then shall summon the cardinal clergy to join them; and afterwards the rest of the clergy and people shall give their assent to the new election. That, lest the disease of venality creep in by any means, godly men shall take the chief part in the election of the pontiff, and the others shall follow their lead. This method of election is regular and in accordance with the rules and decrees of the Fathers . . . especially with the words of St. Leo: "No argument," he says, "will permit them to be considered bishops who have not been elected by the clergy, nor demanded by the people, nor consecrated by the bishops of the province with the approval of the metropolitan." But since the Apostolic See is raised above all churches in the world and therefore can have no metropolitan over it, the cardinal bishops without doubt perform the function of a metropolitan, when they raise the elected pontiff to the apostolic eminence. They shall elect someone from out of this [Roman] church, if a suitable candidate be found; if not, he shall be chosen from another church. Saving the honor and reverence due to our beloved son Henry, who at present is acknowledged King and, it

[1]Pope, 1059–1061.

SOURCE. H. Bettenson, *Documents of the Christian Church* (London: Oxford University Press, 1947), pp. 142–143. Reprinted by permission of the publisher.

is hoped, will be Emperor, by God's grace; as we have granted to him and to such of his successors as obtain this right in person from the apostolic see. But, if the perversity of evil and wicked men shall make it impossible to hold a pure, fair and free election in the city, the cardinal bishops with the godly clergy and catholic laymen, even though they be few, shall have the right and power to elect the pontiff of the Apostolic See in any place which they shall consider most convenient. After an election has been clearly made, if the fierceness of war or the malignant endeavors of any man shall prevent him who is elected from being enthroned on the apostolic chair according to custom, the elected shall nevertheless have authority as Pope to rule the holy Roman Church and to dispose of its resources, as we know that blessed Gregory did before his consecration. . . .

2 FROM *E. F. Henderson*
Select Historical Documents of the Middle Ages

The Dictate of the Pope which Emanated from the Papal Chancery under Gregory VII

That the Roman church was founded by God alone.

That the Roman pontiff alone can with right be called universal.

That he alone can depose or reinstate bishops.

That, in a council, his legate, even if a lower grade, is above all bishops, and can pass sentence of deposition against them.

That the pope may depose the absent.

That, among other things, we ought not to remain in the same house with those excommunicated by him.

That for him alone is it lawful, according to the needs of the time, to make new laws, to assemble together new congregations, to make an abbey of a canonry; and, on the other hand, to divide a rich bishopric and unite the poor ones.

That he alone may use the imperial insignia.

That of the pope alone all princes shall kiss the feet.

That his name alone shall be spoken in the churches.

That this is the only name in the world.

SOURCE. E. F. Henderson, *Select Historical Documents of the Middle Ages* (London: G. Bell & Sons, Ltd., 1965), pp. 366–367. Reprinted by permission of the publisher.

That it may be permitted to him to depose emperors.

That he may be permitted to transfer bishops if need be.

That he has power to ordain a clerk of any church he may wish.

That he who is ordained by him may *preside* over another church, but may not hold a subordinate position; and that such a one may not receive a higher grade from any bishop.

That no synod shall be called a general one without his order.

That no chapter and no book shall be considered canonical without his authority.

That a sentence passed by him may be retracted by no one; and that he himself, alone of all, may retract it.

That he himself may be judged by no one.

That no one shall dare to condemn one who appeals to the apostolic chair.

That to the latter should be referred the more important cases of every church.

That the Roman church has never erred; nor will it err to all eternity, the Scripture bearing witness.

That the Roman pontiff, if he have been canonically ordained, is undoubtedly made a saint by the merits of St. Peter; St. Ennodius, bishop of Pavia, bearing witness, and many holy fathers agreeing with him. As is contained in the decrees of St. Symmachus the pope.

That, by his command and consent, it may be lawful for subordinates to bring accusations.

That he may depose and reinstate bishops without assembling a synod.

That he who is not at peace with the Roman church shall not be considered catholic.

That he may absolve subjects from their fealty to wicked men.

3 FROM E. F. Henderson
Select Historical Documents of the Middle Ages

Gregory VII's Decrees on Lay Investiture[1]

Inasmuch as we have learned that, contrary to the establish-ments of the holy fathers, the investiture with churches is, in many places, performed by lay persons; and that from this cause many disturbances arise in the church by which the Christian religion is trodden under foot: we decree that no one of the clergy shall receive the investiture with a bishopric or abbey or church from the hand of an emperor or king or of any lay person, male or female. But if he shall presume to do so he shall clearly know that such investiture is bereft of apostolic authority, and that he himself shall lie under excommunication until fitting satisfaction shall have been rendered.

2. Decree of March 7th, 1080, forbidding the same

Following the statutes of the holy fathers, as, in the former councils which by the mercy of God we have held, we decreed con-cerning the ordering of ecclesiastical dignities, so also now we decree and confirm: that, if any one henceforth shall receive a bishopric or abbey from the hand of any lay person, he shall by no means be considered as among the number of the bishops or abbots; nor shall any hearing be granted him as bishop or abbot. Moreover we further deny to him the favour of St. Peter and the entry of the church, until, coming to his senses, he shall desert the place that he has taken by the crime of ambition as well as by that of disobedience —which is the sin of idolatry. In like manner also we decree con-cerning the inferior ecclesiastical dignities.

Likewise if any emperor, king, duke, margrave, count, or any one at all of the secular powers or persons, shall presume to per-form the investiture with bishoprics or with any ecclesiastical

---

[1]The text of Gregory's original prohibition against lay investiture, issued in February 1075, has been lost, but the essence of that document was repeated in his two later injunctions published in November 1078 and March 1080.

SOURCE. E. F. Henderson, *Select Historical Documents of the Middle Ages* (London: G. Bell & Sons, Ltd., 1965), pp. 365–366. Reprinted by permission of the publisher.

dignity,—he shall know that he is bound by the bonds of the same condemnátion. And, moreover, unless he come to his senses and relinquish to the church her own prerogative, he shall feel, in this present life, the divine displeasure as well with regard to his body as to his other belongings: in order that, at the coming of the Lord, his soul may be saved.

4 FROM *T. E. Mommsen and K. F. Morrison*
Imperial Lives and Letters of the Eleventh Century

Henry Confesses his Misdeed against the Church and asks Papal Support
(1073)

To the most watchful and zealous Lord Pope, Gregory, distinguished by heaven with the apostolic dignity, Henry, by the grace of God King of the Romans, sends the most faithful expression of due subservience.

Since, in order to continue rightly administered in Christ, the kingship and the priesthood are always in need of the strength which He delegates, it is surely fitting for them, my lord and most loving father, not to disagree with one another, but rather to cleave to each other, inseparably joined with the bond of Christ.

With God's consent we have held the office of kingship for some time now, but we have not shown to the priesthood the proper justice and honor in all things. To be sure, we have not borne in vain the avenging sword of the power given us by God; yet we have not always unsheathed it justly in judicial punishment against wrongdoers. Now, however, through divine mercy, we have been stung in some measure by remorse, and having turned against ourself in self-accusation, we confess our former sins to you, Most Indulgent Father, placing our hopes in the Lord that absolved by your apostolic authority we may be worthy of forgiveness.

Alas, we are guilty and wretched! Partly through the inclination of youthful pleasure, partly through the license of our mighty and imperious power, partly also through the seductive deception of those whose counsels we have followed, all too easily misled, we

SOURCE. T. E. Mommsen and K. F. Morrison, *Imperial Lives and Letters of the Eleventh Century* (New York: Columbia University Press, 1962), pp. 141–142. Reprinted by permission of the publisher and K. F. Morrison.

have sinned against heaven and before you, and now we are not worthy to be called your son. For not only have we usurped ecclesiastical properties, but we have also sold the churches themselves to unworthy men—men embittered with the gall of simony—who entered not by the door but by some other way; nor have we defended the churches as we should have. And now, since alone, without your authority, we cannot reform the churches, we earnestly seek your counsel together with your help in these matters as well as in all our affairs. We stand ready to keep your commands most zealously in every respect. And now especially for the church of Milan, which has fallen into error through our fault, we ask that it be corrected canonically by your apostolic stringency and that your authoritative judgment should then proceed to the correction of other churches.

Therefore, God willing, we will not fail you in anything, and we humbly beg you, O father, actively to stand beside us, showing mercy in all things. In a short time you will receive our letter with our most faithful men, from whom, God granting, you will hear more fully about those of our affairs which await further discussion.

5   FROM   *E. Emerton*
The Correspondence of Gregory VII

Gregory VII's Letter to Henry IV[1]

Gregory, bishop, servant of God's servants, to King Henry, greeting and the apostolic benediction—but with the understanding that he obeys the Apostolic See as becomes a Christian king.

Considering and weighing carefully to how strict a judge we must render an account of the stewardship committed to us by St. Peter, prince of the Apostles, we have hesitated to send you the apostolic benediction, since you are reported to be in voluntary communication with men who are under the censure of the Apostolic See and of a synod. If this is true, you yourself know that you cannot receive

---

[1] In 1075 Gregory wrote to Henry IV advising him to obey the papal decrees and warning him, for the first time threateningly, of the consequences of failing to do so.

SOURCE. E. Emerton, *The Correspondence of Gregory VII* (New York: Columbia University Press, 1932), pp. 86–89. Reprinted by permission of the publisher.

the favor of God nor the apostolic blessing unless you shall first put away those excommunicated persons and force them to do penance and shall yourself obtain absolution and forgiveness for your sin by due repentance and satisfaction. Wherefore we counsel Your Excellency, if you feel yourself guilty in this matter, to make your confession at once to some pious bishop who, with our sanction, may impose upon you a penance suited to the offense, may absolve you and with your consent in writing may be free to send us a true report of the manner of your penance.

We marvel exceedingly that you have sent us so many devoted letters and displayed such humility by the spoken words of your legates, calling yourself a son of our Holy Mother Church and subject to us in the faith, singular in affection, a leader in devotion, commending yourself with every expression of gentleness and reverence, and yet in action showing yourself most bitterly hostile to the canons and apostolic decrees in those duties especially required by loyalty to the Church. Not to mention other cases, the way you have observed your promises in the Milan affair, made through your mother and through bishops, our colleagues, whom we sent to you, and what your intentions were in making them is evident to all. And now, heaping wounds upon wounds, you have handed over the sees of Fermo and Spoleto—if indeed a church may be given by any human power—to persons entirely unknown to us, whereas it is not lawful to consecrate anyone except after probation and with due knowledge.

It would have been becoming to you, since you confess yourself to be a son of the Church, to give more respectful attention to the master of the Church, that is, to Peter, prince of the Apostles. To him, if you are of the Lord's flock, you have been committed for your pasture, since Christ said to him: "Peter, feed my sheep," and again: "To thee are given the keys of Heaven, and whatsoever thou shalt bind on earth shall be bound in Heaven and whatsoever thou shalt loose on earth shall be loosed in Heaven." Now, while we, unworthy sinner that we are, stand in his place of power, still whatever you send to us, whether in writing or by word of mouth, he himself receives, and while we read what is written or hear the voice of those who speak, he discerns with subtle insight from what spirit the message comes. Wherefore Your Highness should beware lest any defect of will toward the Apostolic See be found in your words or in your messages and should pay due reverence, not to us but to Almighty God, in all matters touching the welfare of the Christian faith and the status of the Church. And this we say although our Lord deigned to declare: "He who heareth you heareth me; and he who despiseth you despiseth me."

We know that one who does not refuse to obey God in those matters in which we have spoken according to the statutes of the holy fathers does not scorn to observe our admonitions even as if he had received them from the lips of the Apostle himself. For if our Lord, out of reverence for the chair of Moses, commanded the Apostles to observe the teaching of the scribes and pharisees who sat thereon, there can be no doubt that the apostolic and gospel teaching, whose seat and foundation is Christ, should be accepted and maintained by those who are chosen to the service of teaching.

At a synod held at Rome during the current year, and over which Divine Providence willed us to preside, several of your subjects being present, we saw that the order of the Christian religion had long been greatly disturbed and its chief and proper function, the redemption of souls, had fallen low and through the wiles of the Devil had been trodden under foot. Startled by this danger and by the manifest ruin of the Lord's flock we returned to the teaching of the holy fathers, declaring no novelties nor any inventions of our own, but holding that the primary and only rule of discipline and the well-trodden way of the saints should again be sought and followed, all wandering paths to be abandoned. For we know that there is no other way of salvation and eternal life for the flock of Christ and their shepherds except that shown by him who said: "I am the door and he who enters by me shall be saved and shall find pasture." This was taught by the Apostles and observed by the holy fathers and we have learned it from the Gospels and from every page of Holy Writ.

This edict [against lay investiture], which some who place the honor of men above that of God call an intolerable burden, we, using the right word, call rather a truth and a light necessary for salvation, and we have given judgment that it is to be heartily accepted and obeyed, not only by you and your subjects but by all princes and peoples who confess and worship Christ—though it is our especial wish and would be especially fitting for you, that you should excel others in devotion to Christ as you are their superior in fame, in station and in valor.

Nevertheless, in order that these demands may not seem to you too burdensome or unfair we have sent you word by your own liegemen not to be troubled by this reform of an evil practice but to send us prudent and pious legates from your own people. If these can show in any reasonable way how we can moderate the decision of the holy fathers [at the Council] saving the honor of the eternal king and without peril to our own soul, we will condescend to hear their counsel. It would in fact have been the fair thing for you, even if you had not been so graciously admonished, to make reasonable inquiry of us in what respect we had offended you or assailed your honor, before you proceeded to violate the apostolic decrees. But how little you cared for our warnings or for doing right was shown by your later actions.

However, since the long-enduring patience of God summons you to improvement, we hope that with increase of understanding your heart and mind may be turned to obey the commands of God. We warn you with a father's love that you accept the rule of Christ, that you consider the peril of preferring your own honor to his, that you do not hamper by your actions the freedom of that Church which he deigned to bind to himself as a bride by a divine union, but, that she may increase as greatly as possible, you will begin to lend to Almighty God and to St. Peter, by whom also your own glory may merit increase, the aid of your valor by faithful devotion.

6 FROM *T. E. Mommsen and K. F. Morrison*
Imperial Lives and Letters of the Eleventh Century

Letter from Henry IV to Gregory VII[1]

Henry, King not by usurpation, but by the pious ordination of God, to Hildebrand, now not Pope, but false monk:

You have deserved such a salutation as this because of the confusion you have wrought; for you left untouched no order of the Church which you could make a sharer of confusion instead of honor, of malediction instead of benediction.

[1] Letter of Henry bitterly condemning Gregory for the disorders into which he has thrown the Church and ordering him to give up the papacy (January 1076).

SOURCE. T. E. Mommsen and K. F. Morrison, *Imperial Lives and Letters of the Eleventh Century* (New York: Columbia University Press, 1962), pp. 150–151, 147–149. Reprinted by permission of the publisher and K. F. Morrison.

For to discuss a few outstanding points among many: Not only have you dared to touch the rectors of the holy Church—the archbishops, the bishops, and the priests, anointed of the Lord as they are—but you have trodden them under foot like slaves who know not what their lord may do. In crushing them you have gained for yourself acclaim from the mouth of the rabble. You have judged that all these know nothing, while you alone know everything. In any case, you have sedulously used this knowledge not for edification, but for destruction, so greatly that we may believe Saint Gregory, whose name you have arrogated to yourself, rightly made this prophesy of you when he said: "From the abundance of his subjects, the mind of the prelate is often exalted, and he thinks that he has more knowledge than anyone else, since he sees that he has more power than anyone else."

And we, indeed, bore with all these abuses, since we were eager to preserve the honor of the Apostolic See. But you construed our humility as fear, and so you were emboldened to rise up even against the royal power itself, granted to us by God. You dared to threaten to take the kingship away from us—as though we had received the kingship from you, as though kingship and empire were in your hand and not in the hand of God.

Our Lord, Jesus Christ, has called us to kingship, but has not called you to the priesthood. For you have risen by these steps: namely, by cunning, which the monastic profession abhors, to money; by money to favor; by favor to the sword. By the sword you have come to the throne of peace, and from the throne of peace you have destroyed the peace. You have armed subjects against their prelates; you who have not been called by God have taught that our bishops who have been called by God are to be spurned; you have usurped for laymen the bishops' ministry over priests, with the result that these laymen depose and condemn the very men whom the laymen themselves received as teachers from the hand of God, through the imposition of the hands of bishops.

You have also touched me, one who, though unworthy, has been anointed to kingship among the anointed. This wrong you have done to me, although as the tradition of the holy Fathers has taught, I am to be judged by God alone and am not to be deposed for any crime unless—may it never happen—I should deviate from the Faith. For the prudence of the holy bishops entrusted the judgment and the deposition even of Julian the Apostate not to themselves, but to God alone. The true pope Saint Peter also exclaims,

"Fear God, honor the king." You, however, since you do not fear God, dishonor me, ordained of Him.

Wherefore, when Saint Paul gave no quarter to an angel from heaven if the angel should preach heterodoxy, he did not except you who are now teaching heterodoxy throughout the earth. For he says, "If anyone, either I or an angel from heaven, preach any other gospel unto you than that which we have preached unto you, let him be accursed." Descend, therefore, condemned by this anathema and by the common judgment of all our bishops and of ourself. Relinquish the Apostolic See which you have arrogated. Let another mount the throne of Saint Peter, another who will not cloak violence with religion but who will teach the pure doctrine of Saint Peter.

I, Henry, King by the grace of God, together with all our bishops, say to you: Descend! Descend!

Letter from the German Bishops to Gregory VII[2]

Siegfried, archbishop of Mainz, Udo of Trier, William of Utrecht, Herman of Metz, Henry of Liége, Ricbert of Verden, Bido of Toul, Hozeman of Speier, Burchard of Halberstadt, Werner of Strassburg, Burchard of Basel, Otto of Constance, Adalbero of Würzburg, Rupert of Bamberg, Otto of Regensburg, Egilbert of Freising, Ulric of Eichstätt, Frederick of Münster, Eilbert of Minden, Hezilo of Hildesheim, Benno of Osnabrück, Eppo of Naumburg, Imadus of Paderborn, Tiedo of Brandenburg, Burchard of Lausanne, and Bruno of Verona, to Brother Hildebrand:

When you had first usurped the government of the Church, we knew well how, with your accustomed arrogance, you had presumed to enter so illicit and nefarious an undertaking against human and divine law. We thought, nevertheless, that the pernicious beginnings of your administration ought to be left unnoticed in prudent silence. We did this specifically in the hope that such criminal beginnings would be emended and wiped away somewhat by the probity and industry of your later rule. But now, just as the deplorable state of the universal Church cries out and laments, through the increasing wickedness of your actions and decrees, you are woefully and stubbornly in step with your evil beginnings.

[2]In this letter, undoubtedly written at the command of the Emperor and simultaneously with it (above), the German bishops at the Synod of Worms (January 24, 1076) accuse Gregory of grave crimes and renounce their allegiance/obedience to him.

Our Lord and Redeemer impressed the goodness of peace and love upon his Faithful as their distinctive character, a fact to which there are more testimonies than can be included in the brevity of a letter. But by way of contrast, you have inflicted wounds with proud cruelty and cruel pride you are eager for profane innovations, you delight in a great name rather than in a good one, and with unheard-of self-exaltation, like a standard bearer of schism, you distend all the limbs of the Church which before your times led a quiet and tranquil life, according to the admonition of the Apostle. Finally, the flame of discord, which you stirred up through terrible factions in the Roman church, you spread with raging madness through all the churches of Italy, Germany, Gaul, and Spain. For you have taken from the bishops, so far as you could, all that power which is known to have been divinely conferred upon them through the grace of the Holy Spirit, which works mightily in ordinations. Through you all administration of ecclesiastical affairs has been assigned to popular madness. Since some now consider no one a bishop or priest save the man who begs that office of Your Arrogance with a most unworthy servility, you have shaken into pitiable disorder the whole strength of the apostolic institution and that most comely distribution of the limbs of Christ, which the Doctor of the Gentiles so often commends and teaches. And so through these boastful decrees of yours—and this cannot be said without tears—the name of Christ has all but perished. Who, however, is not struck dumb by the baseness of your arrogant usurpation of new power, power not due to you, to the end that you may destroy the rights due the whole brotherhood? For you assert that if any sin of one of our parishioners comes to your notice, even if only by rumor, none of us has any further power to bind or to loose the party involved, for you alone may do it, or one whom you delegate especially for this purpose. Can anyone schooled in sacred learning fail to see how this assertion exceeds all madness?

We have judged that it would be worse than any other evil for us to allow the Church of God to be so gravely jeopardized—nay rather, almost destroyed—any longer through these and other presumptuous airs of yours. Therefore, it has pleased us to make known to you by the common counsel of all of us something which we have left unsaid until now: that is, the reason why you cannot now be, nor could you ever have been, the head of the Apostolic See.

In the time of the Emperor Henry [III] of good memory, you

bound yourself with a solemn oath that for the lifetime of that Emperor and for that of his son, our lord the glorious King who now presides at the summit of affairs, you would neither obtain the papacy yourself nor suffer another to obtain it, insofar as you were able, without the consent and approbation either of the father in his lifetime or the son in his. And there are many bishops today who were witnesses of this solemn oath, who saw it then with their own eyes and heard it with their own ears. Remember also that in order to remove jealous rivalry when ambition for the papacy tickled some of the cardinals, you obligated yourself with a solemn oath never to assume the papacy both on the plea and on the condition that they did the same thing themselves. We have seen in what a holy way you observed each of these solemn vows. Again, when a synod was celebrated in the time of Pope Nicholas [II], in which one hundred twenty-five bishops sat together, it was decided and decreed under anathema that no one would ever become pope except by the election of the cardinals and the approbation of the people, and by the consent and authority of the king. And of this council and decree, you yourself were author, advocate, and subscriber.

In addition to this, you have filled the entire Church, as it were, with the stench of the gravest of scandals, rising from your intimacy and cohabitation with another's wife who is more closely integrated into your household than is necessary. In this affair, our sense of decency is affected more than our legal case, although the general complaint is sounded everywhere that all judgments and all decrees are enacted by women in the Apostolic See, and ultimately that the whole orb of the Church is administered by this new senate of women. For no one can complain adequately of the wrongs and the abuse suffered by the bishops, whom you call most undeservedly sons of whores and other names of this sort.

Since your accession was tainted by such great perjuries, since the Church of God is imperiled by so great a tempest arising from abuse born of your innovations, and since you have degraded your life and conduct by such multifarious infamy, we declare that in the future we shall observe no longer the obedience which we have not promised to you. And since none of us, as you have publicly declared, has hitherto been a bishop to you, you also will now be pope to none of us.

7 FROM

H. Bettenson
Documents of the Christian Church

Excommunication[1]

Blessed Peter, chief of the apostles, incline thine holy ears to us, I pray, and hear me, thy servant, whom from infancy thou hast nourished and till this day hast delivered from the hand of the wicked, who have hated and do hate me for my faithfulness to thee. . . . Especially to me, as thy representative, has been committed, and to me by thy grace has been given by God the power of binding and loosing in heaven and on earth. Relying, then, on this belief, for the honor and defense of thy Church and in the name of God Almighty, the Father, the Son and the Holy Ghost, through thy power and authority, I withdraw the government of the whole kingdom of the Germans and of Italy from Henry the King, son of Henry the Emperor. For he has risen up against thy Church with unheard of arrogance. And I absolve all Christians from the bond of the oath which they have made to him or shall make. And I forbid anyone to serve him as king. For it is right that he who attempts to diminish the honor of thy Church, shall himself lose the honor which he seems to have. And since he has scorned to show Christian obedience, and has not returned to the Lord whom he has deserted—holding intercourse with the excommunicate; committing many iniquities; despising my warnings, which, as thou art my witness, I have sent to him for his salvation, separating himself from thy Church and trying to divide it—on thy behalf I bind him with the bond of anathema. Trusting in thee I thus bind him that the peoples may know and acknowledge that thou art Peter and that on thy rock the Son of the living God has built His Church and that the gates of hell shall not prevail against it.

---

[1]The strong German attacks on Gregory and his policies were countered by the promised papal pronouncement of excommunication and the deposition of Henry IV (February 1076).

SOURCE. H. Bettenson, *Documents of the Christian Church* (London: Oxford University Press, 1947), pp. 146–147. Reprinted by permission of the publisher.

8 FROM
E. Emerton
The Correspondence of Gregory VIII

Letter to the German Princes[1]

Whereas, for love of justice you have made common cause with us and taken the same risks in the warfare of Christian service, we have taken special care to send you this accurate account of the king's penitential humiliation, his absolution and the course of the whole affair from his entrance into Italy to the present time.

According to the arrangement made with the legates sent to us by you we came to Lombardy about twenty days before the date at which some of your leaders were to meet us at the pass and waited for their arrival to enable us to cross over into that region. But when the time had elapsed and we were told that on account of the troublous times—as indeed we well believe—no escort could be sent to us, having no other way of coming to you we were in no little anxiety as to what was our best course to take.

Meanwhile we received certain information that the king was on the way to us. Before he entered Italy he sent us word that he would make satisfaction to God and St. Peter and offered to amend his way of life and to continue obedient to us, provided only that he should obtain from us absolution and the apostolic blessing. For a long time we delayed our reply and held long consultations, reproaching him bitterly through messengers back and forth for his outrageous conduct, until finally, of his own accord and without any show of hostility or defiance, he came with a few followers to the fortress of Canossa where we were staying. There, on three successive days, standing before the castle gate, laying aside all royal insignia, barefooted and in coarse attire, he ceased not with many tears to beseech the apostolic help and comfort until all who were present or who had heard the story were so moved by pity and

[1]In a letter to the German princes, Pope Gregory described the celebrated incident at Canossa (January 1077). It is not without significance that the letter is addressed to the princes, who, in supporting the pope, had strengthened their own feudal independence, and not to churchmen, who backed the emperor.

SOURCE. E. Emerton, *The Correspondence of Gregory VIII* (New York: Columbia University Press, 1932), pp. 111–112. Reprinted by permission of the publisher.

compassion that they pleaded his cause with prayers and tears. All marveled at our unwonted severity, and some even cried out that we were showing, not the seriousness of apostolic authority, but rather the cruelty of a savage tyrant.

At last, overcome by his persistent show of penitence and the urgency of all present, we released him from the bonds of anathema and received him into the grace of Holy Mother Church, accepting from him the guarantees described below, confirmed by the signatures of the abbot of Cluny, of our daughters, the Countess Matilda and the Countess Adelaide, and other princes, bishops and laymen who seemed to be of service to us.

And now that these matters have been arranged, we desire to come over into your country at the first opportunity, that with God's help we may more fully establish all matters pertaining to the peace of the Church and the good order of the land. For we wish you clearly to understand that, as you may see in the written guarantees, the whole negotiation is held in suspense, so that our coming and your unanimous consent are in the highest degree necessary. Strive, therefore, all of you, as you love justice, to hold in good faith the obligations into which you have entered. Remember that we have not bound ourselves to the king in any way except by frank statement—as our custom is—that he may expect our aid for his safety and his honor, whether through justice or through mercy, and without peril to his soul or to our own.

9 FROM *T. E. Mommsen and K. F. Morrison*
Imperial Lives and Letters of the Eleventh Century

Henry's Oath at Canossa

Oath of Henry, King of the Germans.

Before the date the Lord Pope Gregory is to set, I, King Henry, shall bring about justice according to his judgment or harmony according to his counsel with regard to the complaint and objection now being made against me by archbishops, bishops, dukes, counts, the other princes in the realm of the Germans, and those who follow

SOURCE. T. E. Mommsen and K. F. Morrison, *Imperial Lives and Letters of the Eleventh Century* (New York: Columbia University Press, 1962), p. 156. Reprinted by permission of the publisher.

them by reason of the same objection. If a concrete obstacle hinder me or him, I shall be ready to do the same when that hindrance has been overcome. Also, if the same Lord Pope Gregory should wish to go beyond the mountains to other lands, he, those who are among his retainers or guards, and those who are sent by him or come to him from any region, will be safe in coming, staying, and going thence, from any harm to life and limb and from capture by me and by those whom I can control. Moreover, no other difficulty prejudicial to his honor will occur with my assent; and should any person create one for him, I shall help him [Gregory] in good faith, according to my ability.

Done at Canossa, 28 January, the fifteenth Indiction.

10 FROM   *H. Bettenson*
Documents of the Christian Church

Letter to the Bishop of Metz[1]

Bishop Gregory, servant of the servants of God, to his beloved brother in Christ, Hermann, bishop of Metz, greeting and apostolic benediction. It is doubtless owing to a dispensation of God that, as we learn, thou art ready to endure trials and dangers in defense of the truth. . . . Thy request, indeed, to be aided, as it were, by our writings and fortified against the madness of those who babble forth with impious tongue that the authority of the holy and apostolic see had no authority to excommunicate Henry—a man who despises the Christian law; a destroyer of the churches and of the empire; a patron and companion of heretics—or to absolve anyone from the oath of fealty to him, seems to us to be hardly necessary when so many and such absolutely decisive warrants are to be found in the pages of Holy Scripture. Nor do we believe, indeed, that those who (heaping up for themselves damnation) impudently detract from the truth and contradict it have added these assertions

[1]In a long letter to the Bishop of Metz, Gregory explained and defended his policy and position (1081).

SOURCE. H. Bettenson, *Documents of the Christian Church* (London: Oxford University Press, 1947), pp. 147–155. Reprinted by permission of the publisher.

to the audacity of their defense so much from ignorance as from a certain madness.

For, to cite a few passages from among many, who does not know the words of our Lord and Saviour Jesus Christ who says, in the gospel: "Thou art Peter and upon this rock will I build my church, and the gates of hell shall not prevail against it; and I will give unto thee the keys of the kingdom of Heaven; and whatsoever thou shalt bind upon earth shall be bound also in Heaven, and whatsoever thou shalt loose upon earth shall be loosed also in Heaven?" [Matthew xvi. 18, 19.] Are kings excepted here? Or are they not included among the sheep which the Son of God committed to St. Peter? Who, I ask, in view of this universal concession of the power of binding and loosing, can think that he is withdrawn from the authority of St. Peter, unless, perhaps, that unhappy man who is unwilling to bear the yoke of the Lord and subjects himself to the burden of the devil, refusing to be among the number of Christ's sheep? It will help him little to his wretched liberty that he shake from his proud neck the divinely granted power of Peter. . . .

The holy Fathers, as well in general councils as in their writings and doings, have called the Holy Roman Church the universal mother, accepting and serving with great veneration this institution founded by the divine will, this pledge of a dispensation to the church, this privilege entrusted in the beginning and confirmed to St. Peter the chief of the apostles. And even as they accepted its statements in confirmation of their faith and of the doctrines of holy religion, so also they received its judgments—consenting in this, and agreeing as it were with one spirit and one voice: that all greater matters and exceptional cases, and judgments over all churches, ought to be referred to it as to a mother and a head; that from it there was no appeal; that no one should or could retract or reverse its decisions. . . .

Is it not clearly pitiful madness for a son to attempt to subject to himself his father, a pupil his master; and for one to bring into his power and bind with iniquitous bonds him by whom he believes that he himself can be bound and loosed not only on earth but also in Heaven? This the Emperor Constantine the Great, lord of all the kings and princes of nearly the whole world, plainly understood— as the blessed Gregory reminds us in a letter to the emperor Maurice, when, sitting last after all the bishops in the holy council of Nicaea, he presumed to give no sentence of judgment over them, but addressed them as gods and decreed that they should not be subject to his judgment but that he should be dependent upon their will. . . . Many pontiffs have excommunicated kings or emperors. For, if particular examples of such princes is needed, the blessed pope Innocent excommunicated the emperor Arcadius for consenting that St. John Chrysostom should be expelled from his see. Likewise another Roman pontiff, Zacchary, deposed a king of the Franks, not so much for his iniquities as because he was not fitted to exercise so great power. And in his stead he set up Pepin, father of the emperor Charles the Great, in his place—releasing all the Franks from the oath of fealty which they had sworn him. As, indeed, the holy Church frequently does by its authority when it absolves servitors from the fetters of an oath sworn to such bishops as, by apostolic sentence, are deposed from their pontifical rank. And the blessed Ambrose—who, although a saint, was still not bishop over the whole Church—excommunicated and excluded from the Church the Emperor Theodosius the Great for a fault which, by other priests, was not regarded as very grave. He shows, too, in his writings that gold does not so much excel lead in value as the priestly dignity transcends the royal power; speaking thus towards the beginning of his pastoral letter: "The honor and sublimity of bishops, brethren, is beyond all comparisons. If one should compare them to resplendent kings and diademed princes it would be far less worthy than if one compared the base metal lead to gleaming gold. For, indeed, one can see how the necks of kings and princes are bowed before the knees of priests; and how, having kissed their right hands, they believe themselves strengthened by their prayers." And a little later: "Ye should know, brethren, that we have mentioned all this to show that nothing can be found in this world more lofty than priests or more sublime than bishops."

Furthermore every Christian king, when he comes to die, seeks as a pitiful suppliant the aid of a priest, that he may escape hell's prison, may pass from the darkness into the light, and at the judgment of God may appear absolved from the bondage of his sins. Who, in his last hour (what layman, not to speak of priests), has ever implored the aid of an earthly king for the salvation of his soul? And what king or emperor is able, by reason of the office he holds, to rescue a Christian from the power of the devil through holy baptism, to number him among the sons of God, and to fortify him with the divine unction? Who of them can by his own words make the body and blood of our Lord,—the greatest act in the

Christian religion? Or who of them possesses the power of binding and loosing in heaven and on earth? From all of these considerations it is clear how greatly the priestly office excels in power.

Who of them can ordain a single clerk in the Holy Church, much less depose him for any fault? For in the orders of the Church a greater power is needed to depose than to ordain. Bishops may ordain other bishops, but can by no means depose them without the authority of the apostolic see. Who, therefore, of even moderate understanding, can hesitate to give priests the precedence over kings? Then, if kings are to be judged by priests for their sins, by whom can they be judged with better right than by the Roman pontiff?

In short, any good Christians may far more properly be considered kings than may bad princes. For the former, seeking the glory of God, strictly govern themselves, whereas the latter, seeking the things which are their own and not the things of God, are enemies to themselves and tyrannical oppressors of others. Faithful Christians are the body of the true king, Christ; evil rulers, that of the devil. The former rule themselves in the hope that they will eternally reign with the Supreme Emperor, but the sway of the latter ends in their destruction and eternal damnation with the prince of darkness, who is king over all the sons of pride.

It is certainly not strange that wicked bishops are of one mind with a bad king, whom they love and fear for the honors which they have wrongfully obtained from him. Such men simoniacally ordain whom they please and sell God even for a paltry sum. As even the elect are indissolubly united with their Head, so also the wicked are inescapably leagued with him who is the head of evil, their chief purpose being to resist the good. But surely we ought not so much to denounce them as to mourn for them with tears and lamentations, beseeching God Almighty to snatch them from the snares of Satan in which they are held captive, and after their peril to bring them at last to a knowledge of the truth.

We refer to those kings and emperors who, too much puffed up by worldly glory, rule not for God but for themselves. Now, since it belongs to our office to admonish and encourage everyone according to the rank or dignity which he enjoys, we endeavour, by God's grace, to arm emperors and kings and other princes with the weapon of humility, that they may be able to allay the waves of the sea and the floods of pride. For we know that earthly glory and the cares of this world usually tempt men to pride, especially those in authority. So that they neglect humility and seek their own glory, desiring to lord it over their brethren. Therefore it is of especial advantage for emperors and kings, when their minds tend to be puffed up and to delight in their own glory, to discover a way of humbling themselves, and to realize that what causes their complacency is the thing which should be feared above all else. Let them, therefore, diligently consider how perilous and how much to be feared is the royal or imperial dignity. For very few are saved of those who enjoy it; and those who, through the mercy of God, do come to salvation are not so glorified in the Holy Church by the judgment of the Holy Spirit as are many poor people. For, from the beginning of the world until our own times, in the whole of authentic history we do not find seven emperors or kings whose lives were as distinguished for religion and so adorned by miracles of power as those of an innumerable multitude who despised the world—although we believe many of them to have found mercy in the presence of God Almighty. For what emperor or king was ever so distinguished by miracles as were St. Martin, St. Antony and St. Benedict—not to mention the apostles and martyrs? And what emperor or king raised the dead, cleansed lepers, or healed the blind? See how the Holy Church praises and venerates the Emperor Constantine of blessed memory, Theodosius and Honorius, Charles and Louis as lovers of justice, promoters of the Christian religion, defenders of the churches: it does not, however, declare them to have been resplendent with such glorious miracles. Moreover, to how many kings or emperors has the Holy Church ordered chapels or altars to be dedicated, or masses to be celebrated in their honor? Let kings and other princes fear lest the more they rejoice at being placed over other men in this life, the more they will be subjected to eternal fires. For of them it is written: "The powerful shall powerfully suffer torments." And they are about to render account to God for as many men as they have had subjects under their dominion. But if it be no little task for any private religious man to guard his own soul: how much labor will there be for those who are rulers over many thousands of souls? Moreover, if the judgment of the Holy Church severely punishes a sinner for the slaying of one man, what will become of those who, for the sake of worldly glory, hand over many thousands to death? And such persons, although after having slain many they often say with their lips "I have sinned," nevertheless rejoice in their hearts at the extension of their (so-called) fame. They do not regret what they have done. Nor are they grieved at having sent their brethren down to Tartarus. As long as they do not repent with their whole heart, nor agree to give up what they have acquired or kept through bloodshed, their repentance remains without the true fruit of penitence before God.

Therefore they should greatly fear and often call to mind what we have said above, that out of the innumerable host of kings in all countries from the beginning of the world, very few are found to have been holy; whereas in one single see—the Roman—of the successive bishops from the time of blessed Peter the Apostle, nearly one hundred are counted amongst the most holy. And why is this, unless because kings and princes, enticed by vain glory, prefer, as has been said, their own things to things spiritual, whereas the bishops of the Church, despising vain glory, prefer God's will to earthly things ? . . .

Therefore let those whom Holy Church, of its own will and after proper counsel, not for transitory glory but for the salvation of many, calls to have rule or dominion, humbly obey. And let them always beware in that point as to which St. Gregory in that same pastoral book bears witness: "Indeed, when a man disdains to be like to men, he is made like to an apostate angel. Thus Saul, after having possessed the merit of humility, came to be swollen with pride when at the summit of power. Through humility, indeed, he was advanced; through pride, rejected—God being witness who said: 'When thou wast small in thine own eyes, did I not make thee head over the tribes of Israel?'" And a little further on: "Moreover, strange to say, when he was small in his own eyes he was great in the eyes of God; but when he seemed great in his own eyes he was small in the eyes of God." Let them also carefully retain what God says in the gospel: "I seek not my own glory"; and, "He who will be the first among you shall be the servant of all." Let them always prefer the honor of God to their own; let them cherish and guard justice by observing the rights of every man; let them not walk in the counsel of the ungodly but, with an assenting heart, always consort with good men. Let them not seek to subject to themselves or to subjugate the Holy Church as a handmaid; but above all let them strive, by recognizing the teachers and fathers, to render due honor to the eyes of the Church—the priests of God. For if we are ordered to honor our fathers and mothers after the flesh—how much more our spiritual ones! And if he who has cursed his father or mother after the flesh is to be punished with death— what does he merit who curses his spiritual father or mother? Let them not, led astray by worldly love, strive to place one of their own sons over the flock for which Christ poured forth His blood, if they can find someone who is better and more useful than he: lest, loving their son more than God, they inflict the greatest damage on the Holy Church. For he who neglects to provide to the best of his ability for such a want—and, one might say, necessity—of Holy Mother Church is openly convicted of not loving God and his neighbor as a Christian should.

For if this virtue, love, has been neglected, no matter what good anyone does he shall be without any fruit of salvation. And so by humbly doing these things, and by observing the love of God and of their neighbor as they ought, they may hope for the mercy of Him who said: "Learn of Me, for I am meek and lowly of heart." If they have humbly imitated Him they shall pass from this servile and transitory kingdom to a true kingdom of liberty and eternity.

11 FROM   Z. N. Brooke
Lay Investiture and its Relation to the Conflict of Empire and Papacy

Among the many issues at stake between the ecclesiastical and the secular authorities in the Middle Ages, there is none that has been given so dramatic a history as that of Lay Investiture during the brief period of its existence; its whole story is confined within the space of fifty years, from the first papal prohibition of it in 1075 to the settlement at Worms in 1122. There was a short prologue before 1075: papal decrees in 1059 and 1063, without indeed mentioning the word "investiture," had prepared the way for Gregory VII's decree; and an unofficial attack on it had been opened, probably in 1058, by Cardinal Humbert in his *liber adversus simoniacos*, followed a few years later by Peter Damian. There was no epilogue after 1122. The canonists registered the decrees, and Gratian in his *Decretum* published Gregory VII's canons of 1078 and 1080 and also canons of Paschal II, but by this time it was no longer a live issue. The lay power had surrendered the right to

SOURCE. Z. N. Brooke, "Lay Investiture and its Relation to the Conflict of Empire and Papacy," in *Proceedings of the British Academy*, XXV (1939), pp. 217–244. Reprinted by permission.

invest with ring and staff, and made no effort to revive the practice. Its sudden emergence, its sudden disappearance, alike distinguish it from other topics of controversy between the *regnum* and the *sacerdotium*. But in that controversy it has been given a peculiar, though as I consider a spurious, significance: during the half-century of its existence Empire and Papacy were engaged in almost continuous conflict, and this half-century is known in history as the period of the Investiture Struggle, the War of the Investitures.

Now, so far as the first part of that period is concerned, that is to say down to the death of Henry IV in 1106, it should be obvious that the struggle is not about investitures at all. The utterances of the two protagonists, the pamphlet literature of their supporters, make clear what was at stake. It was a struggle for supremacy between the *regnum* and the *sacerdotium*, between the heads of the secular and ecclesiastical departments, each side claiming that its power derives from God and that it has the right to judge and depose the other, while itself subject to no human judgement but to God alone. The settlement of this issue would automatically carry with it the settlement of all minor issues, such as lay investiture, which, in all their attacks upon one another and justifications of their own conduct, neither Henry nor Gregory troubled to mention, save for a brief reference to it in Gregory's letter to Henry in December 1075. However, a contest fought out over a supreme issue such as ultimate sovereignty will usually be provoked by a concrete case in which that sovereignty is concerned. Was Gregory VII's decree against lay investiture, as has so often been stated, the concrete case which led to the breach between him and the king? This view is undoubtedly a plausible one. The decree was issued in Lent 1075 and it was followed, in less than a year, by open warfare between the two powers. The conflict was practially continuous, for though interrupted by Henry IV's death in 1106 it was resumed almost immediately. The final settlement in 1122 was over the question of investiture; if this was the issue which was settled by the terms of peace, surely this was the issue about which the two powers had come to war.

Plausible as this reasoning is, it is unsound. The crisis in the relations between king and Pope occurred after, but not immediately after, the investiture decree; some nine months intervened, and during six of these at least relations between Gregory and Henry remained quite cordial. The breach happened after the decree, not because of it. Secondly, the interruption at 1106 was of short duration, but of the first importance. It was not a continuous struggle from 1076 to 1122; one contest ended in 1106 and another, a different one, began. The settlement in 1122 was a settlement of the issues raised in 1106, not of the much more important issue that was at stake in 1076. Contemporaries of the second struggle, looking back rightly to Gregory's decree as the source of their quarrel, might regard the contest as a continuous one from that point; contemporaries of the first struggle had no reason to make this mistake, and none of them attributes the cause of their conflict to the investiture decree. The cause was Henry's challenge to papal independence, or, from the other point of view, Gregory's challenge to royal independence. The concrete instance which occasioned the challenge of Henry, and provoked the Pope's counter-challenge, arose out of the situation at Milan; it was the question of the appointment and control of the archbishop of Milan that really provided the *casus belli*.

During the long minority of Henry IV, when the government of the Empire was in the hands of a woman and then of a self-seeking archbishop, the royal authority had been gravely impaired in Germany and had almost disappeared in Italy. The Papacy had attained to a degree of independence hitherto unknown, and every advance it made—the Papal Election Decree of Nicholas II, the alliance with the Normans and the assumption of the overlordship of South Italy, its measures to make the headship of the Church a reality—was viewed with alarm or indignation at the imperial court. Henry IV, when he became his own master in 1067, set himself the task of recovering the ground that had been lost since his father's death, and of all the usurpers of royal rights the Papacy was in his eyes the chief. How clearly does he show his purpose to follow in his father's footsteps when his brief moment of victory is vouchsafed to him; when in 1084 he was able to enter Rome to be crowned Emperor by Pope Clement, his nominee, after he had caused Pope Gregory to be deposed by a synod, thus repeating exactly what his father had done in 1046. But in his earlier days he had to walk warily; his power depended on Germany, and until it was assured there he was careful to keep on good terms with the Pope, even at the expense of some humiliation to the royal dignity. He was remarkably successful in Germany in those early years, and when he crushed a dangerous Saxon revolt it seemed that he had achieved the first part of his programme, and in 1071 could look to Italy, where indeed the situation demanded his close attention.

In 1056, the year of his accession, the revolt of the Pataria broke out in Milan. At first it took the form of an attack on the clerical aristocracy, lax in morals and regardless of the new canons of reform. The powerful alliance of the Papacy was readily obtained, and the Popes were able to carry their reforming campaign into Milan and to make the archbishop subject to their authority. But the revolt of the Pataria was a constitutional as much as a religious movement; it was a revolt against the rule of the archbishop and the feudal nobility, and a commune was formed by the popular classes, including both wealthy merchants and artisans, which, obtaining leaders from among the nobility, took over the government of the city. The king was doubly concerned. His government in the Italian kingdom depended largely on the bishops, chief among whom was the archbishop of Milan; it was directly contrary to royal interests that the archbishop should be subject to the Pope and that the political government of the city should pass into the hands of a commune. This was what happened during the minority, and as ruler he himself had for a time to suffer it to continue. Suddenly, in 1071, just at the moment that he seemed to have become master in Germany, the opportunity came to intervene in Italy. The archbishop of Milan, Guido, died, and the nobles and clergy hastily elected one Godfrey, who was invested by Henry and consecrated at Milan in 1072. But the popular party meanwhile elected, and the Pope consecrated, another candidate, Atto, as archbishop. Pope Alexander II urged Henry to renounce his candidate, and on Henry's refusal excommunicated five of his councillors in 1073, charging them with the responsibility for the king's action. Henry ignored the excommunication, and by continuing to associate with them was himself implicated in the ban. This was the situation at the time of Gregory VII's election: Pope and king were already at schism. Gregory did what he could to heal the breach and induce the king to change his mind, but where his efforts were unavailing the Saxons succeeded. By their revolt in 1073 they so seriously endangered the king's position in Germany that he had no alternative but to make peace with the Pope on the Pope's terms, recognizing Atto and disowning Godfrey. It was not until the summer of 1075, some months after the investiture decree had been passed, that Henry regained the upper hand in Germany and was able once more to turn his attention to Italy. And once more Milan gave him the opportunity. The leader of the commune, Erlembald, was killed in a riot. The nobles and clergy temporarily recovered their former position and proceeded to elect a new archbishop of Milan,

Tedald, whom Henry, regardless of his solemn pledge to the Pope, recognized as archbishop and conferred investiture on him by deputy. The commission sent by him for this purpose to Milan had instructions also to appoint and invest bishops to Fermo and Spoleto, which lay within the papal province, and to seek alliance with the Norman duke, Robert Guiscard; the king's plan was to surround and isolate the Papacy.

So, both in 1071 and in 1075, when the king felt himself in a position to intervene in Italy, the opportunity was provided by the situation at Milan. On the first occasion he was forced to withdraw owing to his disastrous set-back in Germany. In 1075 there was no withdrawal; Gregory took up the challenge to papal independence, and, after bitterly reproaching the king for his breach of faith, counter-attacked with the claim of papal authority over lay rulers, and the great issue was joined. In 1077 Henry made his peace with the Pope at Canossa (when no mention was made of investiture by either side), but after an uneasy truce of three years, the struggle broke out again in 1080, this time on Gregory's initiative, and only ended with Henry's death in 1106. What Henry felt about the investiture decree is impossible to say, as he never mentioned it; it is fair, however, to infer that it was an additional irritant to his mind. But by itself it had no influence on the course of events leading to the breach; they had no direct relation with it, and would have taken place if no decree against lay investiture had been issued. They began in 1071, four years before the investiture decree, and the issue was not whether the king could invest the archbishop of Milan, but whether king or Pope was to decide who was to be archbishop. If Henry had been content to accept the papal candidate, Atto, in 1072, there is no reason to suppose that Pope Alexander II would have objected to Atto receiving investiture from the king; Gregory VII himself in 1073 ordered the new bishop of Lucca, Anselm, to avoid royal investiture only so long as the king remained out of communion with the Pope. In 1075 the papal indignation was expressed not at Henry's investing his new nominee, Tedald, but at his trying to set up a new archbishop in place of Atto, whom he had promised to recognize in 1073. So in this case, where the king himself had chosen his ground of attack, it was the control of appointments that was at stake. This was the immediate question which led to war, the preservation or the abolition of the lay control over the Church.

Lay control had centuries of tradition behind it. The lesser churches were subject to lay patronage, which practically meant lay ownership, the higher offices were usually at the disposal of kings or, in some cases in France, of powerful nobles. From the ecclesiastical point of view, the independence of the Church was at stake, and the newly reformed Papacy had come to recognize that lay control was the chief obstacle to the accomplishment of its programme. But control of the episcopate had become more than a tradition; to the rulers, particularly of Germany, it was both a political and an economic necessity. To maintain this control which was so necessary to them, the kings kept a close hand on elections and took care to see that the persons elected were attached primarily to their service. By the law of the Church, vague and ill-defined as yet, the election of a bishop rested with the clergy and people, as in the early days when the congregation in each town chose its own bishop. The election itself was supposed to be a matter for the clergy, among whom the cathedral clergy were coming to play the principal part, while the laity, often represented by the knights holding episcopal fiefs, were supposed to give their assent and support to the choice of the clergy. What actually happened when a vacancy occurred was that the electors had to obtain the king's leave to elect, and were often told by him whom they were to elect. If they tried to choose a candidate of their own, the king might refuse to ratify the election, and could make his will effective by withholding from such a candidate the temporalities, which during vacancy were in royal hands. First of all, then, the king could ensure an appointment satisfactory to himself, and this without infringing the canon law; for it would appear that the electors usually went through the formality of electing the king's nominee, so that the process approximated closely to the modern *congé d'élire*. Secondly, the king ensured the personal attachment and future services of the bishop-elect in the ceremony in which investiture took place. The king invested the bishop by handing to him the episcopal ring and the episcopal staff, which had been specially brought from the cathedral church of the bishopric, with the words *Accipe ecclesiam*, "Receive the church"; the bishop knelt before the king, did homage, and took an oath of fealty. Finally the bishop-elect was consecrated by the archbishop and bishops of the province. The king's control was thus assured, while the rule of canonical election was in most cases outwardly observed. One rule of the Church, however, was consistently ignored—that a candidate for office, whether priest or bishop, should be examined by his ecclesiastical superior and be rejected if unfit. It was the king and not the archbishop who satisfied himself as to the candidate's fitness for office.

In this customary procedure, then, we see all the parts designed to the end of maintaining royal control over the higher clergy. Lay investiture was one of the parts, but distinct from all the others; it was not the means by which the king maintained his control, but rather the outward sign of that control and of its character. It was not in itself a necessity to the kings; when they renounced it in the twelfth century, their authority remained as binding as it was before. But just because it was the outward sign, it was to the Church reformers the most objectionable feature of the proceedings. Investiture was always the outward and visible sign of a gift from lord to subject, whether of office or land, the necessary formality which made the donation valid. Something had to pass from donor to recipient to typify the donation—a clod of earth, for instance. Investiture of bishops had always differed from that of laymen in the character of the thing that passed—at first a book, then the episcopal staff, later both ring and staff. It can be understood why the kings were reluctant to give up this ceremony, because, even if unnecessary, it was the traditional expression of the validity of their action. Still more comprehensible is the attitude of the reformers. For what the king was giving was the insignia that represented the spiritual functions of the bishop, and when he said "Receive the church" he was clearly giving the spiritual office. When the practice of investing with the episcopal staff began, at the end of the ninth century, it seems to have been introduced intentionally in order to indicate that bishoprics were at the royal disposal. In the period under our consideration there were still some who averred that the consecrated king had the power of conferring spiritual functions. Most of the royal supporters, however, defended the practice by declaring that when the king invested with ring and staff he was in fact only investing with the temporalities of the see. Cardinal Humbert, the first writer to attack lay investiture, dealt trenchantly with this argument, insisting on the significance of the ring and its seal, of the pastoral staff, and of the words "Receive the church." So, too, Peter Damian a few years later, though much more moderate in disposition, cast scorn on the ingenuous defence of the royal supporters. "If the king gave an ordinary staff, well and good; but if he gave the pastoral staff, how is that traffic of episcopal rank to be excused?" "When he placed the staff in your hands, did he say, 'Receive the lands and wealth of the church'? Did he not in fact say, 'Receive the church'?" Logically there was no real answer to this contention. Moreover, long before the king began to invest with the staff, it had been customary in the rite of consecration for the new bishop to receive the episcopal staff from the hands of his consecrator; both ring and staff were now given to him by the king first, and then by the archbishop. Why this duplication? To denote the difference of function, said the imperialists; the king is conferring the temporalities, the archibishop the spiritualities. In both cases, said the Church party, spiritual functions are being bestowed. This is a sacramental act, and even if a layman can administer a sacrament, as he can in the case of baptism, it cannot be reiterated. The king's action makes the archbishop's meaningless and invalid, and this is an additional proof that royal investiture is an improper act.

The abolition of the ceremony of royal investiture, while it would get rid of the manifest appearance of the king conferring ecclesiastical office and functions, would not really touch the heart of the question, for the royal authority over bishops and their appointments would remain unimpaired. But it was the first and most obvious point of attack. It was necessary to start by making clear that spiritual functions, the priestly or the episcopal office, were not, and could not be, given by and received from a layman. In 1059, at Nicholas II's Council at the Lateran, a decree was passed that no cleric or priest was to obtain a church from a layman whether gratis or for money, and this was repeated at a council held in Rome by Alexander II in 1063. This lays down clearly the principle that the church—the spiritual office or function—is not to be given by a layman. Otherwise it is somewhat ambiguous in wording, as it is not clear whether it refers to the lower clergy only, and also whether, as the words seem to imply, it excludes lay patronage altogether. A canon of synods held at Vienne and Tours in 1060 is more precise: "no one henceforth is to receive a church, great or small, from a layman, without the consent of the bishop." The last words seem to indicate that the lesser clergy only are concerned, and that lay patronage is not excluded but confined to its lawful function of presentation. . . .

The investiture decree, therefore, while prohibiting the ceremony of investiture with ring and staff and the accompanying words, says nothing about the temporalities or the homage done by the bishop for them or his oath of fealty. Its purpose was to remove all suggestion that the ecclesiastical office, the spiritual functions, could be conferred by a layman. It was, as has been said, a means towards an end, and the end was the appointment of the right men as bishops. It was only a step in that direction, for Gregory knew that, even if the ceremony of lay investiture was abandoned, secular considerations would still prevail in the creation of a bishop. His mind was set on good appointments, and this meant the upsetting of the first part of the customary procedure. Both of these points are emphasized in a letter he wrote to the clergy and people of Aquileia in September 1077, a letter which shows signs of having been written at the Pope's personal dictation. "That which in the Church has long been neglected owing to sin and corrupted by evil custom, we desire to renew and restore to the honour of God and the salvation of all Christendom, namely that to rule the people of God in every church, when the moment arises such a bishop shall bé elected and in such a way that in accordance with the judgement of Truth he may not be termed a thief and a robber, but be worthy to bear the name and office of shepherd. This is indeed our will, this is our desire, this by the mercy of God will be, so long as we live, our unwearied aim." "But," he goes on to say, "that which pertains to the service and fealty due to the king, we do not wish to contradict or to prevent. And so we are trying to introduce nothing new, nothing of our own invention, but that alone do we seek, which the salvation and need of all men requires, that in the ordaining of bishops in accordance with the common understanding and approval of the holy fathers, first of all the evangelic and canonical authority should be preserved." Notice the words "nothing new, nothing of our own invention." These were the same words as he had used about his investiture decree in his letter to Henry IV in December 1075. It was not new to forbid kings to give ecclesiastical offices; it would have been new, he implies, for him to interfere with the services due to the king for the temporalities. . . .

If this programme in its entirety had been carried into practice, it would have produced almost a revolution in political as well as in ecclesiastical conditions. It left to the king only the right of bestowing the temporalities and receiving due services in return; it denied to him any part in the appointment of those who were to receive the temporalities from him. The effect would be very serious for him, far more serious than that created by the abolition of lay investiture. In spite of this, Gregory no longer feels it necessary to act circumspectly, and to try by negotiation to obtain the king's consent. Doubtless these decrees have special reference to Germany and Italy; in France his legates have the upper hand and the enforcement of canonical regulations is within their power; when their authority extended to Normandy there was friction with William I, but Gregory was anxious to avoid a contest with a king whose appointments were at any rate in keeping with the spirit, if not the letter, of the ecclesiastical regulations. Hitherto he had not denied to the king of Germany some part in appointments, and as late as July 1075, he wrote asking for Henry's assistance in the appointment of a successor to bishop Hermann of Bamberg, who had been deposed for simony. But with the change in the political situation came a complete change in his attitude. He had sat in judgement on the king, and after Canossa, and particularly after the election at Forchheim of Rudolf as rival to Henry, he felt himself to be in a position to lay down the law. He claimed that the decision between the two kings must rest with him, and he continually announced that he would decide for the one with whom was righteousness. The sign of the righteous ruler was, in the teaching of St. Augustine and Gregory the Great, obedience to the commandments of God and therefore by inference to the Church which interprets God's will. So Gregory VII felt that he could now proclaim the complete canonical doctrine and expect obedience. Rudolf's supporters were careful to show how scrupulous their leader was in refraining from interfering with ecclesiastical appointments and from investing with ring and staff, limiting his part to the bestowal of the temporalities after consecration (notice that this is regarded as perfectly lawful), while Henry flagrantly violated the papal decrees. There is every reason to credit their account, for Henry felt himself entirely within his rights in maintaining the customary practice, while Rudolf was anxious to avoid giving any offence to the Pope, whose recognition and support he needed. Probably this was one of the chief considerations which caused Gregory to give his decision at last in 1080, when he declared Henry deposed for ever because of his pride, disobedience, and falsehood, and assigned the kingdom to Rudolf because of his humility, obedience, and truthfulness. The repetition at the same time of the investiture decree, accompanied by the positive statement of the law of the Church on canonical elections, seemed now to be a programme which could be straightforwardly achieved. As events showed, his optimism, both in 1078 and in 1080, was unjustified. As he could not execute his sentence against Henry, he could not carry out his ecclesiastical programme. There was not even a contest about this programme, which, while naturally accepted by the German rebels, was as naturally disregarded by Henry's adherents, who had a Pope of their own. The issue could not become a live one until Henry IV was dead and Empire and Papacy were once more in communion. . . .

The eventual settlements, with the king of England in 1107 and with the Emperor in 1122, were very similar: in effect, both kings agreed to renounce their practice of investing with ring and staff provided that the other canons were not pressed. In England, Paschal II allowed Anselm to consecrate bishops who had done homage, provided the king abstained from investing; this, intended by him to be a temporary concession, was treated as a permanent one by Henry I, and the persistence of the customary procedure is shown in the Constitutions of Clarendon. Calixtus II's concession to Henry V at Worms was a carefully-drawn legal document. In return for Henry's renunciation of investiture, it recognizes the king's share in the elections of German bishops and abbots, especially when the elections were contested; the regalia were to be received from the king by a touch of the sceptre; and the bishop or abbot was to do homage and take the oath of fealty to the king before consecration. The Pope, therefore, obtained the abolition of the objectionable ceremony of investiture with ring and staff, but all the rest of the customary procedure was maintained. Canonical elections took place, but clearly not free elections, since they were to be held in the king's presence; no mention is made of examination by the consecrator; and the additions introduced by Urban II and Paschal II to Gregory's decree against investiture have disappeared. Lay control over appointments and over the personnel of the episcopate remains unchanged. All that has happened is that what Gregory VII forbade in 1075 has been abolished. It is true that Calixtus's concession to Henry V, like Paschal's to Henry I, was intended to be temporary; for it was granted to Henry V only, with no mention of his successors. Henry himself made his renunciation of investiture permanent and binding on his successors, and it may seem strange that he failed to obtain a similarly binding concession from the Pope. Possibly this was done on purpose. The king had to make terms of peace with the Pope, but he did not wish that in the future the customary practice, which he regarded as sanctioned by the law of the German kingdom and was determined to maintain, should seem to be legalized by papal authority. His successor Lothar III, who owed his election largely to ecclesiastical backing, did not uphold the royal rights in elections, but Frederick Barbarossa resumed the customary practice as his lawful right and maintained it throughout his reign, after as well as before his long struggle with the Pope. It was Frederick II who, as part of his bargain with Innocent III, finally renounced the royal rights.

It is instructive here to notice how different was the course of events in France. There was considerable friction but no open conflict, and there was no formal concordat. The royal power was so weak in the eleventh century that Gregory VII was able to establish permanent legates—Hugh bishop of Die and Amatus bishop of Oloron—who held numerous councils, and, in spite of constant opposition from the king, were often able to enforce the execution of their decrees. We have seen that the decree against lay investiture was openly published first in France, and it seems to have had its principal effect there; certainly by the twelfth century the king has ceased to invest with ring and staff. At the same time the king ceased to nominate to bishoprics, so that election in accordance with canonical regulations was becoming the rule. He still exercised an influence on the election, especially when it was contested, and he retained his right of confirming elections, which was certainly no mere formality. In place of investiture he conceded the temporalities of the see, and the bishop took an oath of fealty, usually after his consecration, but did not do homage. The king was thus left with a certain voice in elections, sometimes a decisive voice, though the initiative had passed from him to the electors; it was recognized that the temporalities were held from him, and services were due to him in return. Usually he could count on the loyalty of the bishops, even against the Pope. The situation was much the same in those regions, especially in South France, where the great vassals and not the king exercised control over the Church. Only in Normandy did the legates meet an authority capable of preventing any advance. So in the greater part of the French kingdom a compromise had been worked out in practice which was much more satisfactory to the Papacy than the arrangements negotiated by concordats with Germany and England. Besides the abolition of lay investiture, it had secured greater freedom in elections, and the disappearance of the act of homage.

The year 1122 marks the end of a chapter. The dispute about lay investiture is over; the question is settled once and for all. It only remains to look back over these fifty years of tragic strife and summarize the conclusions of the survey I have been attempting to give. The main purpose of Gregory VII in the early years of his Papacy was that the Church should be properly governed, and therefore that the right men should be appointed to hold office and to have the cure of souls. But the offices were being filled with men whose qualification was their capacity for secular administration. The lay rulers controlled appointments in their own interests and not in that of the Church, and to gain office the clergy canvassed, curried favor, spent large sums of money; against this offence, simony, the reformers had already been fighting a long and apparently unsuccessful battle. Success, Gregory saw, could only be won if lay control, which resulted in bad appointments and encouraged the practice of simony, was abolished. He felt it to be obligatory on him to rescue the Church from the stranglehold of the lay power, so that it could be free to conduct its elections in accordance with its own regulations. He made his first aim not at the means by which that control was exercised and maintained, but at the ceremony which was the outward and visible sign of that control, in which the king invested with ring and staff and so gave the spiritual office. His decree in 1075 prohibited that part of the ceremony and nothing more. It was not an end in itself, but a first step towards the real end of proper appointments to ecclesiastical offices—a necessary step, to make clear that the hold of the laity over the spiritual functions, which this ceremony portrayed, was illegal. It was a grave matter, likely to lead to conflict, though Gregory, misled by the compliant attitude of the king, hoped that it would not and that some composition could be arranged by mutual consent; possibly if Henry received assurances about the *temporalia* he would be willing to abandon the *spiritualia*. However, against Gregory's purpose was set the purpose of Henry IV, determined to relax none of his control but rather to regain what had been lost during his unfortunate minority, when the Papacy which his father had dominated had become independent. As soon as success came to him in Germany, he grasped the opportunity afforded by the situation at Milan and challenged a conflict which involved the major issue between the *regnum* and *sacerdotium*; and while that conflict was raging there was no place for consideration of a subordinate issue such as lay investiture.

So comes the first intermission. Thereafter the Pope, with the impression of victory strong upon him, proceeded to his more positive aim. He abandons the idea of negotiation and begins to enforce his decree. Twice he reissues it, in 1078 and 1080, and couples with it decrees enjoining free canonical election and examination of the candidate by his ecclesiastical superior, which if they could be enforced would ensure that the purpose for which the investiture decree had been promulgated would be achieved. The schism, renewed in 1080, again made the fulfilment of his purpose impossible. With his death in 1085, there is a change of motif. For his successors, while they continually repeated his decree against lay investiture, did not use it for the purpose for which he had intended it. With him it had been the spiritual work of the bishop that mattered, so he had concentrated on the method of appointment; they concentrated on the temporal possessions and services, which he had ignored. They used the decree, not so much as a means to an end of good appointments, but rather as a means towards depriving the king of all control over the bishop when appointed. They added to it decrees forbidding homage to be done by clerics to laymen, and forbidding the clergy to receive their temporalities from lay hands. When the long schism came to an end, this was the situation with which the new king of Germany was faced. Investiture is now of prime importance, its removal an end in itself, since the other decrees are nugatory without it. Its abolition is therefore the one desideratum with the papal party. But by concentrating upon it they lost their ultimate aim. The king had something with which to barter; by renouncing investiture he gave up the shadow and retained the substance—all that part of the customary procedure which ensured his control over the appointment of bishops and over the bishops when appointed. So Gregory's purpose was defeated when what he intended as a means became an end. It was a Pyrrhic triumph for the Papacy when the king was left in possession of the field.

12 FROM

Karl F. Morrison
Canossa: A Revision

One must examine Gregory's thought and actions in a dimension other than the purely constitutional, in which they have generally been set. Gregory was not primarily a legist. However great the work of canonists in his day, however great his encouragement of their work, Gregory cannot be named among the lawyer-popes. In his decrees and letters, there are no such citations of Roman or barbarian law, no such explicit citations of canons from the synods and councils of the early Church, as there are in the declarations of Nicholas I and John VIII or of the popes in the High Middle Ages. His pronouncements are tissues, not of legal sanctions, but rather of moral and ethical assertions.

Gregory's relations to temporal princes are therefore to be seen in a framework of moral instead of juristic thought. One must acknowledge that his claims to supreme authority in temporal affairs were primarily claims over Christian men, not over their offices; and moreover one must attempt to see those claims in the light of Gregory's own metaphysical orientation as parts of the ceaseless warfare between the Church and the world. An examination of Gregory's dealings with Henry IV from that point of view indicates that the recent construction of his hierocratic concept of relations between the spiritual and the temporal power must be modified: it suggests that Gregory's claims that the Pope could judge of candidates for the royal office and depose unworthy kings were relative and not absolute. In establishing the scope of those assertions, one must observe three major limitations: Gregory never claimed for the Papacy the power to grant the kingship, but rather he consistently attributed it to God alone. He never claimed or, as we shall show, attempted to exercise the power of final deposition over kings, for that also fell to heavenly judgment. Finally, and most important, his assertion of headship over temporal government extended only to Christian rulers in communion with the Roman church; outside that communion were pagan or heretical princes, whose titles to the royal office Gregory himself

SOURCE. Karl F. Morrison, "Canossa: A Revision," in *Traditio*, XVIII (1962), pp. 121–148. Reprinted by permission of Fordham University Press, New York, and the author.

acknowledged. For him, the kingship was an office existing independently of the Church, employed for the good of the Church if
the king were a true believer, but removed from that service or
even turned against the faithful if he were not. Consequently,
Gregory did not assert that the Pope could bestow the kingship
but rather that he could sanction the use of the kingly power; he
maintained, not that he could withdraw the royal office, but that
he could withdraw ecclesiastical sanctions from its exercise. To use
the terminology of a later age, Gregory saw papal relations to temporal government in terms of indirect power. . . .

In order to understand more fully Gregory's view of his process
against Henry, one must enquire into the moral context of his
political thought.

From the beginning of the controversy with Henry IV until his
own death, Gregory maintained one major premise: that as Pope
he was the leader of the faithful in active battle against the Devil.
It is sometimes maintained that in Gregory's thought, the Church
had acceded to the territorial and jurisdictional universality of
the Roman Empire, and that as head of the Church, the Pope was
in some sense the successor of the Augusti. But Gregory himself
never claimed the territorial or jurisdictional universality associated with the Empire, nor did he ever describe himself as the heir
of the Caesars. His greatest claims were based upon his belief in the
moral hegemony of the Papacy over orthodox Christendom, and
the earnest conviction that the successor of St. Peter must lead the
forces of God against the enemies of God.

The importance of this "political manichaeism" in Gregory's
political thought can scarcely be overemphasized, for the concept
is distinct in all his judgments upon problems of temporal and
spiritual discipline. He complains repeatedly that the Devil has
become lord of the world, and that kings, nobles, and even clerics
have joined him in undermining the Christian religion, in striving
"against the Lord and against His Christ." All who professed to
be Christians and still refused to obey the Roman See joined the
body of the Devil, for they had fallen into the sin of idolatry, into
heresy, into paganism, and could no longer be numbered among
the true believers. By virtue of their heresy, they were one with the
Jews and Saracens, the enemies of God.

Between them and the true believers there was an actual state of
war, "the war of God." And it was the duty of the Pope to lead the
sons of God against His foes, fighting with the sword of the Holy

Spirit even unto death. Nor was the warfare to be entirely spiritual. Gregory himself aspired to lead armies against pagans and heretics; he encouraged the Spanish princes in the Reconquista; he urged King Sven II of Denmark and the German princes to lift the material sword "against the profane and the enemies of God" on behalf of the Roman Church; and he commanded the use of secular arms to eject condemned bishops from their former sees. The threat of armed revolt or invasion may also have been intended when Gregory wrote of King Philip I, of France, that if the King should persist in disobedience towards the Roman See, the Pope would "by every measure attempt with the help of God to snatch the kingdom of France from his tenure."

In this struggle, the Pope was the commander-in-chief, "dux et pontifex," of the faithful; Christian kings were his adjutants. His claims to authority over them were sweeping and comprehensive. In the Church, among the orthodox, the Pope bore secular burdens as well as spiritual, and all in communion with the true Church owed him their absolute subjection. There were to Gregory's mind several major duties of the Christian king: to feed the poor, to defend the widowed and the orphaned, and to guard the laws of peace and the judgment of equity. But none of them was more important than reverence for the priesthood, and obedience to the See of Peter. In some instances. Gregory added or attempted to add, juristic sanctions to that duty of obedience by requiring oaths of homage from temporal rulers; in them, the princes obliged themselves to obey the Roman see in all things and to render it military assistance in time of need. Those oaths did not, however, impose any general duties other than those Gregory expected of all Christian rulers; whether they were bound to his obedience juristically or not, orthodox rulers were subject to the direction and moral jurisdiction of Rome. It is in this context of relationships within the body of the faithful that Gregory's famous letter to William the Conqueror must be set. Just as all the world is illumined by two lights, the sun and the moon, so, he wrote, creation is governed by two divers offices, the apostolic (i.e., episcopal or papal) and the royal; and the Christian religion is so ordered that the royal office is governed by the apostolic and by God. It has been suggested that this statement accompanied a demand that William render an oath of homage to the Papacy. But it concerns us more that the basis of the statement and of the supposed demand was the same: obedient to the judgment of the

Apostolic See, William had waged war against Harald of England, vanquishing him and acceding to his office with the blessing of St. Peter. It is indicative of his thought that Gregory should address his claim for the supremacy of the spiritual office over the temporal in the Christian commonwealth to a ruler who, on papal commission, had fought against and conquered an excommunicate King.

Gregory's concept of his struggle with Henry IV turns entirely upon the premise that Henry had joined the forces of the Devil, and that Gregory was consequently obliged to rouse the Church against him. In 1076, as he proceeded to the first excommunication of Henry, Gregory compared the King to the serpent of evil and declared that he must raise the sword of vengeance and strike "the enemy of God and of the Church." Defending that action, he wrote that Henry had fallen into the hands of the Devil, and that those who (like Henry) refused to heed the command of God were members of Antichrist and must be chastened for their disobedience. He had earlier complained that the simoniac Lombard bishops sought to prostitute the bride of Christ with the Devil, and now he describes Henry and his supporters, principally Wibert of Ravenna (the Antipope Clement III), as members of the Devil, as members of Antichrist, or as Antichrist himself; and the Synod of Brixen, where Henry declared Gregory deposed and secured the election of Wibert, was for Gregory "the assembly of Satan." Through them, the world had come to be ruled by the Devil; through them, Satan's conquests were daily increased; through them, the return of the Church to her proper honor, free, chaste, and orthodox, was hindered.

A king—or indeed any person—who lapsed from the true faith into heresy, into the "sin of paganism," must be severed from the body of the faithful. He must lose the title "Christian." That is clear; but in losing it, must he of necessity lose the title "king" or the royal office itself? Gregory took three measures against Henry: he excommunicated him; he denied him government, and he forbade Christians bound by oath to Henry to honor those oaths. In other words, he severed Henry from the body of the Church, declared that by ecclesiastical sentence he was no longer king, and separated Christian allegiants from their heretical ruler. Christian orthodoxy and legal tenure of the royal office, however, were discrete in Gregory's mind, and as we shall attempt to show later, removal from one did not invariably produce removal from the other. To be sure, the only true kings were, for Gregory, Christian kings; and only kings who honored the Church obtained their office rightly (recte).

But not all kings were Christian: Gregory acknowledges Saracen kings and pagan princes and emperors. Though they might not govern rightly, as Christians, they nevertheless governed lawfully, as kings. This distinction is implicit in Gregory's letter to Herman of Metz, justifying his second excommunication and deposition of Henry. There, acknowledging Henry as "King," he at the same time wrote: "In short, any good Christians are to be viewed as kings more suitably than evil princes. For seeking the glory of God, they rule themselves firmly; but seeking their own rather than what is God's the latter, enemies to themselves, oppress others tyrannically. The former are the body of Christ, the true King, but the others are the body of the Devil." Gregory does not in this passage or in any other declare that wicked princes might not be lawful rulers; he is rather concerned to say that such princes are incapable of that moral rectitude (*justitia*) which for him characterized true kingship, kingship patterned on that of Christ, the heavenly King. Saracen, pagan, and heretical princes were under "the prince of darkness, who is king over all the sons of pride," but they were still effectual rulers. In short, Gregory did not maintain, as did the later canonist Johannes Teutonicus, that "there is no empire outside the Church," for to his eyes there were two empires on earth, that of God and that of Satan. . . .

If, in Gregory's judgment, Henry deserved to be permanently removed from the royal office, and if the papal powers were insufficient to secure his removal, one must ask what power could effect the just deposition of an unjust king. It seems probable that Gregory believed such a deposition could be performed only by divine action or by the judgment of St. Peter, who "Jesus Christ, the King of glory, established as prince over the kingdoms of the world." For Gregory, although there was a close relationship between the comprehensive power of St. Peter and papal authority, the two were not identical. But, casting his decrees in the form of letters to St. Peter (the second was addressed to St. Paul as well), whose vicar he was, Gregory sought the final ratification of his action by heavenly judgment. He acknowledged circumstances under which the pope might rely in vain upon the merits of St. Peter, and stated the premise that divine judgments often differed from those of men. Just as he himself sometimes overturned the judgments of his own vicars, so, he appears to have thought, St. Peter might reverse the decisions of his.

In fact, Gregory explicitly appealed to St. Peter for final

corroboration of his sentence, perhaps in battle or, as evidence from the 1083–4 negotations suggests, in trial by ordeal. In 1075, he had warned Henry to observe the example of Saul, whom God, "in whose hand and power is all kingdom and empire," cast down; again, after issuing the first edict against the King, he threatened him with "wrath and vengeance of divine judgment." And the words with which he concluded the second decree make his meaning plain. Addressing SS. Peter and Paul, he prayed:

"Act now, I ask, Fathers and Most Sacred Princes, that all the world may perceive and understand that, if you can bind and loose in Heaven, you can on earth withdraw from and grant to anyone according to his merits empires, kingdoms, principalities, duke-doms, marquisates, countships and the possessions of all men. For you have often taken patriarchates, primacies, archiepiscopacies, and episcopacies from the wicked and unworthy, and have given them to religious men. If you judge of spiritual things, what must one believe of your powers in secular matters? And if you will judge the angels who rule in all proud princes, what can you do with regard to their servants? Let kings and all princes of the world now heed how great you are and what you can do, and let them fear to disregard the command of your Church. Implement your judgment as regards the said Henry so quickly that all may know he falls not by chance, but by your power; may he be confounded— O that it were to repentance—that his soul may be saved in the day of the Lord!"

In this prayer, Gregory attributed the power to dispose of temporal as well as spiritual offices to SS. Peter and Paul, but he did not claim it for the Pope, their vicar. It is clear that Gregory left the definitive deposition of Henry to divine judgment.

We are now in a position to sum up the major points of Gregory's thought concerning Church–State relations and, addressing our-selves to the original problem, to assess the meaning of the specific measures Gregory took against Henry IV and of his actions at Canossa.

Gregory's political and ecclesiological thought was cast entirely in terms of a conflict between the forces of Antichrist and the forces of God, whose earthly leader was the Pope. Within the Christian community, the Pope held directive power over all persons and consequently over all offices exercised by Christians, including the kingship. But temporal offices were in the last analysis discrete from the Church; they were like threads which might be woven into the fabric of Christendom or pulled out from it, retaining their integrity in either case. The power to grant or to withdraw the legal powers of the kingship was attributed, therefore, not to the Papacy, but to divine judgment. The Church might cast wicked rulers out from the body of the faithful; but, having acknowledged them as members of the Devil, it had no further power over them, no power to depose them from the offices which they exercised wrongfully, but, at the same time, lawfully.

Of the three measures Gregory took against Henry, excommunication is surely the easiest to understand. It was simply the removal of a recalcitrant sinner from the Church, and it had no intrinsic political implications. Gregory had considered Henry excommunicate in 1074, before the beginning of their dispute, but he did not then regard his royal title as being tainted in any way. Indeed, the distinction between this religious sanction and the political measures he adopted is illustrated by Gregory's own statement that at Canossa he restored the King to communion but neither restored him to the kingship nor enjoined his subjects to resume their obedience to him. The second measure, the release of Christian subjects from their vows of fidelity to Henry, is a logical, but as we have said, not a necessary, elaboration. On the apparent principle that Christians ought not to be subject to the "synagogue of Satan," Gregory freed them from the necessity of obeying a heretical ruler. Subjects had, therefore, the option of rejecting their ruler or rejecting their faith. Just as Gregory released subjects of simoniac bishops and priests from their obligation of obedience—without, it should be added, encouraging them to rebellion—so he also attempted to preserve the spiritual welfare of Christians from the moral danger of wicked kings by delivering them from their subjection. The final measure, deposition, was, as we have attempted to show, a declarative act, rather than a definitive one, and indicated that the king against whom it was directed was no longer a true king in the eyes of the Church; it was in fact a moral, not a juristic, sentence.

In the context of Gregory's thought, therefore, as well as in the context of history, Canossa cannot be viewed as an unique event, but rather as one stage in a legal process which lasted almost a decade. The final confirmation or withdrawal of the kingship, which was the object of that process, was not a real question at Canossa. Gregory appeared there in two capacities: He was the earthly head of the Church, and at the same time he was the judge whom both Henry and the Saxons had elected to arbitrate their dispute. By virtue of his prelatical office, he had full authority to receive a penitent sinner back into orthodox communion. He therefore freed Henry from the ban of excommunication. In his second capacity, however, he could take no action until both parties in the dispute were present and a full hearing could be held. While acknowledging Henry's title as king, Gregory consequently withheld ecclesiastical sanctions from his rule pending settlement of the case which had been appealed to him. Henry had shown himself morally worthy to return to Christ's flock, but his worthiness of the royal office in the eyes of the Church had not been cleared by the judgment of the German electors, who alone had the power to elevate to the king-ship, and of the Pope. At Canossa, when he forbade Henry to use the royal insignia and at the same time he acknowledged him as King, Gregory indicated clearly that he considered Henry sus-pended, but not irrevocably deposed, from the kingship. For Gregory, the importance of the interview was that negotiations leading to a just settlement of the dispute might be renewed directly between Henry and himself, since Henry had been delivered from the hands of the Devil back among the sons of God. Canossa was not, therefore, the testing ground of extreme hierocratic theories, but it was simply the beginning of a new stage in a legal process.

Canossa, however, has a higher value for the historian, for the resolution of its ambiguity leads directly to the resolution of the apparent ambiguity which consistently marks Gregory's part in the Investiture Conflict. As Fliche and Arquillière have shown, the essence of that ambiguity is that Gregory acknowledged a man whom he himself had declared deposed to be a lawful king. That ambivalence, one of the invariables in the controversy, was the result, not of indecisiveness, but of settled convictions in Gregory's mind.

It exists even in those most crucial acts, the edicts of deposition against Henry. We have seen that, in the correspondence which followed the first edict, Gregory declared that he had deposed Henry and urged the Germans to receive him back as king should he repent. On the other hand, it has been shown that Gregory prayed for Henry's reconciliation with the Church and continued to negotiate with him and to acknowledge his royal title. And in the later history of the conflict, there is much—Gregory's Easter prophecy of 1080, continued willingness to negotiate with Henry, offer to surrender the imperial crown to him, retraction of the second edict of excommunication, and steadfast acknowledgment of Henry's royal title—to indicate that Gregory himself did not regard his second deposition as a definitive juristic act.

In 1076 as well as in 1080, the emphasis in Gregory's mind was constantly on moral, instead of juristic considerations. His two decrees of excommunication and deposition against Henry were provoked by insupportable challenges to the moral prestige of the Papacy itself. The first was prompted by the Synod of Worms (1076) where, at Henry's instigation, the German episcopacy declared Gregory unworthy of the Papacy, renounced its obedience to him, and denied the supreme jurisdiction of Rome in diocesan affairs. The second followed quickly upon the discovery that Henry had bribed the papal legate Ulrich of Padua, to render false reports to his papal master. Gregory's anger was so great that he deposed Ulrich on the spot; immediately thereafter, he moved the deposition of Henry and the recognition of Rudolf.

In the more usual circumstances of the controversy, however challenging, Gregory without exception recognized Henry's royal title, and declared his eagerness for the King's reconciliation with the true Church, which latter was the condition for renewed negotiations in 1074, the preliminary condition satisfied at Canossa, the condition Gregory set for his coronation of Henry in 1084, and the condition upon which, in his last days, Gregory provisionally lifted the ban of excommunication against the King. However, Gregory's constant acknowledgment of Henry's royal title and his refusal of his own power to set another in Henry's place was as frequent an element in the history of the conflict as were Gregory's insistent and prayerful entreaties that Henry turn from his wrongful government and accept once again the direction of the Roman Church. From the penance Henry rendered to papal legates in 1074 to his first excommunication, from the first ban to Canossa, from Canossa to the second ban, and from the second decree to the time of Gregory's death the tacit rejection of absolute powers over temporal government and the determined assertion of Rome's moral headship within the body of the faithful were Gregory's Scylla and Charybdis.

It was the combination of political and moral thought which produced the apparent ambivalence in Gregory's whole conduct in the dispute, and which was epitomized in his actions at Canossa.

At the important interview, he was able to acknowledge Henry as king, since he was in fact lawfully king; he was able, at the same time to observe that he did not restore Henry to the kingship, since it was beyond his competence to bestow the royal power. Henry's definitive deposition or restoration did not fall to the Papacy, but to divine judgment as manifested in war or in full judicial process. The seeming inconsistency between the Pope's thought and his actions, which appears if one assumes him to have been an absolute papal supremist in theory, is therefore resolved if one sees his thought in moral terms, in terms of the struggle between the world and the Church which allowed him to recognize a wrongful king as a lawful king.

PART FIVE

Henry II and Archbishop Thomas Becket

As the twelfth century advanced, the principles of the Gregorian Reformers—freedom from lay control and the supremacy of *sacerdotium* over *regnum*—clashed with the emerging goal of secular powers—the development of strong centralized states. At the same time, strong secular authorities sought to elevate patterns of society from an arrangement based on personal relationships and feudal custom to a system of government founded on clearly articulated and written law. These ideals and goals are clearly seen in the most celebrated conflict between temporal and spiritual powers in English history, the struggle between King Henry II (1154–1189) and Archbishop Thomas Becket (1162–1170).

The long-range causes of this trial are many: the unusual circumstances of Becket's appointment to the see of Canterbury; the perhaps inevitable clash between two strong-willed and determined personalities; and the clear resolution of King Henry to draw to himself all the powers of the State. In his apparent desire to control all the elements of feudal military power and to possess ultimate authority over the instruments of justice in England (the courts, both ecclesiastical and lay), Henry sought a kind of jurisdiction which in hindsight seems much in advance of his time. His jurisdiction would have amounted to the realization of the concept which modern political theorists call sovereignty. The Constitutions of Clarendon (1164) were an attempt to formulate in a written statement what the king believed to be the proper and traditional royal control not only over "criminous clerks" but over all English–papal relations as well. Henry insisted that he was establishing nothing new. In fact, except for Chapter Seven, the principles of the Constitutions *had* been the practices of his grandfather, Henry I (1100–1135); Henry II was arguing from the pre-Gregorian conditions that existed in the days of William the Conqueror (1066–1087).

But Thomas Becket, as a strong if unexpected defender of Church privileges and the newly codified canon law, could not accept the precepts of Clarendon. He, too, could justifiably argue from precedent, since the dike erected by William I against papal authority in England had been burst by the flood of Roman influence during the weak government of King Stephen (1135–1154). Hence the dispute, which was aggravated by the archbishop's flight to France and his appeal to Pope Alexander III (1159–1190), was not settled until his murder in Canterbury Cathedral. Becket's martyrdom so inflamed public opinion that he achieved more dead than he probably ever would have done alive.

The course of the controversy may be traced, first, in the account of Becket's contemporary, Roger of Pontigny, which although written from hindsight and with the undoubted intention of magnifying the virtues of the dead archbishop, reveals some of the hesitations which were felt about his qualifications for the primatial see of Canterbury. This chronicle also suggests, inadvertently, that Becket may have deceived the king into promoting him to the office. The document containing the issues around which the conflict centered is the all-important Constitutions of Clarendon (January 1164). Thirdly, the description of the Council of Northampton (October 1164) by the eyewitness William Fitz Stephen beautifully illustrates the positions of both sides; the events at that council point up the confused loyalties of high ecclesiastics who are also feudal barons. The murder of Archbishop Thomas Becket in Canterbury Cathedral (December 29, 1170) was the most dramatic moment in English religious history; the picture presented here helps explain why public opinion was so aroused that Henry II had to retreat and the victory went to the Church. Z. N. Brooke emphasizes Becket's posthumous victory with the full impact of canon law operative in England after his death. Charles Duggan takes some exception to Brooke's thesis, and in a lucid commentary sets the problem against the background of domestic and international developments in the twelfth century.

1 FROM

David C. Douglas and
George W. Greenaway
English Historical Documents

Roger of Pontigny on Becket's Election to the Primacy[1]

About the same time, on the death of Theobald, archbishop of Canterbury, the king designed to make Thomas his successor, for he judged him to be most worthy of so great an honour and trusted that he would be fully prepared to do his will and consult his interests in everything. For Thomas had made a point of showing great severity towards the persons and interests of ecclesiastics in order by this means to remove all mark of suspicion from himself and, under cover thereof, to meet more easily the king's wishes, of which he had intimate knowledge. The king, therefore, believed that his design against the Church could be most effectively carried out through Thomas, whom indeed he had found by experience was most loyal to him in everything and well disposed to his wishes. Accordingly he took the irrevocable decision to promote him archbishop of Canterbury.

The king therefore sent two bishops [to Canterbury], accompanied by a certain trusty magnate of his named Richard of Lucé,

[1]Shortly after Becket's death, this description of his election was written by Roger, a monk of Pontigny where the archbishop passed part of the years of his exile. Roger was Becket's personal servant at Pontigny.

SOURCE. David C. Douglas and George W. Greenaway, eds., *English Historical Documents*, Volume II, "Materials for the History of Thomas Becket" [London: Eyre & Spottiswoode (Publishers) Ltd.; New York: Oxford University Press, 1961], pp. 709–712. Reprinted by permission of the publishers.

giving them letters of mandate to convene the chapter of Canterbury for the election of an archbishop. Arriving at Canterbury, they entered the chapter-house, and having first expatiated at great length on the generosity and condescension of the king, they charged Richard of Lucé with the delivery of the royal mandate, who thereupon addressed the assembly as follows: "Since the lord bishops have signified their pleasure that I should declare unto you the king's wishes, be it known of a truth to all of you, that our lord, the king, as you have already heard from the bishops, is most zealous in everything which concerns the things of God and displays the utmost devotion towards holy Church, especially towards this church of Canterbury, which he recognizes in all humility, loyalty and filial affection as his particular mother in the Lord. Wherefore, that she be not in any way oppressed or thrown into disorder by remaining long bereft of a shepherd, be it known to you that the king accords you full freedom of election, provided, however, that you choose a man worthy of so great an office and equal to the burden thereof. For it is not unknown to you that our lord, the king, is wont to endeavour nothing in such a matter save what he believes to be well-pleasing to God and profitable to his Church. For the rest, then, it is incumbent on you, and wholly expedient, to elect one under whose protection you may rejoice before God and men. For if king and archbishop be joined together in the bond of affection and cherish each other in all friendship, there is no doubt that the times will be happy and the Church will preserve her estate in joy and tranquillity. But if, which God forbid, things should turn out otherwise, the dangers and confusion, the labours and tumults, and, in the end, the loss of property and the peril to souls which may result therefrom, are not, I imagine, hidden from your reverences."

When Richard had made an end of speaking and the bishops had declared their approval, the prior of Canterbury first gave thanks to God and then with due reverence expressed his deep gratitude to the king for his kindness and solicitude on their behalf. And so, with the permission of the bishops, he summoned to him certain of the older and wiser monks and retired with them. But after they had been in session together to consider the message they had received, they came to the conclusion that nothing could be decided without the advice of Richard of Luce and the bishops, who were fully acquainted with the king's wishes, on which the whole question of the election must depend. Accordingly they now called in the royal commissioners, namely Bartholomew, bishop of Exeter, Hilary, bishop of Chichester, and Richard. And when the latter had entered and discussed the proposed election with the monks at some length, they all, both monks and bishops, with one voice and one mind elected the chancellor to be the shepherd and bishop of their souls. The monks indeed had for some time hesitated over the election, not because they failed to recognize that Thomas was a virtuous man, but because he did not wear the habit of religion; for up to that time the church of Canterbury had almost always had for pastors men who wore the religious habit and observed the monastic rule. For St. Augustine, the monk sent by the blessed and apostolic Pope Gregory, who first preached the faith of Christ to the English people, settled and established the church of Canterbury and many others in these parts under regular and monastic discipline, and this custom had hitherto been more carefully observed in the church of Canterbury than elsewhere, especially in the choice of an archbishop. Nevertheless, when the monks came to set this feature which they disliked in the character of their choice against the other virtues and graces which shone so brightly in him, they unanimously elected him with one heart and will.

The bishops, therefore, whom the king had sent for this purpose, appointed a day for the prior and monks of Canterbury to meet them in London, in order that whatever remained necessary to complete the formalities of the election might be publicly performed before all the bishops and abbots of the realm and in the presence of the young king. For the king, his father, had now given over his kingdom to him and, as stated above, had caused the homage and fealty of the realm to be paid to him at the hand of his chancellor. The king had also written to him about the election to the archbishopric of Canterbury, signifying that whatever might be done in that matter in his son's presence, he would himself consent to, confirm and ratify for all time. Accordingly, the aforesaid bishops, by virtue of the king's mandate, summoned all the bishops and abbots of the realm, together with the priors of the conventual churches, the earls and magnates and all the king's officers of State to assemble in London on the appointed day. When that day came and they were all gathered together, the prior of Canterbury reverently manifested, in the presence and hearing of all the bishops, the form of election which had taken place at Canterbury with the king's consent and by his mandate before the three bishops whom he had dispatched for that very purpose; affirming that by the inspiration of the Holy

Spirit Thomas, the chancellor of the realm, had been unanimously and canonically elected archbishop. The bishops also, who had been sent by the king and had witnessed the election at Canterbury, were warm in their commendation both of the form of the election and of the person of the elect, whereupon all present gave their assent and with one accord raised their voices to God in thanksgiving.

Only Gilbert Foliot, bishop of London, opposed and murmured against the election, but when he saw that the others were unanimous in their assent and that of his own malice he could effect nothing, he likewise gave his consent. He was a man advanced in years, of considerable learning, and a monk by profession, who by repute had himself long since aspired to the archbishopric. . . . But Henry, bishop of Winchester, famous no less for his lineage than for his prudence and piety, thus addressed the young king: "The lord chancellor, our archbishop-elect, has now for a long time enjoyed the highest place in the household of the king, your father, and in the whole realm, which he has entirely under his governance, nor has anything been done in the kingdom during his time save at his command. We demand therefore that he shall be handed over to us and God's Church free and absolved from all ties and service to the court, and from all suits, accusations or any other charges, and that from this hour and henceforward he may be at liberty and leisure to pursue freely the service of God. For we know full well that the king, your father, has delegated his authority to you in this matter, and will gladly ratify whatever you shall do therein." The young king willingly accepted this petition and released Thomas freely and absolutely from all secular obligations in accordance with the bishop of Winchester's request. But Thomas himself, from the first moment that his promotion was mooted, opposed it by every means in his power; knowing full well that it was impossible for him to serve two masters at once, whose wills were so much at variance, and that whoever was made archbishop of Canterbury would be sure soon to offend either God or the king. Nevertheless, God had ordained otherwise, and Henry of Pisa, cardinal-priest and legate of the apostolic see, and a monk of Cistercian Order, encouraged and urged him by every means to undertake the office. So finally his election was completed in the way we have briefly described.

On the day fixed for the consecration the bishops assembled at Canterbury and with them an immense number of abbots, monks and clergy of the land, desirous of being present at the consecration of the archbishop and of hearing his first Mass and receiving his blessing. Thomas also arrived, attended by a large body of monks and other religious personages. The bishops went out to meet him, together with the monks and clergy and a vast concourse of the people, acclaiming him with heartfelt joy and high honour; so great was their devotion and exultation that it cannot be expressed in words. But Thomas paid no heed to these manifestations, but advanced on foot with great humility and contrition, the tears flowing from his eyes, as he thought less of the honour vouchsafed to him than of the burden imposed on him. So he was ordained and consecrated archbishop at the hands of the venerable Henry, bishop of Winchester. . . . It was in the eighth year of the king's reign that Thomas was consecrated archbishop of Canterbury.

2 FROM *Carl Stephenson and*
Frederick George Marcham
Sources of English Constitutional History

The Constitutions of Clarendon (1164)

In the year 1164 from the Incarnation of the Lord, in the fourth year of the papacy of Alexander [III], and in the twelfth year of Henry II, most illustrious king of the English, there was made, in the presence of the said king, this record and recognition of a certain portion of the customs and liberties and rights of his ancestors—namely, of King Henry his grandfather and of others—which ought to be observed and held in the kingdom. And on account of the dissensions and disputes that had arisen between the clergy and the justices of the lord king and the barons of the realm concerning [such] customs and rights, this recognition was made in the presence of the archbishops, bishops, clergy, earls, barons, and magnates of the realm. Furthermore, Thomas, archbishop of Canterbury,[1] and Roger, archibishop of York, and Gilbert, bishop of London, and Henry, bishop of Winchester, and Nigel, bishop of

[1]At this Council at Clarendon (January 1164), Becket yielded to pressure and attached his name, although not his seal, to the document. He later regarded this act as a grave sin and did penance for it.

SOURCE. Carl Stephenson and Frederick George Marcham, eds. and trans., *Sources of English Constitutional History* (New York: Harper & Brothers, copyright, 1937; renewed 1965 by Frederick G. Marcham and James and Richard Stephenson), pp. 73–76. Reprinted by permission of Harper & Row, Publishers.

Ely, and William, bishop of Norwich, and Robert, bishop of Lincoln, and Hilary, bishop of Chichester, and Jocelyn, bishop of Salisbury, and Richard, bishop of Chester, and Bartholomew, bishop of Exeter, and Robert, bishop of Hereford, and David, bishop of St. David's, and Roger, [bishop] elect of Worcester, have granted and steadfastly promised, *viva voce* and on their word of truth, that the said customs, recognized by the archbishops, bishops, earls, and barons, and by the nobler and more venerable men of the realm, should be held and observed for the lord king and his heirs in good faith and without evil intent, these being present . . . and many other magnates and nobles of the realm, both clerical and lay.

Now a certain part of the recognized customs and rights of the kingdom are contained in the present writing, of which part these are the chapters:—

1. If controversy arises between laymen, between laymen and clergymen, or between clergymen, with regard to advowson and presentation to churches, it shall be treated or concluded in the court of the lord king.

2. Churches of the lord king's fee may not be given in perpetuity without his assent and grant.

3. Clergymen charged and accused of anything shall, on being summoned by a justice of the king, come into his court, to be responsible there for whatever it may seem to the king's court they should there be responsible for; and [to be responsible] in the ecclesiastical court [for what] it may seem they should there be responsible for—so that the king's justice shall send into the court of Holy Church to see on what ground matters are there to be treated. And if the clergyman is convicted, or [if he] confesses, the Church should no longer protect him.

4. Archbishops, bishops, and parsons of the kingdom are not permitted to go out of the kingdom without the licence of the lord king. And should they go out [of it], they shall, if the king so desires, give security that, neither in going nor in remaining nor in returning, will they seek [to bring] evil or damage to the king or to the kingdom.

5. Excommunicated men should not give security for all future time (*ad remanens*) or take an oath, but [should] merely [provide] security and pledge of standing by the judgment of the church in order to obtain absolution.

6. Laymen should not be accused except through known and

lawful accusers and witnesses in the presence of the bishop, [yet] so that the archdeacon shall not lose his right or anything that he should thence have. And if the guilty persons are such that no one wishes or dares to accuse them, the sheriff, on being asked by the bishop, shall have twelve lawful men from the neighbourhood, or the vill, placed on oath before the bishop to set forth the truth in the matter according to their own knowledge.

7. No one who holds of the king in chief, nor any of his demesne ministers, shall be excommunicated; nor shall the lands of any of them be placed under interdict, unless first the lord king, if he is in the land, or his justiciar, if he is outside the kingdom, agrees that justice shall be done on that person—and in such a way that whatever belongs to the king's court shall be settled there, and whatever belongs to the ecclesiastical court shall be sent thither to be dealt with there.

8. With regard to appeals, should they arise—they should proceed from the archdeacon to the bishop, and from the bishop to the archbishop. And if the archbishop fails to provide justice, recourse should finally be had to the lord king, in order that by his precept the controversy may be brought to an end in the court of the archbishop; so that it should not proceed farther without the assent of the lord king.

9. If a claim is raised by a clergyman against a layman, or by a layman against a clergyman, with regard to any tenement which the clergyman wishes to treat as free alms, but which the layman [wishes to treat] as a lay fee, let it, by the consideration of the king's chief justice and in the presence of the said justice, be settled through the recognition of twelve lawful men whether the tenement belongs to free alms or to lay fee. And if it is recognized as belonging to free alms, the plea shall be [held] in the ecclesiastical court; but if [it is recognized as belonging] to lay fee, unless both call upon the same bishop or [other] baron, the plea shall be [held] in the king's court. But if, with regard to that fee, both call upon the same bishop or [other] baron, the plea shall be [held] in his court; [yet] so that, on account of the recognition which has been made, he who first was seised [of the land] shall not lose his seisin until proof [of the title] has been made in the plea.

10. If any one in a city, castle, borough, or demesne manor of the lord king is summoned by an archdeacon or a bishop for some offence on account of which he ought to respond to the said persons, and if he refuses satisfaction on their summons, he may

well be placed under an interdict; but he should not be excommunicated until the chief minister of the lord king in that vill has been called upon to bring him to justice, so that he may come for satisfaction. And if the king's minister defaults in the matter, he shall be in the mercy of the lord king, and the bishop may then coerce that accused man through ecclesiastical justice.

11. Archbishops, bishops, and all persons of the realm who hold of the king in chief have their possessions of the king as baronies and are answerable for them to the king's justices and ministers; also they follow and observe all royal laws and customs, and like other barons they should take part with the barons in the judgments of the lord king's court, until the judgment involves death or maiming.

12. When an archbishopric, bishopric, abbey, or priory within the king's gift becomes vacant, it should be in his hands; and he shall thence take all revenues and income just as from his own demesne. And when it comes to providing for the church, the lord king should summon the greater parsons of the church, and the election should be held in the king's own chapel by the assent of the lord king and by the counsel of those parsons of the kingdom whom he has called for that purpose. And there the man elected should, before being consecrated, perform homage and fealty to the lord king as to his liege lord, for life and limbs and earthly honour, saving the rights of his order.

13. If any of the magnates of the realm forcibly prevent an archbishop, bishop, or archdeacon from administering justice, either by himself or through his men, the lord king should bring them to justice. And if perchance any forcibly prevent the lord king from [administering] his justice, the archbishops, bishops, and archdeacons should bring them to justice, so that they may satisfy the lord king.

14. Chattels of those who have incurred royal forfeiture should not be withheld in any church or churchyard against the king's justice; for they are the king's own, whether they are found inside churches or outside them.

15. Pleas of debt, owed under pledge of faith or without pledge of faith, belong to the king's justice.

16. Sons of peasants should not be ordained without the assent of the lord on whose land they are known to have been born.

Now the [present] record of the aforesaid royal rights and customs was made at Clarendon by the archbishops, bishops, earls, and barons, and by the more noble and venerable men of the realm, on the fourth day before the Purification of the Blessed Virgin Mary, in the presence of the lord Henry, together with his father, the lord king. There are, moreover, other rights and customs, both many and great, of the Holy Mother Church, of the lord king, and of the barons of the realm, which are not contained in this writing; they are to be saved to Holy Church, to the lord king and his heirs, and to the barons of the realm, and are inviolably to be observed forever.

3 FROM *David C. Douglas and*
George W. Greenaway
English Historical Documents

The Council of Northampton[1]

The king decreed that another general council should be held at Northampton on Tuesday, 6 October, being the Octave of St. Michael. On the day appointed we came to Northampton. . . .

The archbishop began by speaking of the case of William of Courcy who had occupied one of his lodgings, and he asked the king to order him to vacate possession. The king gave the order. Next the archbishop intimated that he had come to meet the summons taken out against him by John the marshal. This John demanded from the archbishop a piece of land which was part of the archiepiscopal township of Pagham. And when several days had been set aside for the hearing of the suit, he had come to the archbishop's court with a writ from the king. When he could obtain no advantage there, being supported by no right, he contended, as the law then permitted, that a defect existed in the archbishop's court; but he used for taking the oath a book of tropes, which he produced from under his cloak, though the judges of the archbishop's court

[1]The fullest account of the significant events of the Council of Northampton was written by William fitz Stephen, who is regarded as the most reliable of Becket's biographers.

SOURCE. David C. Douglas and George W. Greenaway, eds., *English Historical Documents*, Volume II, "Materials for the History of Thomas Becket" [London: Eyre & Spottiswoode (Publishers) Ltd.; New York: Oxford University Press, 1961], pp. 724–733, 761–768. Reprinted by permission of the publishers.

declared that he ought not to have brought such a book with him nor used it to such purpose. Having returned to the king, he obtained a summons citing the archbishop to answer him in the king's court, the day fixed for the hearing of the suit being the Feast of the Exaltation of the Holy Cross. The archbishop, however, did not appear on that day, but sent to the king four knights with letters from himself and the sheriff of Kent, bearing witness both to the wrong done by John and the inconclusive nature of his evidence. But to what profit? The king, being angry that the archbishop had not come in person to answer the citation and to prove his allegation, evil entreated his messengers with anger and threats for bringing a false, hollow and useless excuse in answer to a summons to the *curia regis*, and would scarcely let them depart, even when they had given sureties. And at the instance of the said John he fixed another day for the case to be heard (that is, the first day of the council), and sent out his letter to the sheriff of Kent summoning the archbishop. For he would not then, nor for a long time before, write to him in person, because he would not give him the customary word of greeting. Nor had the archbishop any other summons to the council, legal in form and directed to him in person, according to ancient custom.

The archbishop, I say, announced that he had come at the king's command concerning the case of John; to which the king replied that John was engaged on his service in London, but would arrive on the morrow, and then he himself would take cognizance of their suit. . . .

On the second day, when the bishops, earls and all the barons of England, as well as many of Normandy, had taken their seats—except the bishop of Rochester, who had not yet arrived, and one other, who was absent—the archbishop was accused of contempt of the crown because, although, as related above, he had been summoned by the king at the suit of John, he had neither come nor given a valid excuse. The archbishop's defence was not accepted, when he declared the wrongs committed by John and maintained the validity and integrity of the jurisdiction of his own court in this matter. The king demanded judgment and the archbishop's defence was wholly rejected. It seemed to all that, considering the respect due to the king and the oath of liege homage which the archbishop had taken, and the maintenance of his lord's earthly honour, to which he had sworn, he had little defence or excuse; because, when summoned by the king, he had neither come nor pleaded sickness or imperative business in respect of his ecclesiastical office.

They therefore declared that he should be condemned to forfeit all his goods and movables at the king's mercy.

A diversity of opinion then arose between the bishops and the lay magnates concerning the pronouncement of sentence, each party trying to impose this duty upon the other, while excusing themselves. The barons said, "You, the bishops, ought to pronounce sentence; this is not our province, for we are laymen. You are ecclesiastics like him, fellow-priests and brother-bishops with him." To this one of the bishops retorted, "Nay rather, it is your office, not ours; for this is a secular judgment, not an ecclesiastical. We sit here, not as bishops, but as barons. You and we are equally barons here. In vain you rely upon our order for an.argument, for if now you have regard for our ordination you ought likewise to do so in the archbishop's case. Because we are bishops, we cannot presume to judge one who is both our archbishop and our lord." What followed? The king, having listened to this argument concerning the pronouncement of sentence, was moved to anger, and soon put an end to the dispute. At his command the bishop of Winchester, though very unwillingly, finally pronounced the sentence.

The archbishop, because it was not lawful to gainsay the sentence and the declaration of the king's court of England, submitted by the advice of the bishops; and bail being granted him (as the custom is at court) to make satisfaction in respect of the judgment that had been pronounced, all the bishops stood surety for him, with the exception of Gilbert of London, who refused when asked to be security for him; which peculiarity made him conspicuous.

Later on the same day the archbishop was sued for 300 pounds which he had received as keeper of the castles of Eye and Berkhamsted. Having previously refused to answer the suit on the ground that he had not been cited therein, the archbishop said, not, however, in formal pleading, that he had used this money and much more besides to defray the expenses of repairing the Tower of London and the castles in question, as it was plain to see. The king denied that this had been done on his authority and demanded that judgment should be given. Whereupon the archbishop agreed for the king's sake to restore this money, since he was wholly unwilling that a mere question of money should occasion a quarrel between them. He therefore put forward as sureties certain laymen, the earl of Gloucester, William of Eynsford and a third person, all of whom were vassals of his.

On the third day the archbishop was interrogated by messengers

[from the king] concerning a loan of 500 marks in connexion with
the war of Toulouse and another 500 marks borrowed from a
certain Jew on the king's security. He was next arraigned by action
of wardship for all the proceeds of the archbishopric while vacant,
and of other bishoprics and abbacies vacant during his chancellorship; and he was ordered to give an account of all these to the king.
The archbishop replied that for this he had not been summoned,
nor was he prepared for it. Furthermore, if he were charged at the
proper time and place, he would render the satisfaction due by
right to his lord, the king. The king thereupon demanded the safe-
guard of sureties from him. He answered that on this matter he
ought to take the advice of his suffragans and his clergy. The king
stuck to his point, and the archbishop retired. From that day forth
the barons and the knights no longer came to see him in his lodging,
for they had well understood the mind of the king.

On the fourth day came all the ecclesiastics to the lord archbishop's lodging. He had separate conversations with the bishops
and the abbots, and took counsel on the matter with each in turn.
By the advice of the noble Henry, bishop of Winchester, who had
consecrated him and now promised him substantial aid, an attempt
was made to discover if the king could be pacified with money. The
archbishop offered him 2000 marks, but the king refused it. There
were certain of the clergy who told the archbishop that on account
of his office he was bound to protect the Church, to pay heed to his
own person and dignity, and to honour the king in all things,
saving the reverence due to God and the honour of the Church; he
need fear no opposition, since no crime or infamy could be laid to
his charge. He had been given to the church of Canterbury free of
the chancellorship and from every secular suit of the king, just as
any vacant abbey would not elect and receive as abbot a monk of
another house unless he were sent to it freed from all obedience to
his abbot. But others, who were more in touch with the secret mind
and ear of the king, showed a far different opinion, and said, "Our
lord the king is grievously angry with him. From certain indications
we interpret his mind to be this, that the lord archbishop should in
everything, and above all by resigning the archbishopric, throw
himself utterly on the king's mercy." . . .

The fifth day, which was Sunday, was wholly employed in consultations. . . .

On the sixth day a sudden weakness seized him, so that he could
not go to court. ... .

Then all the bishops were summoned to the king and remained within for some time. With them was Roger, archbishop of York, who had been the last to come to court in order to make a more distinguished entry and not to appear to be of the king's' counsel. He had his own cross carried before him, albeit outside his province, as though "threatening blow for blow." He had been forbidden by the lord pope in letters dispatched to him to have his cross borne before him in the province of Canterbury; but, on receipt of this prohibition, he lodged an appeal on a plea of false allegations on the part of the archbishop of Canterbury, and thereby considered himself safe. No wonder that grief and groaning and contrition of heart beset the archbishop; for it had been told him that on that day he would either be made a prisoner by some sentence or other, or, if he escaped this, he would be slain by a conspiracy of wicked men formed against him, as though without the king's knowledge. Meanwhile, as they sat silent, Herbert, his master in Holy Scripture, said privately to the archbishop, "My lord, if they lay impious hands on you, you may launch a sentence of excommunication against them on the spot, so that the spirit may be saved in the day of the Lord." To whom William fitz Stephen, who was sitting at the archbishop's feet, said in a little louder tone so that the archbishop might hear, "Far be it from him: not so did God's holy apostles and martyrs when they were seized and lifted up on high; rather, should this occur, let him pray for them and forgive them, and possess his soul in patience. For if it should come to pass that he suffer for the cause of justice and the freedom of the Church, by God's providence his soul will be at rest and his memory blessed. If he should pronounce sentence against them, it would appear to all men that from anger and impatience he had done his utmost to avenge himself. And without doubt he would be acting contrary to the canons." . . .

The archbishop listened to these remarks and pondered them in his heart. A little while after, the same William fitz Stephen—desirous of speaking with the archbishop and being forbidden to do so by one of the king's marshals, who stood beside him with his rod and said that no one was to speak to him—after a short space looked at the archbishop and, raising his eyes and moving his lips, made a sign to him that he should gaze upon the Cross and on the image of the Crucified which he held, and spend his time in prayer. The archbishop well understood the sign and did so, taking comfort in God. Many years afterwards, when the archbishop was an exile in France at St. Benedict's house on the Loire, he met the said William, who was then on his way to the pope, and reminded him of this among other memories of his distresses. . . .

Then the bishops, as they talked within with the king, told him that, when they had come to the archbishop that day, they had been reprimanded by him because they had, together with the barons, recently treated him in a hostile manner and judged him with unjust severity and in an unheard-of fashion, since for a single absence he should not have been adjudged contumacious or condemned at the king's mercy to the forfeiture of all his movables. For by this means the church of Canterbury might be ruined, if the king saw fit to harden his heart unmercifully against him, and a similar captious judgment might in a like case be given against the bishops and barons themselves. Then [the archbishop maintained] that it was laid down that in every shire a fixed sum of money should be paid by those condemned to pecuniary forfeiture at the king's mercy. In London it was fixed at 100 shillings. In Kent, which through its proximity to the sea has to ward off pirates from the English coast and claims the right to strike the first blow in war against a foreign enemy, and where, since the burden is the greater, the greater is the freedom, there a fine of 40 shillings is fixed for those in such wise condemned. Wherefore he, having his residence and see in Kent, ought at least to have been judged and fined by the law of Kent. Furthermore, the bishops said, on that very day, within ten days of the sentence being passed, the archbishop had summoned them to the lord pope, and had forbidden them on the pope's authority to judge him in future on any secular charge brought against him in respect of the time prior to his appointment as archbishop.

Then the king was wroth and sent to him his earls and many of his barons to inquire of him whether he was indeed responsible for this appeal and prohibition; especially in view of the fact that he was the king's liegeman and bound to him by the common oath and the particular covenant made at Clarendon in word of truth that he would preserve the royal privileges in good faith, lawfully and without guile. Among them was one that the bishops should take part in all the king's trials, save only in judgments involving shedding of blood. They were also to ask him if he would give pledges for rendering an account of his chancellorship and stand therein to the judgment of the king's court. Whereupon he, gazing upon the image of the Crucified, steadfast in mind and countenance, and remaining seated in order to preserve the dignity of an archbishop, delivered an address after this manner, clearly and smoothly, without stumbling over a single word:

"Men and brethren, earls and barons of the lord king, I am indeed bound to the king, our liege lord, by homage, fealty and oath; but the oath of a priest hath justice and equity for its fellows to a peculiar degree. In honour and fealty to the lord king am I bound in all due and devoted submission to offer him for God's sake obedience in all things, saving my obedience to God, my ecclesiastical rank and my personal honour as archbishop. I decline this suit since I received my summons neither to render accounts nor for any other cause save only for the cause of John; neither am I bound to answer or to hear judgment at the suit of another. I confess and recall that I received many commissions and dignities from the lord king, wherein I served him faithfully both here and overseas, and also, after I had joyfully expended all my own revenues, I became bound on his behalf as a debtor for a considerable sum of money. Furthermore, when, by divine permission and the favour of the lord king, I was elected archbishop and awaited consecration, I was dismissed by the king and given free to the church of Canterbury, quit and loosed from every secular suit of the king, although now he angrily denies it: but this many of you well know, and all the ecclesiastics of the realm. And you who know the truth of this I pray, beseech and adjure to bring this to the king's notice, against whom it were not safe, even if it were lawful, to produce witnesses; nor indeed will there be any need, for I will not litigate in this affair. After my consecration I set myself to sustain the honour and responsibility I had assumed with all my strength, and to be of some service to the Church of God over which I was placed. If it is not given me to make any progress or achieve any profit through the blasts of adversity, I impute this not to the lord king nor to any other man, but chiefly to my own sins. God is able to give the increase of grace to whom and when he will.

"I cannot give sureties for rendering an account. I have already bound all the bishops and friends of mine who could help me here; neither should I be compelled thereto, for it has not been so judged against me. Nor am I being impleaded concerning this account, for I was not summoned for that cause nor for any other suit, save that of John the marshal. But as to the prohibition and appeal which the bishops have this day alleged against me, I remember indeed that I did say to my brother-bishops that they had condemned me for a single absence, and not for contumacy, with undue severity and contrary to custom and age-long precedent. For this I have appealed against them and forbidden them, while this appeal is pending, to judge me again in any secular suit arising from the time prior to my assumption of the archiepiscopal dignity. I still appeal, and I place both my person and the church of Canterbury under the protection of God and the lord pope." He ended his speech, and some of the magnates returned in silence to the king, pondering and weighing his words. Others said, "Behold, we have heard the blasphemy proceeding out of his mouth." . . .

The king, having received the archbishop's answer, approached the bishops, commanding and conjuring them by the homage and fealty due to him and sworn by them, to join the barons in pronouncing sentence upon the archbishop. They began to excuse themselves by citing the archbishop's prohibition. The king was not satisfied, asserting that this single prohibition would not hold in face of what had been determined and sworn at Clarendon. The bishops, on the other hand, represented to the king that the archbishop might lay a heavy hand upon them if they did not obey his prohibition and respect his appeal; they urged that they desired and felt obliged for the king's good and the welfare of the kingdom to agree to the prohibition. When at length they had succeeded in persuading the king, they returned to the archbishop. Robert of Lincoln was weeping, and some of the others could scarce restrain their tears. Then the bishop of Chichester spoke thus, "My lord archbishop, saving your favour, we have much to complain of against you. You have gravely injured us, your bishops. You have shut us up in a trap by your prohibition, you have placed us, as it were, between the hammer and the anvil; for if we disobey, we are ensnared in the bonds of disobedience; if we obey, we infringe the constitution and trespass against the king. For recently, when we were assembled together with you at Clarendon, we were required by our lord the king to observe his royal dignities and, lest perchance we should be in any doubt, he showed us in writing the royal customs of which he spoke. At length we pledged our assent and promised to observe them, you in the first place, and we, your suffragans, afterwards at your command. When, furthermore, the lord king exacted an oath from us as security and required the impression of our seals, we told him that our oath as priests, sworn to him in the word of truth, to observe his royal privileges in good faith, lawfully and without guile, ought to suffice. The lord king was persuaded and agreed. You now compel us to act contrary to this, forbidding us to take part in the trial, as he requires of us. From this grievance and whatsoever further injury you may add to it, we appeal to the lord pope and for the present obey your prohibition."

The archbishop made answer, "I hear what you say, and if it please God I will meet your appeal. But at Clarendon no concession was made by me, or by you through me, except *saving the honour of the Church*. For, as you yourselves affirm, we made there these three reservations, *in good faith, lawfully and without guile*, whereby these privileges are saved to our churches, since we have them by canon law. For whatsoever is contrary to the faith we owe to the Church and to the laws of God cannot be observed 'in good faith' and 'lawfully.' Besides, it is not to the dignity of a Christian king that the liberty of the Church, which he has sworn to defend, shall perish. Moreover, these same articles, which you call the royal privileges, the lord king has transmitted to the pope for confirmation, but they have been sent back rejected rather than approved. He has given us an example for our learning that we should also do likewise, being ready with the Roman Church to receive what he receives and to reject what he rejects. Besides, if we fell at Clarendon (for the flesh is weak) we ought to take fresh courage and strive in the strength of the Holy Spirit against the ancient enemy. . . . If, under covenant in the word of truth, we there yielded or swore what was unjust, you well know that an unlawful oath is not binding."

Then the bishops returned to the king and, having been excused by him from judging the archbishop, they took their seats apart from the barons; nevertheless the king demanded judgment concerning the archbishop from the earls and barons. Certain sheriffs and barons of the second rank, men full of years, were also summoned to take part in the judgment. After some little delay the magnates returned to the archbishop. Robert, earl of Leicester, who in age and rank excelled the others, tried to depute the pronouncement of sentence to certain others, but when they refused, he began to recapitulate the business enacted at Clarendon point by point . . . and signified to the archbishop that he must hear the sentence. But the archbishop could endure no more and said, "What is this which you would do? Have you come to judge me? You have no right to do so. Judgment is a sentence given after trial. This day I have said nothing in the way of pleading. For no suit have I been summoned hither save only at the suit of John, who has not come to prove his charge. With respect to this you cannot give sentence. Such as I am, I am your father; you are magnates of the household, lay powers, secular personages. I will not hear your judgment." The magnates then retired. After a short interval the archbishop arose and, bearing his cross, made for the door, which had all day been securely fastened, but now opened as though of its own accord. A certain man pursued him, slandering him as he went forth, calling him a perjurer; another cried out that he fled like a traitor and carried the king's sentence with him. In the hall, which was full of servants, he stumbled over a bundle of faggots, but did not fall. He came to the gate where were his horses. Mounting his steed, he took with him Master Herbert, who could not secure his own horse so quickly on account of the crowd thronging him, and carried him to his lodging at the monastery of St. Andrew. O how great was the martyrdom he bore in spirit that day! But he returned the happier from the examination of the council, since he had been deemed worthy there to suffer shame for the Name of Jesus.

The murder of Thomas Becket[2]

So then the aforesaid men,[3] no knights forsooth but miserable wretches, as soon as they landed, summoned the king's officials, whom the archbishop had already excommunicated, and by falsely proclaiming that they were acting with the king's approval and in his name, they got together a band of knights and their followers. For they were easily persuaded to this crime by the knights' statement that they had come to settle the affair by order of the king. They then collected in a body, ready for any impious deed, and on the fifth day after the Nativity of Christ,[4] that is, on the morrow of the Feast of the Holy Innocents, they gathered together against the innocent. The hour of dinner being over, the saint had already withdrawn with some of his household into an inner chamber to transact some business, leaving the crowd awaiting his return in the hall without. The four knights with one attendant forced their way in. They were received with respect as servants of the king and well known to the archbishop's household; and those who had waited on the archbishop, being now themselves at dinner, invited

[2]The eyewitness Edward Grim describes the murder of Thomas Becket in Canterbury Cathedral on December 29, 1170.

[3]The four knights were Reginald fitz Urse, William "de Traci," Hugh of Morville, and Richard Brito; they had recently arrived in England from the king's court in Normandy.

[4]December 29, 1170.

them to share their table. They scorned the offer, thirsting rather
for blood than for food. By their order the archbishop was informed
that four men had arrived who wished to speak with him on behalf
of the king. On his giving consent, they were permitted to enter. For
a long time they sat in silence and neither saluted the archbishop
nor spoke to him. Nor did the man of wise counsel salute them
immediately they came in, in order that, according to the Scriptures,
"By thy words shalt thou be justified," he might discover their
intentions from their questions. After a while, however, he turned
to them and, carefully scanning the face of each, he greeted them in
a friendly manner; but the unhappy wretches, who had made a pact
with death, straightway answered his greeting with curses and
ironically prayed that God might help him. At these words of bitter-
ness and malice the man of God flushed deeply, for he now realized
that they had come to work him injury. Whereupon fitz Urse, who
seemed to be their leader and more prepared for the crime than the
others, breathing fury, broke out in these words: "We have somewhat to say to thee by the king's command; say if thou wilt that we
tell it here before all." But the archbishop knew what they were
about to say and answered, "These things should not be spoken in
private or in the chamber, but in public." Now these wretches so
burned for the slaughter of the archbishop that if the door-keeper
had not called back the clerks—for the archbishop had ordered
them all to withdraw—they would have killed him with the shaft of
his cross which stood by, as they afterwards confessed. When those
who had gone out returned, he, who had before reviled the archbishop, again addressed him saying, "When the king made peace
with you and all disputes were settled, he sent you back to your own
see, as you requested; but you, in contrary fashion, adding insult
to injury, have broken the peace, and in your pride have wrought
evil in yourself against your lord. For those, by whose ministry the
king's son was crowned and invested with the honours of sovereignty,
you with obstinate pride have condemned with sentence of suspen-
sion. You have also bound with the chain of anathema those
servants of the king by whose counsel and prudence the business of
the kingdom is transacted. From this it is manifest that you would
take away the crown from the king's son if you had the power. But
now the plots and schemes you have hatched in order to carry out
your designs against your lord the king are known to all men. Say
therefore whether you are prepared to come into the king's presence
and make answer to these charges." The archbishop replied, "Never

was it my wish, as God is my witness, to take away the crown from
my lord the king's son or to diminish his power; rather would I wish
him three crowns and help him to obtain the greatest realms of the
earth, so it be with right and equity. . . . Moreover, it was not by me,
but by the lord pope that the prelates were suspended from office."
"It was through you," said the infuriated knights, "that they were
suspended; do you absolve them?" "I do not deny," he answered,
"that it was done through me, but it is beyond my power and utterly
incompatible with my dignity to absolve those whom the lord pope
has bound. . . ."

"Well then," said these butchers, "this is the king's command,
that you depart with all your men from the kingdom and the lands
which own his dominion; for from this day forth there can be no
peace betwixt him and you or any of yours, for you have broken the
peace." To this the archbishop answered, "Cease your threats and
still your brawling. I put my trust in the King of Heaven who for his
own suffered on the Cross; for from this day forth no one shall see
the sea between me and my church. I have not come back to flee
again . . . "Such were the king's commands," they replied, "and
we will make them good, for whereas you ought to have shown
respect to the king's majesty and submitted your vengeance to his
judgment, you have followed the impulse of your passion and basely
thrust out from the Church his ministers and servants." At these
words Christ's champion, rising in fervor of spirit against his
accusers, exclaimed, "Whoever shall presume to violate the decrees
of the holy Roman see or the laws of Christ's Church, and shall
refuse to come of his own accord and make satisfaction, whosoever
he be, I will not spare him, nor will I delay to inflict ecclesiastical
censures upon the delinquent."

Confounded by these words, the knights sprang to their feet, for
they could no longer bear the firmness of his answers. Coming close
up to him they said, "We declare to you that you have spoken in
peril of your head." "Are you then come to slay me?" said he. "I
have committed my cause to the great Judge of all mankind; wherefore I am not moved by threats, nor are your swords more ready to
strike than is my soul for martyrdom. . . .". As they retired amidst
tumult and insults, he who was fitly surnamed 'the bear' brutishly
cried out, "In the king's name we command you, both clerks and
monks, to seize and hold that man, lest he escape by flight ere the
king take full justice on his body." As they departed with these
words, the man of God followed them to the door and cried out

after them, "Here, here will you find me"; putting his hand on his neck, as though marking beforehand the place where they were to strike.

The archbishop then returned to the place where he had before been seated, consoled his clerks and exhorted them not to fear; and, so it seemed to us who were present, he sat there waiting as unperturbed, although his death alone was sought, as if they had come to invite him to a wedding. Ere long back came the murderers in full armour, with swords, axes and hatchets, and other implements suitable for the crime on which their minds were set. Finding the doors barred and unopened at their knocking, they turned aside by a private path through an orchard till they came to a wooden partition, which they cut and hacked and finally broke down. Terrified by the noise and uproar, almost all the clerks and the servants were scattered hither and thither like sheep before wolves. Those who remained cried out to the archbishop to flee to the church; but he, mindful of his former promise that he would not through fear of death flee from those who kill the body, rejected flight. For in such case it were not meet to flee from city to city, but rather to set an example to those subject to him, so that every one of them should choose to die by the sword rather than see the divine law set at naught and the sacred canons subverted. Moreover, he who had long since yearned for martyrdom, now saw that the occasion to embrace it had seemingly arrived, and dreaded lest it should be deferred or even altogether lost, if he took refuge in the church. But the monks still pressed him, saying that it was not becoming for him to absent himself from vespers, which were at that very moment being said in the church. He lingered for a while motionless . . . deliberately awaiting that happy hour of consummation which he had craved with many sighs and sought with such devotion; for he feared lest, as has been said, reverence for the sanctity of the sacred building might deter even the impious from their purpose and cheat him of his heart's desire. For, being confident that after martyrdom he would pass from this vale of misery, he is reported to have said in the hearing of many after his return from exile, "You have here a martyr, Alphege, beloved of God and a true saint; the divine compassion will provide you with yet another; he will not tarry." But when he would not be persuaded by argument or entreaties to take refuge in the church, the monks seized hold of him in spite of his resistance, and pulled, dragged and pushed him; without heeding his opposition and his clamour to let him go, they brought him as far as the church. But the door, which led to the monks' cloister, had been carefully barred several days before, and as the murderers were already pressing on their heels, all hope of escape seemed removed. But one of them, running forward, seized hold of the bolt, and to the great surprise of them all, drew it out with as much ease as if it had been merely glued to the door.

After the monks had retreated within the precincts of the church, the four knights came following hard on their heels with rapid strides. They were accompanied by a certain subdeacon called Hugh, armed with malice like· their own, appropriately named Mauclerc, being one who showed no reverence either to God or his saints, as he proved by his subsequent action. As soon as the archbishop entered the monastic buildings, the monks ceased the vespers, which they had already begun to offer to God, and ran to meet him, glorifying God for that they saw their father alive and unharmed, when they had heard he was dead. They also hastened to ward off the foe from the slaughter of their shepherd by fastening the bolts of the folding doors giving access to the church. But Christ's doughty champion turned to them and ordered the doors to be thrown open, saying, "It is not meet to make a fortress of the house of prayer, the Church of Christ, which, even if it be not closed, affords sufficient protection to its children; by suffering rather than by fighting shall we triumph over the enemy; for we are come to suffer, not to resist." Straightway these sacrilegious men, with drawn swords, entered the house of peace and reconciliation, causing no little horror to those present by the mere sight of them and the clash of their armour. All onlookers were in tumult and consternation, for by this time those who had been singing vespers had rushed up to the scene of death.

In a spirit of mad fury the knights called out, "Where is Thomas Becket, traitor to the king and the realm?" When he returned no answer, they cried out the more loudly and insistently, "Where is the archbishop?" At this quite undaunted, as it is written, "The righteous shall be bold as a lion and without fear," he descended from the steps, whither he had been dragged by the monks through their fear of the knights, and in a perfectly clear voice answered, "Lo! here am I, no traitor to the king, but a priest. What do you seek from me?" And whereas he had already told them that he had no fear of them, he now added, "Behold, I am ready to suffer in His Name who redeemed me by His Blood. Far be it from me to

flee from your swords, or to depart from righteousness." Having
thus said, he turned aside to the right, under a pillar, having on one
side the altar of the blessed Mother of God, Mary ever-Virgin, on
the other, that of the holy confessor, Benedict, by whose example
and prayers, having crucified the world and its lusts, he endured
whatsoever the murderers did to him with such constancy of soul,
as if he were no longer in the flesh. The murderers pursued him.
"Absolve," they cried, "and restore to communion those whom
you have excommunicated, and the functions of their office to the
others who have been suspended." He answered, "There has been
no satisfaction made, and I will not absolve them." "Then you shall
die this instant," they cried, "and receive your desert." "I, too,"
said he, "am ready to die for my Lord, that in my blood the Church
may obtain peace and liberty; but in the name of Almighty God I
forbid you to harm any of my men, whether clerk or lay." Thus did
the noble martyr provide piously for his followers, and prudently
for himself, in that no one standing near should be hurt nor the
innocent oppressed, lest any serious mishap befalling any that
stood by him should dim the lustre of his glory as his soul sped up
to Christ. Most fitting was it that the soldier-martyr should follow
in the footsteps of his Captain and Saviour, who, when the wicked
sought to take him, said, "If ye seek me, let these go their way."

Then they made a rush at him and laid sacrilegious hands upon
him, pulling and dragging him roughly and violently, endeavoring
to get him outside the walls of the church and there slay him, or
bind him and carry him off prisoner, as they afterwards confessed
was their intention. But as he could not easily be moved from the
pillar, one of them seized hold of him and clung to him more
closely. The archbishop shook him off vigorously, calling him a
pandar and saying, "Touch me not, Reginald; you owe me fealty
and obedience; you are acting like a madman, you and your
accomplices." All aflame with a terrible fury at this rebuff, the
knight brandished his sword against that consecrated head. "Neither
faith," he cried, "nor obedience do I owe you against my fealty to
my lord the king." Then the unconquered martyr understood that
the hour was approaching that should release him from the miseries
of this mortal life, and that the crown of immortality prepared for
him and promised by the Lord was already nigh at hand. Whereupon, inclining his head as one in prayer and joining his hands
together and uplifting them, he commended his cause and that of
the Church to God and St. Mary and the blessed martyr, St. Denys.

Scarce had he uttered the words than the wicked knight, fearing lest he should be rescued by the people and escape alive, leapt suddenly upon him and wounded the sacrificial lamb of God in the head, cutting off the top of the crown which the unction of the sacred chrism had dedicated to God, and by the same stroke he almost cut off the arm of him who tells the story. For he, when all the others, both monks and clerks had fled, steadfastly stood by the saintly archbishop and held his arms around him, till the one he opposed to the blow was almost severed. Behold the simplicity of the dove, the wisdom of the serpent in his martyr who presented his body to the strikers that he might preserve his head, that is to say, his soul and the Church, unharmed, nor would he take any forethought or employ any stratagem against those who slay the body whereby he might escape. O worthy shepherd, who gave himself so boldly to the wolves, in order that his flock might not be torn to pieces! Because he had cast away the world, the world in seeking to crush him unconsciously exalted him.

Next he received a second blow on the head, but still he stood firm and immovable. At the third blow he fell on his knees and elbows, offering himself a living sacrifice and saying in a low voice, "For the Name of Jesus and the protection of the Church I am ready to embrace death." But the third knight inflicted a terrible wound as he lay prostrate. By this stroke the sword was dashed against the pavement and the crown of his head, which was large, was separated from the head in such a way that the blood white with the brain and the brain no less red from the blood, dyed the floor of the cathedral with the white of the lily and the red of the rose, the colours of the Virgin and Mother and of the life and death of the martyr and confessor. The fourth knight warded off any who sought to intervene, so that the others might with greater freedom and licence perpetrate the crime. But the fifth—no knight he, but that same clerk who had entered with the knights—that a fifth blow might not be wanting to the martyr who in other things had imitated Christ, placed his foot on the neck of the holy priest and precious martyr and, horrible to relate, scattered the brains and blood about the pavement, crying out to the others, "Let us away, knights; this fellow will rise no more."

In all his sufferings the illustrious martyr displayed an incredible steadfastness. Neither with hand nor robe, as is the manner of human frailty, did he oppose the fatal stroke. Nor when smitten did he utter a single word, neither cry nor groan, nor any sound indicative of pain. But he held motionless the head which he had bent to meet the uplifted sword until, bespattered with blood and brains, as though in an attitude of prayer, his body lay prone on the pavement, while his soul rested in Abraham's bosom.

4 FROM *Z. N. Brooke*
The English Church and the Papacy from the Conquest to The Reign of John

The Victory of Canon Law

Becket won a victory in his lifetime that might or might not have been lasting. But by his death he won a much more striking victory for the freedom of the Church, which was a permanent one; it was a victory, however, rather for the Pope than for the archbishop. The clause about criminous clerks was repealed, though not apparently the other clauses affecting the ecclesiastical courts. But Henry also promised to allow freedom of appeals for the future, which meant the discarding of the old barriers between England and Rome, and therefore the nullification of the main purpose of the Constitutions. As a result of the concessions of Henry II, canon law becomes at last completely valid in this country; in the full practice of the law the English Church is able to take its place with the rest of the Church. Neither the knowledge nor the desire had been lacking before, but only the power. The king's authority had stood in the way. Now he withdraws his opposition and allows free intercourse between Rome and England, and the working of the law is able to take its normal course. There had been an approximation to this in the reign of Stephen, but only an approximation, as I have already shown.

The change after the death of Becket is especially illustrated in the canon law itself. For in the *Decretales* of Gregory IX are included over 400 decretals of Alexander III, and the remarkable thing about them is that he addressed to this country more decretals than to all the rest of Europe put together. I made, in the

SOURCE. Z. N. Brooke, *The English Church and the Papacy from the Conquest to the Reign of John* (Cambridge: Cambridge University Press, 1952), pp. 211–214. Reprinted by permission of the publisher.

article mentioned above, an analysis of them and of the points on which particular instruction was given to Englishmen. These decretals of Alexander III to England reveal a number of important facts: that appeals from England at once became numerous and regular as in other countries; that English bishops were applying to the Pope for advice on numerous points of canon law; that Englishmen were entering into the study of canon law with an enthusiasm unknown before, and were showing themselves especially zealous in the collection of papal decretals, particularly the recent ones; and, finally, that the Pope was taking advantage of the cases coming from England to give solemn judgments on points which were either not dealt with in the law or were not decided definitely by papal authority. Even Gratian had left a number of points rather indecisive, and there was no complete code of law, procedure, and jurisprudence; a great deal that was customary was not written down, and the Roman customs had to be explained and enforced. This was particularly necessary in the case of England, and of course the majority of these decretals are concerned with questions of jurisdiction. The number of Alexander's decretals to England is especially accounted for by the need of instructing a part of the Church which up till then had not been experienced in the full practice of the law as worked at Rome. To take one instance to show what I mean. Enormous readjustments were required when appeals to Rome became lawful and common. The Bishop's court became much less important, and so did his functions as judge ordinary; on the other hand, he commonly had to act on papal instructions as judge delegate. This was a new field of practice, the details of which had to be carefully elaborated, and thirteen of Alexander's decretals to England deal with this topic. The point, then, is that now at last we can see the canon law in full working order in England, and therefore the normal exercise of papal authority. This does not mean that the royal authority was of no effect in the Church, or that all the rules of canon law were implicitly adhered to. The king exercised a very considerable control in certain respects, and in the clash of legislations and jurisdictions the secular often won a victory over the ecclesiastical. But this was the case in every country in Europe. The papal authority and the canon law have the same validity and the same efficacy in England as elsewhere, but the boundaries between the two authorities could never be accurately defined, so that disputes were bound to occur everywhere.

Charles Duggan
From the Conquest to the Death of John

A Victory for Both Sides

There is no doubt that Henry selected Becket as primate in the expectation that the former association of William I and Lanfranc, to their mutual advantage, would be re-created; and this was natural in recollection of the important political role which had been filled by English prelates down to that time, while contemporaries noted how in a wider canvass the German rulers enjoyed a similar relationship with the archbishops of Mainz and Cologne as imperial chancellors. But this expectation was not to be realized. The conflict which ensued will not be understood if the vision is narrowed to the particular points at issue at any given stage of the controversy. If this were done, it would be possible to argue that personal differences between Becket and Henry were of primary importance; or that material interests, such as the Canterbury properties, dominated Becket's policies; or that primatial notions of prestige and power in the English Church lay at the root of Becket's relations with the English episcopate. All these elements are present in the story and have their importance; but they could not explain why, for instance, Alexander III, despite the difficulties of his own position and his reluctance at times to be committed to the full rigour of Becket's logic, nevertheless associated Becket with Lucas of Gran as the twin buttresses of the Church's liberties.

This is not to make a moral judgment for or against the archbishop or the king: both their policies are explicable in the framework of their thought processes. It is possible in retrospect to sympathize either with the one or the other, while fully accepting and understanding the views of both. On the one hand, there is the background of relentlessly advancing canon law and papal ideology already described, together with the spiritual and religious climate reflected in the dynamic monastic movements of the period; on the other, there are the concepts of medieval kingship and the increasingly self-conscious theories of royal justice and its practical realiza-

SOURCE. Charles Duggan, "From the Conquest to the Death of John," in C. H. Lawrence, ed., *The English Church and the Papacy in the Middle Ages* (New York: Fordham University Press, 1965; copyright 1965 by Burns & Oates, Ltd.), pp. 87–93. Reprinted by permission of the publishers, the editors, and the author.

tion. Both these major streams of development were swelling and flowing more swiftly through the century. The intellectual ferment of the age must also be considered, especially the legal and theoretical strands of the so-called twelfth-century renaissance, which was reaching in these respects a peak of achievement in the second half of the century: an intensively creative period in the history of law, whether of canon law and Roman law, or of the regional laws of the various kingdoms. It was virtually inescapable that difficulties, in various forms, would arise as the separate concepts of jurisdiction and legal systems clashed at their many points of overlapping interests.

Henry, in his coronation charter of 1154, had promised to preserve the freedom of the Church. And, while Theobald lived, an open conflict was averted; but there is ample evidence that the aged archbishop was increasingly disquieted by indications of a firmer royal policy. Meanwhile, Henry had thrown his support on the side of Alexander III in the papal schism which opened in 1159; and, in the early phase of Becket's rule, the English Church was seen in harmonious relationship with the exiled pope: both archbishops, of Canterbury and York, attended the Council of Tours in 1163, with a number of English bishops. A widening area of disagreement between Becket and the king rose, however, to a crisis over the question of criminous clerks in 1163, and culminated in Henry's sixteen points programme in the Constitutions of Clarendon in 1164. By these clauses Henry sought formal recognition of the customs regulating relations between royal and ecclesiastical interests as established by the Norman kings. These were the *avitae consuetudines*, the customs of his grandfather; and there is general agreement that his claim was valid on almost all points as to the matter of historical fact. Some of the clauses necessarily involved relations with the papacy, others dealt more specifically with politico-ecclesiastical questions within the kingdom. One vital clause aimed to make the departure of ecclesiastics from England to the continent subject to the king's consent; a further clause cut short the appellate system of ecclesiastical courts at the provincial level, so that recourse should not be had to the papal Curia except at the will of the king; the famous third clause embodied the royal plan to ensure the secular constraint of criminous clerks; yet another clause dealt with ecclesiastical vacancies and electoral procedure. There is no doubt that Henry made a tactical mistake in seeking to extort a sealed acceptance of these requirements, which could not be reconciled with the existing state of the Church's law. He would almost certainly have been able to enforce his will, at least on several points, in practice. Becket, for his part, was adamant in his refusal to agree to such conditions, apart from a temporary vacillation under heavy pressure. For Becket the appeal to custom was quite irrelevant. Echoing directly the words of Gregory VII in the previous century, he argued that Christ had said "I am the truth"; He had never said "I am the custom."

In canon law there is little doubt that Becket was fully justified in the attitude he assumed in opposing the constitutions. But the English bishops, though basically in agreement with him, were not prepared, for various reasons, to support him *in extremis*. The pope, too, was in a perilous phase of his struggle with Barbarossa, and would doubtless have preferred to avoid the English issue altogether at that moment. Nevertheless, when confronted directly with Henry's constitutions, he condemned ten outright, while being prepared to tolerate six. The archbishop's exile, his absence in France for six years filled with difficult negotiations and abortive attempts to work out a solution of the quarrel, the final reconciliation and return to England, his martyrdom at Canterbury in 1170, and his canonization by Alexander III in 1173: all these are very familiar details. Relations between England and the papal Curia continued at a high and sometimes anxious level of activity throughout. Alexander's rulings varied in their precision and firmness in some proportion to his own fluctuating fortunes in his struggle with Frederick I; and Henry was not averse to exploiting Alexander's difficulties by the threat of defecting to Pascal III. Constantly, letters were exchanged between both parties in the English dispute on the one hand and the Roman Curia on the other; paradoxically the quarrel increased this intercommunication, which Henry made no attempt to curtail. Meanwhile, Alexander had also to deal diplomatically with the re-emergence of the Canterbury and York dispute, which was brought to a pitch of crisis by Roger of York's coronation of the young king, Henry's son, in 1170 while Becket was still in exile, in derogation of Becket's rights and in opposition to the papal prohibitions. And all the while the routine contacts were maintained, to some extent, between English religious houses and ecclesiastical judges and the papal Curia.

Henry averted the threat of serious papal reprisals for Becket's murder, and his reconciliation with the Church was achieved in two main stages. The Compromise of Avranches in 1172 included royal promises of acts of penance in atonement for the outrage, which Henry swore he had neither wished nor contrived, and policy undertakings in connection with specified points in dispute during the quarrel. He promised to repeal the customs introduced in his time against the Church in his kingdom, though he protested to Bartholomew of Exeter that he considered these very few or even none at all; and he promised also to allow freedom of appeals to the Curia unless injury to his own position was thereby threatened. There was no explicit reference to the Clarendon Constitutions, nor was there mention of the subject of criminous clerks. A letter of Alexander III to Henry, recording the terms of agreement, survives in transcription, from which it is clear that the pope was much concerned to have them officially registered for future reference. Three years later, the legate Pierleoni arrived in England in 1175, and further disputed points were settled by the following year. On this occasion a letter of Henry II to Alexander is extant, agreeing to the elimination of various outstanding abuses touching vacancies and the persons and rights of clerks, and most significantly accepting the principle of clerical immunity from secular justice, with the exceptions of charges relating to lay fees or transgressions of the forest law. Meanwhile, other facets of Anglo-papal relations were revealed by Henry's appeal for papal support in his period of great danger during the rising of 1173–4, and by the young king's dealings with the pope in an attempt to assert his royal position, *vis à vis* his father. In many ways Henry continued to keep a firm grip on the English Church, in spite of several important concessions. Three of his most loyal aides in the contest with Becket were elected to the sees of Winchester, Norwich and Ely in the years of the post-Becket settlement: they were respectively Richard of Ilchester, John of Oxford and Geoffrey Ridel. In such ways as these, Henry was seen to achieve some of the vital objects which he had pursued at Clarendon in 1164. Nor did he faithfully fulfil the promises he had made to the papal legates in 1172 and 1175–6, as the prolongation of episcopal vacancies affords striking testimony.

Historians have variously assessed the results of the compacts between Henry II and the papacy after Becket's martyrdom. For Zachary Brooke, the main theme was a posthumous victory for the archbishop, with the defeat of Henry's attempt to reconstruct the barrier policy of his ancestors, and the opening up of England for the first time to the full impact of canon law after a period of isolation. For Cheney, the Compromise of Avranches settled nothing, in the sense that royal policy seemed not significantly changed by the precise terms of the agreement; and he has adduced impressive evidence in support of the thesis that the period after Avranches was one of "effective adjustment, with give and take between the two jurisdictions." For Morey, the importance of the settlement was rather that it permitted the English Church to go forward participating fully in the overall advance of the Western Church, whereas this result might otherwise have been imperilled. In two respects, Brooke's thesis is no longer acceptable, since the English Church had clearly not been isolated before the compromise; and his use of decretal evidence as the main element of proof in his argument is now known to have been misconceived. Apart from this important proviso, the various views are not as irreconcilable as they may seem at first consideration, and are in fact complementary facets of a single whole.

The twelfth century was not an age of unconditional surrender: victory of Church or monarchy on one point did not necessarily entail the same result on others. In this respect, Cheney's view is clearly valid: each side gained some points and surrendered others. It is difficult not to believe that the Church, under papal guidance, gained a great victory in the matter of routine appeals to the Roman Curia: the striking evidence of the decretals which poured into England from the early 1170's (as they did into other countries also) and the ever-expanding jurisdiction of the papal judges delegate prove that the two-way traffic between the English courts Christian and the Curia had now become a constant factor and altogether a matter of course, whatever evidence there may be of royal curtailment of it in specific instances. On the vexed question of criminous clerks, the Church gained recognition of a highly-prized principle, but conceded certain exceptions in return. On other debated matters, the Church failed utterly to establish its position against secular opposition. The question of advowsons, the *ius praesentandi*, affords a significant example of the secular law in practice winning a victory over the law of the Church; and in many other ways, as already indicated, the English king was able to canalize or curtail its full operation. But the canon law in England made dramatic strides forward in the decades following Becket's death: the activities of the English judges delegate and of the canonists in the circles of distinguished English bishops were unsurpassed in some respects elsewhere in Europe at that period, of which developments the work of the English decretal collectors provides a major and permanently important illustration. Papal legislation then flowed into England: Archbishop Richard cited Alexander's decretals in his provincial council of 1175; the canons of the 1179 Lateran Council, which English bishops attended, were brought back immediately into England, and transcribed in numerous manuscripts within a year or two of their promulgation; papal decretal letters enforced some of the Lateran rulings in England before Alexander's death in 1181; swift and frequent interchange between the schools of English and continental canonists is abundantly recorded in the manuscripts surviving from the period. Archbishops Richard and Baldwin are frequently judged inadequate successors to Becket, from an ecclesiastical or papal viewpoint, but in the application of canon law throughout the kingdom there is irrefutable evidence of its steady and effective growth throughout their time.

PART SIX

The Culmination of the Gregorian Reform Movement : The Pontificate of Innocent III

The pontificate of Innocent III (1198–1216) is justifiably considered the high point of medieval papal influence. It was the period when Rome became, in fact, the center of the legal and ecclesiastical machinery of the Church; when the papacy achieved real jurisdiction over the clergy and sometimes guided the policies of lay rulers. To a degree far surpassing his medieval predecessors and his modern successors, Innocent dominated the political, diplomatic, and ecclesiastical stage of Europe for eighteen years. Insofar as the goals of the Gregorian reformers were ever completely achieved, the pontificate of Innocent III marks the culmination of that movement.

Innocent intervened frequently in matters that could ordinarily be considered strictly within the province of temporal powers. For example, he played a vigorous role in the disputes over the imperial crown of Germany; he claimed the right to interfere in the feudal conflicts that developed between Kings John of England (1199–1216) and Philip Augustus of France (1180–1223); he stressed the appellate jurisdiction of the Roman Curia and encouraged appeals from all over Europe on matters relating to the clergy, marriage, wills, and issues summarized under the vague and highly elastic term "cure of souls."

The theories of papal authority enunciated by Pope Innocent have been subjected to a great variety of interpretations. The problem arises essentially from the fact that, while he issued what are undoubtedly the most sweeping general assertations of papal power ever made, he justified his actual interventions in secular affairs, his disputes with civil authorities, on the ground that it was his duty as the Vicar of Christ to correct and punish sin, to promote peace among Christian countries, and to preserve the fidelity of Christian oaths. Contemporary rulers disagreed violently and considered Innocent's words only a pious camouflage to conceal his political ambitions. The viewpoints of subsequent students likewise represent many shades of opinion.

Papal statements and decretals illustrate Innocent's dynamic application of original Gregorian ideas, his apparent belief that the Bishop of Rome, as Vicar of Christ and supreme representative of the Church, possessed the "plenitudo potestatis," the fullness of power over both Church and State. First is a passage from a sermon delivered on the morning of his coronation (February 22, 1198). In the Decretal *Per Venerabilem*, Innocent used the opportunity of an ordinary request by Count William of Montpellier for the legitimization of his two bastard sons to expand on his theory of papal power. Third, the Decretal *Novit Ille*, which sought to bring about peace between Philip Augustus and John, had the most far-reaching consequences. While Innocent acknowledged that he had no jurisdiction in ordinary feudal disputes, he insisted that his competence did exist in matters involving sin; and what political deeds do not contain some moral aspects? Innocent justified his right to participate in the election of the German emperor in the Decretal *Venerabilem Fratrem* partly on the precedent set by the coronation of Charlemagne.

The commentaries which follow reflect some of the diversity of interpretations about the man, his theories and his motives. The severely critical viewpoint of Geoffrey Barraclough sees Innocent as a ruthless practitioner of power politics and as partially responsible for the retarded development of the German monarchy. Brian Tierney, a leading scholar of medieval canon law, places Innocent's Decretal *Per Venerabilem* in the context of the legal and canonical developments of the twelfth century.

1 FROM *J. P. Migne*
Sermo II. In Consecratione Pontificis Maximi

Innocent III—Sermons on the Consecration of a Pope, February 22, 1198

Who am I, or what was the house of my father, that I am permitted to sit above kings, to possess the throne of glory? For it is to me that the words of the prophet apply: "I have established you above kings in order that you will uproot and destroy, and also that you will build and plant" (Jeremiah 1:10). It was to me that the words were addressed, "I will give you the keys of the kingdom of heaven, and all that you bind on earth will be bound in heaven" (Matthew 16:19). See then who is this servant who commands all the family. This is the Vicar of Jesus Christ, the successor of St. Peter . . . established as the mean between God and man: less than God, but greater than man.

The Roman Church that I have espoused . . . has brought me a dowry, the plenitude of spiritual powers and the breadth of temporal ones. Only Peter was called to assume the fullness of power. She (the Church) has brought to me the mitre, the symbol of my religious responsibilities, and she had given me the crown, the sign of my temporal authority.

SOURCE. From "Sermo II In Consecration Pontificis Maximi," in J. P. Migne, *Patrologiae Latinae*, Volume 217 (Paris, 1855), cols. 657–658, 665. Translated for this volume by Bennett D. Hill.

2 FROM *Sidney Z. Ehler and John B. Morrall*
Church and State Through the Centuries

The Decretal *"Per venerabilem,"* September 7, 1202

Through our venerable brother, the Archbishop of Arles, who had betaken himself to the Apostolic See, your humility requested us that we deign to adorn your sons with the title of legitimation in order that the objection of (illegitimate) birth should not do harm to their succession to you. From the fact that the Apostolic See, after investigation of various pleas, has dispensed some illegitimate sons, not only natural sons but also those born from adultery, legitimating them for spiritual functions so that they could be promoted to be bishops, from this fact it is evident that the Apostolic See has full power in this matter. Consequently, it is believed as the more probable and reputed as the more credible that it is entitled to legitimate such children for secular functions, particularly since they do not know among men any one superior to the Roman Pontiffs who would have the power of legitimating; because, as for spiritual things both a greater precaution and higher fitness and authority are required, that which is conceded in major things appears as lawful also in minor ones.—

Inspired by these considerations, we conceded the favour to the king (Philip II of France) as we had been requested, holding it both from the Old and from the New Testament that it is not only in the States of the Church—where we have full power in temporal matters—but also in other countries that we can occasionally exercise the temporal jurisdiction in certain cases, after having previously examined them. This does not mean that we want to prejudice the rights of anybody else or usurp any power which does not belong to us because we do not ignore that Christ replied in the Scripture: "Render to Caesar the things that are Caesar's and to God the things that are God's"; consequently, when He was asked to divide an inheritance between two claimants, He said: "Who hath appointed me judge or divider over you?" But in Deuteronomy the following is contained: "If thou perceive that there be among you a

SOURCE. Sidney Z. Ehler and John B. Morrall, eds. and trans., *Church and State Through the Centuries* (Glen Rock, N.J.: Newman Press, 1954), pp. 67–72. Reprinted by permission of the publisher.

hard and doubtful matter in judgment between blood and blood, cause and cause, leprosy and leprosy; and thou see that the words of the judges within thy gates do vary: arise, and go up to the place, which the Lord thy God shall choose. And thou shalt come to the priests of the Levitical race, and to the judge, that shall be at that time; and thou shalt ask of them, and they shall show thee the truth of the judgment. And thou shalt do whatsoever they shall say, that preside in the place which the Lord shall choose, and what they shall teach thee according to His law; and thou shalt follow their sentence: neither shalt thou decline to the right hand nor to the left hand. But he that will be proud, and refuse to obey the commandment of the priest, who ministereth at that time to the Lord thy God, and the decree of the judge: that man shall die, and thou shalt take away the evil from Israel." Thus, if interpreting the second law of Deuteronomy, it proves on the strength of its wording and in relation to this passage that what is determined there should also be observed in the New Testament. For the place which the Lord has chosen is obviously the Apostolic See because the Lord Himself has established it, having laid its foundation stone. For when Peter, on his flight from Rome, was leaving the City the Lord, wanting him to return to the place which He had chosen and being asked by him "Lord, where are you going?" replied: "I am going to Rome to be crucified again." Understanding that this was meant for him Peter immediately returned. For the priests of the Levitical tribe are our brothers who function according to the Levitical law as our coadjutors in the discharge of our sacerdotal office. A priest or judge exists, superior to them, to whom the Lord said in the person of St. Peter: "Whatsoever thou shalt bind upon earth, it shall be bound also in Heaven; and whatsoever thou shalt loose upon earth, it shall be loosed also in Heaven"; he is the vicar of Him Who is priest in eternity according to the law of Melchizedek, and established by God to be judge over the living and the dead. For in fact three kinds of justice are to be distinguished: first between blood and blood by which the criminal and the civil law are meant; last between leprosy and leprosy by which the ecclesiastical and the criminal law are understood; and a middle one is between cause and cause which refers to both laws, ecclesiastical as well as civil; in these if anything were difficult or ambiguous, recourse is to be had to the Apostolic See and if any one in his pride would disregard its sentence with contempt, he shall precipitate himself into death and shall take away the evil from Israel, i.e. he shall be separated, as if dead, from the communion of the faithful by a sentence of excommunication. St. Paul, too, writing to the Corinthians in order to explain the plenitude of power, said: "Know you not that we shall judge angels? How much more things of this world!" Consequently, the office of the secular power is exercised sometimes and in some matters directly by him, but other times and in other cases through others.

Thus, although we have decided that justice should be done to the sons of the often-mentioned king of France when it was doubted whether they had been legitimate from the start; because both the Mosaic and Canon law hates children born in adultery, as the Lord is witness: "A mamser, that is to say, one born of a prostitute" and a bastard "shall not enter into the church of the Lord, until the tenth generation"; as the Canon law forbids them to be promoted to the holy orders; and as secular laws not only exclude them from paternal succession but even deny them allowances for sustenance ("alimenta"), we have thought it right so far to supersede the aforesaid petition and we do not meet now your prayer in this matter with consent until, if possible, both a lesser guilt and a more liberal jurisdiction may appear; although we embrace your person with arms of a special affection and are prepared to show to you special favour in any matters in which we could extend it in accordance with God and honesty.

The Decretal "Novit Ille," 1204

He knows, Who ignores nothing and Who, knowing the secrets, is searcher of hearts, that we love our illustrious son in Christ, Philip, king of the French, with pure heart, good conscience and unpretended fidelity; we genuinely favor his honor, success and prosperity, pondering on the growth of the French kingdom and the exaltation of the Apostolic See and wishing that this kingdom, blessed by God, may always remain in devotion to Him and never depart—as we hope—from this devotion; for, although sometimes, here and there, the influence of the wicked angels appear, we shall endeavour—not ignoring the astuteness of Satan—to prevent his temptations hoping that the said king will not allow himself to be tempted by his fallacies.

No one, therefore, may suppose that we intend to disturb or diminish the jurisdiction or power of the illustrious king of the French just as he himself does not want to and should not impede our jurisdiction and power; as we are insufficient to discharge all our jurisdiction, why should we wish to usurp that of someone else? But the Lord said in the Gospel: "If thy brother shall offend against thee, go, and rebuke him between thee and him alone. If he shall hear thee, thou shalt gain thy brother. And if he will not hear thee, take with thee one or two more, that in the mouth of two or three witnesses every word may stand. And if he will not hear them, tell the church. And if he will not hear the church, let him be to thee as the heathen and publican." And the king of England is prepared—so he says—to prove sufficiently that the king of the French sins against him, that he himself tried to correct him according to the Evangelic rule and then, when he had no success, he told the Church about it. And how could we, who have been called by the Highest disposition to the government of the whole Church, fail to obey the Divine mandate and not to proceed according to its form unless, perhaps, he produces in our presence or in the presence of our Legate a sufficient plea to the contrary? For we do not intend to render justice in feudal matters, in which the jurisdiction belongs to him, unless something may be detracted from the common law by some special privilege or contrary custom, but we want to decide in the matter of sins, of which the censure undoubtedly pertains to us and we can and must exercise it against any one.—

In this, indeed, we do not lean on human constitutions, but much more on Divine law, because our power is not from man but from God: any one who has a sound mind knows that it belongs to our office to draw away any Christian from any mortal sin and, if he despises the correction, to coerce him with ecclesiastical penalties.—

That we can and also must coerce, is obvious from the words which the Lord said to the prophet who was one of the priests of Anathot: "Lo, I have set thee this day over the nations and over kingdoms, to root up and to pull down, and to waste, and to destroy, to build, and to plant." It is, indeed, obvious that what is to be rooted up, pulled down and destroyed is all mortal sin. Besides, when the Lord handed over the keys of the kingdom of Heaven to St. Peter, He told him: "Whatsoever thou shalt bind upon earth, it shall be bound also in Heaven; and whatsoever thou shalt loose upon earth, it shall be loosed also in Heaven." Nobody will certainly doubt that he who commits mortal sins is bound before God. If therefore Peter is to imitate the Divine justice, he must bind on earth those who are known to be bound in Heaven. Somebody might, perhaps, say that the kings are to be dealt with differently from the others. But, as we know, it is written in the Divine law: "There shall be no difference in persons; you shall hear the little as well as the great; neither shall you respect any man's person, because it is the judgment of God"; . . . We are thus entitled to wield the power to proceed in this manner in any criminal sin, in order to recall the sinner back from vice to virtue and from error to truth, and particularly so if sins are committed against peace which is the bond of charity.—

As the treaties of peace should be ultimately renewed between the two kings and as they had been confirmed on both sides by duly sworn oaths, but not fulfilled within the fixed time, could we not examine these religious oaths—which undoubtedly pertain to the jurisdiction of the Church—in order to cause the broken peace treaties to be restored? Lest we seem to favour hypocritically such a discord, to conceal the destruction of sacred places and to neglect the ruin of Christian people, we gave the instruction to the above-said Legate, our beloved son the Abbot of Casamari, that, unless the king (of France) re-establishes a solid peace with the afore-mentioned king (of England), or concludes an adequate truce, or at least remains humbly passive, this Abbot and our venerable brother, the Archbishop of Bourges, should extrajudicially investigate whether the complaints, which the king of the English raised against him before the Church, are just, or whether that his defence against the plaintiff is substantiated, which he had expressed in the letter he sent to us, not omitting to observe the procedure that we had fixed for him. And we enjoin to you all by this Apostolic letter and clearly order in virtue of your obedience that when the said Abbot shall have carried out the Apostolic instructions in this matter, you should accept his sentence—which will be actually our sentence—in a humble manner, observe it and make it to be observed by others, knowing that if you depart from it, we will punish your disobedience.

Given at the Lateran, in the year VII [sc. of our Pontificate, i.e. in 1204.]

The Decretal "Venerabilem fratrem," March, 1202

We have kindly received our venerable brother, the Archbishop of Salzburg, and our beloved son the Abbot of Salmansweiler, and the noble margrave of the East, who were sent by some princes as envoys to the Apostolic See, and we decided to grant them a bene-volent audience. The letter which had been dispatched through them by some noble princes, we caused to be read carefully and we have noted everything which it contained. Among other things some princes use chiefly the objection that our venerable brother, the Bishop of Palestrina and Legate of the Apostolic See, behaved either as an Elector or as a judge; if as Elector, he threw his sickle in a stranger's harvest and, interfering with the election, disparaged the dignity of Electors; if as judge, it seems obvious that he proceeded wrongly because one of the parties was absent, was not called upon and thus should not have been judged as contumacious.

Just as we—who owe justice to particular persons according to the service connected with the Apostolic office—do not want our justice to be usurped by others, so we do not wish to vindicate to ourselves the rights of the princes. Wherefore we recognize, as we should, the right and power of those princes to whom it is known to pertain by right and ancient custom to elect a king who is subsequently to be promoted to the dignity of Emperor; and particularly so as this right and power has come to them from the Apostolic See, which had transferred the Roman Empire from the Greeks to the Germans in the person of Charlemagne. But, on the other hand, the princes should recognize, and they actually do recognize, that the right and authority to examine the person elected as king—who is to be promoted to the office of Emperor—belong to us, who anoint, consecrate and crown him. For it is usually and generally observed that the examination of the person appertains to him to whom belongs the laying-on of hands. Consequently, if the princes not only by divided votes but even unanimously elected as king a sacrilegious or excommunicated man, a tyrant or an idiot, a heretic or a pagan, should we anoint, consecrate and crown such a man? Certainly not!—

And it is obvious both from law and precedent that, if in an election the votes of the princes are divided, we can favour, after due warning and adequate waiting, one of the two parties, the more so as the unction, consecration and coronation will be demanded of us and it has often happened that both parties demanded it. For if the princes, after having been warned and granted a delay, either can not or will not agree, the Apostolic See would have no advocate and defender and, therefore, would not their fault result in penalizing her?—

As we can not be diverted from our intention by any occasion, we shall keep to it most persistently and as you had often suggested to us not to support that duke (i.e. Philip of Hohenstaufen), we now

admonish your Nobility and enjoin by this Apostolic letter that—
since you rely on our favour and we hope for your devotion—you
abandon entirely the cause of the aforesaid duke Philip in spite of
any oath that you might have taken towards him with regard to the
kingdom; because, as he can not obtain the Imperial dignity, having
been rejected, such oaths need not to be observed. But adhere, openly
and effectively, to king Otto whom we intend to call—with the
Lord's help—to the Imperial crown; if, following this our admonition, you adhere to him, you shall deserve particularly and among
the. first to obtain his favour and benevolence and in this you shall
have, for the love of your Nobility, our full support.

Given at the Lateran.

3   FROM   *Geoffrey Barraclough*
              The Origins of Modern Germany

Innocent III, the Master of Power Politics

With the accession of Innocent III to the papal throne in 1198, it
was immediately clear how unwise was the failure of Henry VI to
grasp the opportunity of conciliation and a final settlement with the
church, which had never been beyond the bounds of possibility
since the death of Alexander III in 1181. The reaction after
Alexander's death against a political papacy had been real and had
offered real prospects of settlement; but the reaction in 1198 with
the accession of a young, energetic, politically-minded pope was to
the other extreme. There is no doubt that Innocent III's main
object was to restore the temporal power of the papacy, assailed
ever since Frederick Barbarossa had embarked on a policy of
territorial reconstruction in central Italy after the peace of Constance, and doubly threatened since the consummation of the union
of Sicily with the Empire. Hence from beginning to end, despite
all pretence of standing above parties, and despite also the tergiver-
sations forced on him by events, he was an unbending opponent of
the Hohenstaufen dynasty, determined to destroy for all time the
connection of Sicily and the Empire and the position in central

SOURCE. Geoffrey Barraclough, *The Origins of Modern Germany* (Oxford: Basil
Blackwell, 1952), pp. 206–208. Reprinted by permission of the publishers and the
author.

Italy, for which the Hohenstaufen stood, at no matter what cost to Germany. Two little-noted facts illustrate his ruthless determination. The one was the severe rebuke issued in 1200 to the great German patriot, archbishop Conrad of Mainz—once the staunchest supporter of Alexander III, now (in the twilight of his life) the altruistic sponsor of peace in Germany—because his attempts to reconcile the German factions threatened to create a common German front and thus to deprive the pope of the influence which German divisions gave him in imperial affairs. The other, in the same year, was the instructions issued to the papal legate in the west, authorizing him to annul the peace concluded between England and France, because the withdrawal of English and French support from the contending parties was likely to put an end to German discords and leave the Hohenstaufen in control of a united people who would not brook papal interference. To get his way, in short, to enforce his own conception of the relations of church and state, Innocent was prepared not only to destroy the internal peace of Germany, but also to set the states of Europe at war with one another. Against these facts it matters little that he protested—too often, perhaps, and too vehemently—that he had imperial interests at heart and had no intention of oppressing or destroying the empire. His protests were doubtless sincere; but when he spoke of the empire, he meant an empire of his own conception and not the historical Empire which had been raised from the dust of the Investiture Contest by the genius of the Hohenstaufen. His praise of Lothar II, the church's nominee, revealed the direction of his thoughts, which led back directly to the ideas of Gregory VII: an emperor selected by the free choice of the princes but unqualified to rule until, after due examination at the Holy See, he had secured the approval and confirmation of the pope. Innocent's claims were, therefore, not new—new only was the rigorous logic with which he argued that the disposal of the German throne was *principaliter et finaliter* a prerogative of the Holy See—but they were claims which, after the revival of the principles of hereditary monarchy in the twelfth century, not one of the peoples of western Europe would willingly accept, and least of all the successors of Frederick Barbarossa. The clash of principles and ideas is nowhere more clearly revealed than in the letter, firm in tone and worthy in content, which Philip of Swabia's adherents dispatched to the pope from Speyer on May 28th, 1199. Instead of asking for papal confirmation of Philip's election, they simply notified the pope in dignified words of the facts, announced that their election itself. constituted an indefeasible right to the imperial throne, and, warning Innocent to attempt nothing against the honour of the empire, informed him that they would appear shortly in Rome to complete the formality of coronation. Here in the declaration of Speyer the age-old conception of the Empire, revived by Barbarossa, found its ultimate expression against the novel pretensions of the papacy: "he who is chosen by the election of the princes alone is the true emperor, even before he has been confirmed by the pope."

4 FROM   *Brian Tierney*
"Tria Quippe Distinguit Iudicia . . ." a note on
Innocent III's decretal
Per Venerabilem

Innocent as Highest Judge

In 1202 Count William of Montpellier persuaded the archbishop of Arles to intercede with the pope concerning the legitimization of the count's bastard children. It was not that he wanted his boys to be eligible to become priests, the usual reason for a papal dispensation *ex defectu natalium*; the count was anxious that his children should enjoy all the rights of legitimate offspring in the temporal sphere as well. Pope Innocent III had recently granted this privilege to the children of King Philip II by Agnes de Meran, and Count William hoped to obtain a similar favor.

The pope refused this request. He had just reached an agreement with Philip about the king's matrimonial difficulties and no doubt did not wish to provoke him anew by an officious intervention in a case that evidently pertained to the royal jurisdiction. But Innocent III was not content to leave the matter at that. He wanted there to be no doubt that the pope did have extensive powers in secular affairs even though he was not choosing to exercise them in this particular case. Hence his reply to Count William was cast in the

SOURCE. Brian Tierney, "'Tria Quippe Distinguit Iudicia . . .' A Note On Innocent III's Decretal *Per Venerabilem*," in *Speculum*, XXXVII; I (January 1962), (copyright #B 955234), pp. 48–59. Reprinted by permission of *Speculum* (Mediaeval Academy of America).

form of the famous decretal *Per Venerabilem* in which Innocent took advantage of this relatively trivial occasion to inject into the mainstream of mediaeval canon law a series of far-reaching pronouncements concerning the juridical rights of the pope in secular disputes. The decretal was included first in the unofficial compilation of Alanus and then in the officially promulgated collection of canons known as the *Compilatio Tertia*. Innocent ensured that no jot or tittle of his carefully chosen terminology should pass into oblivion or lack adequate canonistic exegesis when he sent a copy of this compilation to the university of Bologna with instructions that henceforward it was to be used "tam in iudiciis quam in scholis." The pope's phrases were indeed discussed eagerly in the schools by generations of mediaeval canonists; more recently their implications have been debated with almost equal vigor by modern historians.

The decretal was full of meat. Innocent's apparently innocuous, incidental comment that the king of France recognized no temporal superior provided a canonical basis for a whole theory of the independence of national kingdoms from the empire, which in turn has given rise to an elaborate controversy among modern historians about the origins of national sovereignty in Europe. As for the immediate occasion of the letter, the pope held that authority to legitimize for spiritual functions necessarily included a capacity to legitimize in the temporal sphere as well "because for spiritualities greater care and authority and worthiness are required." This also gave rise to an important canonical controversy. But the greatest significance of the decretal for students of mediaeval political theory lies in the fact that, having made these points and having protested that he had no wish to usurp the jurisdiction of another, Innocent went on to give a more general explanation of the pope's right to intervene in secular affairs:

"Persuaded, therefore, by these reasons, We have granted the request asked [of us] by the king, taking justification from both the Old and New Testaments, because We exercise temporal jurisdiction not only in the patrimony of the church (over which We have full power in temporal matters), but also in other territories, in certain cases, where we exercise this power depending on circumstances."

The Old Testament proof was a passage from Deuteronomy (xvii. 8–12), "If thou perceive that there be among you a hard and doubtful matter in judgment between blood and blood, cause and cause, leprosy and leprosy; and thou see that the words of the judges within thy gates do vary: arise and go up to the place which the Lord thy God shall choose. And thou shalt come to the priests of the Levitical race and to the judge that shall be at that time . . . And thou shalt do whatsoever they shall say." The New Testament was cited (Matthew xvi. 19, "Whatsoever thou shalt bind on earth it shall be bound in heaven") to demonstrate that in the new dispensation the apostolic see was evidently the "chosen place" of God, and the pope himself the judge who presided there. And so Innocent reached his conclusion:

"Wherefore, one can distinguish three types of cases: First between blood and blood, for which reason it is understood as criminal, and civil. The last [is] between leper and leper for which reason it is known as Ecclesiastical, and also criminal. In the middle between case and case, which is referred to both, as much to the Ecclesiastical as to the civil; when there develops something difficult or ambiguous in these matters, it ought to be referred to the judgment of the See Apostolic: he who in his pride neglects to observe this sentence, is condemned to death, that is to be separated from the communion of the faithful by the sentence of excommunication as one dead."

The interpretation of this passage is of crucial importance for the whole much-controverted question whether Pope Innocent III was essentially "dualistic" or "hierocratic" in his theory of the relations of church and state. It was already well established that in the strictly ecclesiastical sphere all "hard and doubtful matters," the so-called *causae arduae*, were to be referred to the apostolic see for decision. The question is whether Innocent was simply extending that claim to the sphere of secular jurisdiction or whether his words were intended to convey some other meaning. It happens that the two outstandingly superior textbooks on medieval political theory in current use offer distorted interpretations of the pope's words and that the distortion has not been discussed, nor the passage adequately analysed in any of the recent specialist works on Innocent's political theory. A note of correction therefore seems in order.

A. J. Carlyle saw in *Per Venerabilem* only a claim that "in cases of conflict between the spiritual and temporal jurisdiction, the spiritual power is to decide." C. H. McIlwain similarly supposed that the "third judgment" referred only to those matters that were "in the first instance concurrently within the jurisdiction of both temporal and spiritual courts." With his usual discernment, however, McIlwain added that this was not the only possible interpretation of the passage. "If the words 'in these' . . . refer back to all three kinds of jurisdiction, then the interpretation above is wrong, and Innocent IV later added practically nothing to the claim of his predecessor."

Innocent III's grouping of clauses does suggest that he intended the "in quibus" to refer particularly to the third type of judgment. But it seems quite certain that he did not intend to exclude the first two types of cases from papal jurisdiction, and there can be no reasonable doubt that, in the third class of cases, he intended to include all lawsuits, whether ecclesiastical or secular, and not merely those cases that had an ecclesiastical as well as a secular aspect.

As to the first point, one has only to consider the nature of the first two types of judgment. One of them was "ecclesiasticum et criminale." That is to say it had reference to criminal cases that fell within the jurisdiction of the spiritual courts, such as heresy or sacrilege. Obviously the pope was not intending to exclude himself from the role of judging such cases; the very essence of the papal position was to be supreme judge, *iudex ordinarius omnium*, at least in spiritualities. The other class of criminal cases mentioned, "inter sanguinem et sanguinem," was defined as "criminale . . . et civile." That is to say it referred to crimes like murder or assault normally cognizable before a secular judge. But Innocent could not have intended to exclude matters of this kind from the sphere of papal judgment for, in the decretal *Novit* (1204), he explicitly claimed the right to intervene in such cases *ratione peccati* [because of sin]. A crime of violence was also a sin, and all cases involving sin pertained to the papal jurisdiction according to Innocent. . . .

I do not think that there can be any question here of a "hierocratic" distortion of Innocent III's original meaning. No other meaning had been suggested. The mid-thirteenth-century canonists were merely giving concrete examples to illustrate an interpretation that had been taken for granted by their predecessors. The principal reason why a modern reader might suppose that the third type of jurisdiction was intended to apply only to mixed cases lies in the fact that the immediate occasion of the decretal was a matter of legitimization, which did fall into this category. But, . . . Innocent III had turned aside from the issue of Count William's offspring to offer some general observations about the nature and extent of papal jurisdiction. It was not the habit of the canonists to relate such observations solely to the subject matter of the decretal in which they occurred; rather they sought to educe from them general rules of law. . . . Innocent III himself was of course well aware of this decretalist technique. In general, it seems to me, the argument that Innocent's true meanings were misunderstood or distorted by the canonists of the next generation should be viewed with extreme caution. The pope was himself a trained canonist and a legislator of genius. He knew exactly what legal implications the canonists would find in the terms he chose to use, and we must surely suppose that he had a shrewd understanding of the effects they were likely to have on the long-range growth of canonical thought.

A new period in the study of Innocent's political ideas began with the publication in 1940 of Maccarrone's *Chiesa e stato*, the first work that seriously attempted to analyse his thought within its canonistic framework. Subsequently major contributions by Mochi Onory, Kempf, Stickler, and Tillmann have clarified our understanding of many doubtful points. It seems arguable, however, that all of these writers have been unduly influenced in their exegesis of *Per Venerabilem* by a natural inclination to defend Pope Innocent III against the charge of seeking worldly power as an end in itself. They are anxious, that is to say, to establish that the great pope was not actuated by motives of gross worldly ambition, but that all his interventions in the political sphere were inspired "by motives of a spiritual order" (a favorite phrase of Mochi Onory). Let us acknowledge at once that Innocent's intentions were probably of the best. It is, heaven knows, no mean task to try to build the City of God on earth. But it also remains true that, after his pontificate, many theologians and some popes did become committed to a doctrine of papal temporal power that was repugnant to the consciences (as well as the interests) of most mediaeval princes and prelates, that this papal claim produced a destructive tension in mediaeval Catholicism, and that Innocent III's decretals played a significant part in its development. The problem of whether he had good intentions is one issue, primarily psychological; the problem of what exactly he did claim in the secular sphere is another, primarily canonical. Both are important, but to endeavor to solve the second problem merely on the basis of a conviction about the first leads only to confusion.

This seems especially the fault of Mochi Onory. Above all he failed to see—and this is true of Maccarrone too—that there was a radical difference between a papal claim to exercise indirect power in temporal affairs and a claim to exercise direct power in certain exceptional cirumstances which the pope himself undertook to define. It was quite consistent with the dualist theory to emphasize that an exercise of spiritual jurisdiction by the pope might sometimes, indirectly, produce effects in the temporal sphere. A sentence of excommunication launched against a king for some specifically ecclesiastical offense like sacrilege might, for example, have political repercussions. But it was surely not consistent with the dualist position for a pope to claim that he could exercise jurisdiction in secular cases whenever the case happened to be a "difficult and ambiguous" one (as was claimed in *Per Venerabilem*) or whenever the temporal judge was negligent or suspect or the office of emperor vacant (as Innocent suggested in the decretal *Licet*):

> *Si vacat imperium, si negligit, ambigit, an sit*
> *Suspectus iudex . . .*

As Hostiensis put it, summarizing Innocent III's doctrine.

It is hard to see how a pope could claim to judge secular cases even in such circumstances, or to enforce his sentences with coercive sanctions, unless he supposed that the nature of his office was such as to include jurisdiction over the purely temporal issues involved. Helene Tillmann is the only modern writer who has emphasized the important distinction between indirect power and direct power exercised *in certis causis*, but even she obscured its full implications by maintaining that the papal claim was rooted in the mediaeval doctrine of necessity. Innocent III certainly did know the Roman law tag, "Necessitas legem non habet," and he could have used it as the basis of a claim to temporal jurisdiction in exceptional circumstances. But the fact is that he did not choose to do so. The legal doctrine of necessity, if applied to the transfer of cases between secular and ecclesiastical courts, might have had uncomfortable consequences. It could after all have worked both ways. No thirteenth-century pope would have conceded that the emperor could judge a spiritual case (on the ground that "necessitas legem non habet") whenever the ecclesiastical judges found the matter "difficult and ambiguous" or when the papacy happened to be vacant. Innocent III, therefore, preferred to base his claim on the quite different ground that he was the vicar of one who was a priest after the order of Melchisedech—and Melchisedech was of course both priest and king. On this theory the pope could judge secular cases when he considered it appropriate to do so simply because regal jurisdiction inhered in his office (and, correspondingly, the emperor could not judge spiritual cases because he possessed no spiritual jurisdiction).

Friedrich Kempf avoided this conclusion in his discussion of *Per Venerabilem* by stressing the voluntary nature of the jurisdiction involved. He did not argue that Innocent was claiming merely *iurisdictio voluntaria* in the most technical sense of that term (as opposed to *iurisdictio contentiosa*) but he did maintain that, in *Per Venerabilem*, Innocent asserted the right to judge a secular case only when all the parties in the case voluntarily selected him as an arbitrator. There seems nothing in the decretal itself to support such a view. Its tone is quite different—"cum aliquid fuerit difficile vel ambiguum ad iudicium est sedis apostolicae recurrendum cuius sententiam qui superbiens contempserit observare mori praecipitur. . . ." Kempf also argued that *Per Venerabilem* must be interpreted in the light of Alexander III's decretal *Cum Sacrosancta,* and so understood in a dualist sense. In this earlier decretal Alexander replied to a series of questions from the archbishop of Rheims. The last one enquired whether an appeal from a secular judge to the pope was valid and the pope replied: ". . . etsi de consuetudine ecclesiae teneat (appellatio), secundum iuris rigorem credimus non tenere." Kempf sees in this a definitive acknowledgment by the papacy of the autonomy of secular jurisdiction. Alexander did not, however, make any pronouncement at all in his decretal on the essentially theological issue of the inherent temporal power which might, or might not, be attributed to the papacy on the basis of such scriptural texts as Matthew xvi. 19. He indicated only that, as a matter of law, there was no adequate basis in the existing canons for a general right of appeal (though the custom of a local church sufficed to make the appeal valid). It was quite open to a future pope, who held on theological grounds that Christ had conferred on the papacy a supreme temporal jurisdiction, to enact such canons as he thought necessary to define the circumstances in which that jurisdiction would in fact be exercised. That is exactly what Innocent III did.

A. M. Stickler has insisted that the very occurrence in canonistic works of lists of "exceptional" cases in which secular jurisdiction would be exercised directly by the pope proves that, even in mid-thirteenth century, the canonists acknowledged in principle the autonomy of the secular power; and he suggested that the presence of such lists in the writings of extreme hierocrats like Tancred and

Hostiensis reflects an unresolved tension in their thought. It is true that some dualist writers did hold that the fact of papal jurisdiction in secular cases being exercised only occasionally and in exceptional circumstances constituted an argument in favor of their own point of view. But their position was a very uneasy and illogical one, and it was natural enough that, after a generation's discussion of Innocent III's legislation, a major shift had occurred in canonistic thinking from the prevailing dualism of the late twelfth century to the dominant hierocratism of the mid-thirteenth. As we have argued, some of the "exceptional" cases were consistent with a dualist position, but some were not. On the other hand, the detailed definition of specific cases in which papal jurisdiction would be exercised directly in temporal affairs was entirely consistent with the most extreme hierocratic theories. Any court that claims a supreme appellate jurisdiction needs to define the circumstances in which it will in fact entertain appeals. It is quite possible to possess jurisdiction legitimately without exercising it in all cases; it is not possible to exercise jurisdiction legitimately in any case without posessing it. We may add that the listing of these exceptional cases occurs not only in the works of the canonists (whose technique of presenting scattered comments on a given topic in widely separated contexts could easily lead to inconsistencies) but also in the orderly exposition of the hierocratic theme by a systematic philosopher like Giles of Rome, who evidently saw no inconsistency in this procedure. Giles maintained that all power, spiritual and temporal, was vested in the pope, that sometimes he wielded his temporal authority directly but more commonly permitted it to be exercised by secular rulers. He went on to mention seven specific cases (based on the canonical exceptions) where the pope actually exercised the universal temporal jurisdiction that pertained to his office, one of them being the "hard and doubtful" matter referred to in the decretal *Per Venerabilem*. Once again there is no question here of a hierocratic distortion of the pope's original meaning. Innocent himself had indeed spelled out precisely the same doctrine towards the end of *Per Venerabilem* itself: "Paul also, that he might expound the plenitude of power, wrote to the Corinthians saying 'Do you not know that you shall judge angels? How much more the things of this world.' And so [the pope] is accustomed to exercise the office of secular power sometimes and in some things through himself, sometimes and in some things through others."

Innocent did not consider it appropriate or desirable to exercise his jurisdiction over spiritual affairs and over temporal affairs in precisely the same fashion, and he pointed this out in *Per Venerabilem*. In the ecclesiastical sphere he was *iudex ordinarius omnium*; in the temporal sphere he had no intention of burdening the papal curia with a mass of petty feudal litigation that, by legitimate custom, belonged to the courts of secular rulers. He did want to ensure that the temporal jurisdiction of the papacy could be invoked whenever a secular case had political implications involving the peace and good order of Christendom, and his various decretals provided a canonical basis for appeals in all such cases. Again, Innocent did take it for granted that, under the pope, secular rulers had a permanent and necessary role to play in the governance of Christian society, and that this role was a part of the divinely ordered scheme of things. He assumed that two hierarchies of administration were necessary for the government of the Christian world but, in his view, both hierarchies culminated in the pope. If this constitutes dualism, as some modern students of Innocent's thought seem to suppose, then all the mediaeval popes and all the most papalist of mediaeval theologians were dualists. It did not occur to Innocent III or his successors that it lay within their competence simply to abolish the offices of all secular rulers and themselves assume the exercise of all temporal power. But it also lay quite outside their competence, in the ecclesiastical sphere itself, to abolish the office of bishop and rule all the affairs of the church through papal delegates. Either innovation would have grievously perturbed "the general state of the church," which was not permitted to a pope or any human legislator.

The recent work on Pope Innocent III has been much concerned with relating his ideas to their mediaeval background. This is all to the good. It needs to be emphasized that the theory of papal power he propounded bore little resemblance to modern positivist theories of sovereignty and still less to modern totalitarian theories of despotism. We shall, however, eventually come to a full understanding of Innocent's position, not by minimizing his plainly stated claim to temporal power, but by relating that claim to the complex of doctrines concerning natural law, counsel and consent, *status ecclesiae*, and customary rights that mediaeval popes as well as their critics took for granted.

PART SEVEN

Philip the Fair and Boniface VIII :
Origins of the National State

More than one medievalist has called the thirteenth century the "greatest of centuries." Leaving aside that question-begging and probably insoluble problem, the thirteenth century was a period of rising legalism and pervasive professionalism; it was the golden age of towns with their incipient capitalism; it was the period which witnessed the long conflict between the papacy and the Emperor Frederick II (1212–1250) in which the Church used secular and sometimes military weapons to gain its goals; and it was the time when the monarchs of France and England were gaining increasing control over all their subjects. The century between the accession of Innocent III and that of Boniface VIII (1294–1303) witnessed very great changes, perhaps greater ones than during any comparable period in the Middle Ages. Consequently, any understanding of the conflict between Pope Boniface and the rulers of France and England must be seen against this background of political centralization, and social and economic transition.

The famous conflict between Pope Boniface VIII and King Philip the Fair of France (1285–1314) was the result of many complicated and interrelated factors: royal hostility to the enormous land holdings of the Church; the contradictory slant and orientation of the sophisticated canon law of the Church and the newly codified laws of the secular State; the age-old contest for the ultimate loyalty of the clergy; a contest of mutually exclusive ideologies; a clash of strong personalities; and, underlying all of these issues, the subordination of the temporal power to the spiritual authority. None of these issues was new at the end of the thirteenth century; they were the same problems that had divided Charlemagne and Leo III, Henry IV and Gregory VII, Henry II of England and Thomas Becket, Philip Augustus and John and Innocent III. The novelty at the end of the thirteenth century rested in the fact that this was the first medieval conflict between the Christian Church and the State which can be described as a dispute over national sovereignty.

There is no need to rehearse again the history of the controversy. It began as a dispute over the right of secular rulers to tax their clergies, a right which, although prohibited by a canon of the Fourth Lateran Council (1215), except in the instance of the "just war," had long been tacitly accepted by the papacy. The conflict intensified when King Philip the Fair, probably as a deliberate provocation, arrested a French bishop and caused a general crisis on royal jurisdiction over the clergy. The struggle culminated in a contest over the supremacy of the State over the Church in which Philip gained the victory and the papacy suffered a serious defeat.

In the bull *Clericis laicos* (1296), Pope Boniface denied that lay governments had national jurisdiction over the clergy and ordered the clergies of France and England to disobey their kings. When Philip of France and Edward of England, who were at war with each other and needed the tax to finance the war, retaliated with strong measures against the clergy in their countries, Boniface was compelled to back down.

The most famous papal letter of all time, *Unum Sanctum* (1302), marks the culmination of the Church's attitude toward secular power after the Gregorian Reformation. It was published after Philip's arrest of Bernard Saisset, Bishop of Pamiers, Boniface's call for a general council at Rome, and Philip's summons of the French Estates General to consolidate public opinion against papal claims. *Unam Sanctam*, as Brian Tierney has emphasized, while it did thoroughly treat the subordination of temporal jurisdiction to the spiritual, was a patchwork of extracts from earlier sources and was fundamentally concerned with the theological question of church unity; it set forth little that was new.[1]

The commentaries which follow provide not only significant background developments against which the controversy should be seen but offer important interpretations of the contest. In his excellent article, Gaines Post shows the importance of the Roman legal idea of "reason of state" for the development of the modern national State and the influence of this idea in Philip IV's conflict with Boniface. Joseph R. Strayer's classic achievement, "The Laicization of French and English Society in the Thirteenth Century," reveals the intellectual and political forces at work which caused a shift of basic loyalties from the Church to the State, and thus contributed to Philip's success. Finally, Pope Boniface's strengths and weaknesses are evaluated in a sensitive but critical study by F. M. Powicke.

[1] Brian Tierney, *The Crisis of Church and State* (Englewood, New Jersey: Prentice Hall, 1964), pp. 182–183.

1 FROM

H. Bettenson
Documents of the Christian Church

The Clericis Laicos Bull, 1296

Boniface Bishop, servant of the servants of God, for the perpetual record of the matter. That laymen have been very hostile to the clergy antiquity relates; and it is clearly proved by the experiences of the present time. For not content with what is their own the laity strive for what is forbidden and loose the reins for things unlawful. Nor do they prudently realize that power over clerks or ecclesiastical persons or goods is forbidden them: they impose heavy burdens on the prelates of the churches and ecclesiastical persons regular and secular, and tax them, and impose collections: they exact and demand from the same the half, tithe, or twentieth, or any other portion or proportion of their revenues or goods; and in many ways they try to bring them into slavery, and subject them to their authority. And, we regret to say, some prelates of the churches and ecclesiastical persons, fearing where there should be no fear, seeking a temporary peace, fearing more to offend the temporal majesty than the eternal, acquiesce in such abuses, not so much rashly as improvidently, without obtaining authority or license from the Apostolic See. We therefore, desirous of preventing such wicked actions, decree, with apostolic authority and on the advice of our brethren, that any prelates and ecclesiastical persons, religious or secular, of whatsoever orders, condition or standing, who shall pay or promise or agree to pay to lay persons collections or taxes for the tithe, twentieth, or hundredth of their own rents,

SOURCE. H. Bettenson, *Documents of the Christian Church* (London: Oxford University Press, 1947), pp. 159–161, 161–163. Reprinted by permission of the publisher.

or goods, or those of the churches, or any other portion, proportion, or quantity of the same rents, or goods, at their own estimate or at the actual value, under the name of aid, loan, relief, subsidy, or gift, or by any other title, manner, or pretext demanded, without the authority of the same see:

And also whatsoever emperors, kings, or princes, dukes, earls, or barons, powers, captains, or officials, or rectors, by whatsoever names they are called, of cities, castles, or any places whatsoever, wheresoever situate, and all others of whatsoever rank, eminence or state, who shall impose, exact, or receive the things aforesaid, or arrest, seize, or presume to take possession of things anywhere deposited in holy buildings, or to command them to be arrested, seized, or taken, or receive them when taken, seized, or arrested, and also all who knowingly give aid, counsel, or support, openly or secretly, in the things aforesaid, by this same should incur sentence of excommunication. Universities, too, which may have been to blame in these matters, we subject to ecclesiastical interdict.

The prelates and ecclesiastical persons above mentioned we strictly command, in virtue of their obedience, and on pain of deposition, that they in no wise acquiesce in such things without express leave of the said see, and that they pay nothing under pretext of any obligation, promise, and acknowledgment whatsoever, made in the past, or in existence before this time, and before such constitution, prohibition, or order come to their notice, and that the seculars aforesaid do not in any wise receive it; and if the clergy do pay, or the laymen receive, let them fall under sentence of excommunication by the very deed.

Moreover, let no one be absolved from the aforesaid sentences of excommunications and interdict, save at the moment of death, without authority and special leave of the Apostolic See, since it is part of our intention that such a terrible abuse of secular powers should not be carried on under any pretense whatever, any privileges whatsoever notwithstanding, in whatsoever tenors, forms or modes, or arrangement of words, conceded to emperors, kings and the others aforesaid; and we will that aid to be given by no one, and by no persons in any respect in contravention of these provisions.

Let it then be lawful to none at all to infringe this page of our constitution, prohibition, or order, or to gainsay it by any rash attempt; and if anyone presume to attempt this, let him know that he will incur the indignation of Almighty God, and of his blessed apostles Peter and Paul.

Given at Rome in St. Peter's on the 25th of February in the second year of our Pontificate.

The Bull Unam Sanctam, *1302*

We are obliged by the faith to believe and hold—and we do firmly believe and sincerely confess—that there is one Holy Catholic and Apostolic Church, and that outside this Church there is neither salvation nor remission of sins. . . . In which Church there is one Lord, one faith, one baptism. At the time of the flood there was one ark of Noah, symbolizing the one Church; this was completed in one cubit and had one, namely Noah, as helmsman and captain outside which all things on earth, we read, were destroyed. . . . Of this one and only Church there is one body and one head—not two heads, like a monster—namely Christ, and Christ's vicar is Peter, and Peter's successor, for the Lord said to Peter himself, "Feed My sheep." "My sheep" He said in general, not these or those sheep; wherefore He is understood to have committed them all to him. Therefore, if the Greeks or others say that they were not committed to Peter and his successors, they necessarily confess that they are not of Christ's sheep, for the Lord says in John, "There is one fold and one shepherd."

And we learn from the words of the Gospel that in this Church and in her power are two swords, the spiritual and the temporal. For when the apostles said, "Behold, here" (that is, in the Church, since it was the apostles who spoke) "are two swords"—the Lord did not reply, "It is too much," but "It is enough." Truly he who denies that the temporal sword is in the power of Peter, misunderstands the words of the Lord, "Put up thy sword into the sheath." Both are in the power of the Church, the spiritual sword and the material. But the latter is to be used for the Church, the former by her; the former by the priest, the latter by kings and captains but at the will and by the permission of the priest. The one sword, then, should be under the other, and temporal authority subject to spiritual. For when the apostle says "there is no power but of God, and the powers that be are ordained of God" they would not be so ordained were not one sword made subject to the other. . . .

Thus, concerning the Church and her power, is the prophecy of Jeremiah fulfilled, "See, I have this day set thee over the nations and over the kingdoms," etc. If, therefore, the earthly power err, it shall be judged by the spiritual power; and if a lesser power err, it shall be judged by a greater. But if the supreme power err, it can only be judged by God, not by man; for the testimony of the apostle is "The spiritual man judgeth all things, yet he himself is judged of no man." For this authority, although given to a man and exercised by a man, is not human, but rather divine, given at God's mouth to Peter and established on a rock for him and his successors in Him whom he confessed, the Lord saying to Peter himself, "Whatsoever thou shalt bind," etc. Whoever therefore resists this power thus ordained of God, resists the ordinance of God . . . Furthermore we declare, state, define and pronounce that it is altogether necessary to salvation for every human creature to be the subject to the Roman pontiff.

2 FROM *Gaines Post*
Law and Politics in the Middle Ages

This public right of the king to decide on actions for the defense of the state meant that he should use "right reason," that is, the "reason" of the public welfare, not the "reason" of his own private rights or selfish aggrandizement. "Reason of state," in fact, was becoming a principle of public law. What was "reason of state" in the Middle Ages, and how did it hasten the development of the political authority of the royal government?

As early as the middle of the twelfth century, Hugo of St. Victor, theologian and mystic, said that when *reason* and *necessity* concurred, the royal authority had the right to tax the clergy. John of Salisbury, that great classical humanist of the twelfth century, included public *ratio* in his general theory that the state is a "work of art." His premise is that God, by means of nature and the natural law, approves human society. Organized society, however, the state and its government, is the product of human reason and skill. Because God and nature endowed men with the faculty of reason, above all it is the duty of the king as head of the corporate body of the realm

SOURCE. Gaines Post, "Law and Politics in the Middle Ages," in Katherine Fischer Drew and Floyd Seyward Lear, eds., *Perspectives in Medieval History*, a Rice University Semicentennial Publication (Chicago: The University of Chicago Press, 1963), pp. 68–72. Reprinted by permission of William Marsh, Rice University, and the author.

to imitate nature by using reason in all public or political business. By steadily practicing the art or skill of governing with the aid of reason, the king is engaged in making the state a work of art. How, then, should the prince use reason and skill in the science of politics? John, good Christian that he was, believed that the king should use his reason above all in obeying the command of God to be just and rule according to the highest principles of justice and equity. He should therefore protect all lawful rights of people and churches and maintain the law in his courts. In other words, John says, the prince should take care of the welfare of the republic and always submit his will to reason and the common good. Indeed, John says literally, the "reason of the common welfare" is itself a principle of law and equity; and it demands that the king should possess no more horses, servants, and baggage than the "reason of necessity or utility" requires for the "reason" of the good of the people. . . . In brief, according to John, "reason of state" is the right reasoning in the public interest of the realm and of the people. God commands it—and the state itself becomes a positive good rather than a necessary evil.

Essentially the same principle, if more down to earth, was a commonplace in the ideas of the lawyers trained in the new legal science. They held that the just war of defense was a supreme reason and necessity for extra ordinary taxation. At least two decretists as early as 1200 spoke of the "reason" of the defense of the fatherland. The legists agreed, and Accursius even said that if a son unavoidably, in battle, killed his father among enemies who were attacking the fatherland, he was not guilty of patricide. "Fight for the fatherland!"—"Pugna pro patria!" Such was the frequently stated imperative. To die for the fatherland, it follows, was to win eternal glory. (Let me remind you that the independent realm of France or England was already, in the thought of some lawyers, the "common fatherland," that is to say, a fatherland that superseded all local loyalties. . . .

The "reason" of defense, moreover, justified deceit against the enemy and made *dolus bonus,* "good deceit" (the "Holy Pretence" of a later age), a lawful principle of government. The moral law of God was always fundamental. But *casualiter,* in cases of necessity, of dire emergency, or of the "just cause," when either the *status regni* or the *status Ecclesiae* was in danger, a compromise (the choice of a lesser evil or a lesser good for the sake of the greater good) was lawful. Indeed, according to the canonists as well as St. Bernard of Clairvaux, the necessity of preserving the "state of the Church" gave the pope supreme authority over the Church and the clergy. A famous secular theologian, Gérard d'Abbeville (about 1260), went so far as to assert that if the emperor were a Saracen who threatened the faith, the pope could grant dispensation to a nun from the vow of chastity and from the "religious habit" in order that she might marry and convert the infidel and thereby prevent the destruction of the Church and the faithful. This the pope could do *ratione utilitatis communis*, by reason of the common utility.

No doubt Gérard's lesson in "reason of the Church" was purely academic, a classroom exercise, so to speak. But even a purely hypothetical *casus*—this was true casuistry—shows how important the reason of necessity and utility was for the authority of any prince. The magistracy, in fact, said the glossators, was a supreme necessity in itself, else the state and law and justice could not exist. Is it surprising, then, that well before 1200 we encounter the words *ratio status regis*? And first, literally, as far as I know, in England, when the great Henry II was consolidating the central government. Richard Fitzneale, in the *Dialogue of the Exchequer*, exalted the *ratio status regis* as the "reason of the public powers" of the king. By reason of this "state of the king" all subjects should serve him with their wealth. Consequently, by reason of his public estate, the "estate royal," the prince was above the law with respect to his duty and right to preserve the state of the realm, *ratione publicae utilitatis*. As early as the twelfth century, then, the double reason of *status regis* and *status regni* was a general reason of state—the *raison d'être* of the public authority of a king was governing with reason in the public interest.

Not only did the reason of the public welfare in cases of necessity give the ruler the right to ask for subsidies and wage a just war. According to the Bolognese jurist Azo, the king of France, Philip Augustus, could allege the "reason of the public utility" of making peace as a justification for sacrificing the private, feudal rights of Arthur of Britanny to King John. Whether Philip actually did so is not certain. But kings were learning from the public law how to make feudalism bow to the interest of the state—of course, they still had a long way to go!

A part of the process of defeating feudalism was the use of the Roman legal theory that special privilege or franchise, accompanied by jurisdiction, was not an immunity, in the old feudal sense, but a delegation of powers that remained subordinate to the royal authority. Such franchises, like the County Palatine of Chester or the French *apanage*, were granted not for the private utility of the great lord but for the "reason of the public welfare" of the whole realm. A distinguished scholar, Helen M. Cam, has, in fact, shown how the royal prerogative in England remained superior in jurisdiction and in policies related to the safety of the community of the realm. All lawful privileges, so canonists and legists were saying, were a recognition of the special merits of those who had served and would continue to serve the state. Privileges were lawful only if granted *ratione publicae utilitatis*. . . .

By 1250, it is now evident, the medieval doctrine of reason of state was well formulated. . . . At the end of the thirteenth century, it is almost needless to say, the principle was repeated over and over when powerful, national monarchs were challenging the universalism of the church under Pope Boniface VIII. If "necessity" was the more frequent word, the publicists and legists sometimes said "*ratio*" too. So Pierre Dubois repeated the old theme that the "reason of necessity" permitted the king to tax the clergy in order to finance the proposed great Crusade. Pierre de Belleperche, an able French legist who became one of Philip the Fair's advisers, specified a demonstrably lawful *ratio* and *causa* for the confiscation of property in order to feed a hungry royal army. The French monarch skilfully employed the principle against Pope Boniface VIII, who obviously was threatening the "state" of the whole corporate body of France—so said the king in his propaganda. And everyone knows how Edward I spoke of the dire emergency that, in Philip the Fair's alleged threat of aggression against England, touched the *status regni* and all the people, clergy and laity, in common; and how, at the same time, Philip was arousing the French with emotion-stirring accusations against the English. What could poor Boniface VIII do but tacitly admit that both kings were fighting a just war of defense against each other and that in such a dire and immediate emergency and necessity they could go ahead and tax the "national" clergy without waiting for his approval? Even the champion of the papacy, Giles of Rome, like Hugo of St. Victor, agreed to this. In the early thirteenth century, a canonist had said: "But nowadays all wars are unjust!" By 1300, the triumph of "reason of the necessity" of the safety of the state had forced the pope to admit that all wars between national states were just. In other words, the new national states, under the leadership of kings and jurists who skilfully used "reason of state" as a political weapon, were beginning to disrupt the ideal of Christian unity within the Church.

3 FROM *J. R. Strayer*

The Laicization of French and English Society in the Thirteenth Century

Students of mediaeval society have long been aware of a sharp change in attitudes and values which took place in the thirteenth century. During that period, while Europe remained sincerely and completely Catholic, the church lost much of its influence. Though it perfected its organization and carried on its religious activities with great energy, the standards which it had set for secular activities were increasingly disregarded. The forces released by the great revival of civilization in the twelfth century could no longer be controlled by the church. They broke out of the old channels and either found new courses for themselves or dissipated their energy in the swamps and backwaters of uncoördinated endeavour. This secularization of European society is apparent in every field of human activity, in art and literature as well as in politics and economics. But while the fact of secularization is undisputed, the reasons for this great change in European opinion and the way in which the change was brought about are not clear. It is a problem which is well worth studying, not only because it is the key to much of the later history of the middle ages, but also because it is an interesting example of the ways in which public opinion is changed.

This paper is an attempt to study one aspect of secularization, the laicization of French and English society in the thirteenth century. Laicization may be defined as the development of a society in which primary allegiance is given to lay governments, in which final decisions regarding social objectives are made by lay governments in which the church is merely a private society with no public powers or duties. When society has been laicized leadership has passed from the church to the state. In the modern period this assumption of leadership by the state is usually manifested in attempts to control social services, such as education, to regulate family relationships, and to confiscate all, or part of the church's property. These particular manifestations of the idea of laicization

SOURCE. J. R. Strayer, "The Laicization of French and English Society in the Thirteenth Century," in *Speculum*, XV, 1 (January 1940) (copyright # B443992), pp. 76–86. Reprinted by permission of *Speculum* (Mediaeval Academy of America) and the author.

should not be confused with the idea itself. There was no demand for government regulation of marriage and divorce in the thirteenth century and very little protest against church control of education. There were efforts to limit the church's acquisition of new property, but only a few fanatics advocated confiscation of what the church already possessed. Yet during the thirteenth century leadership passed from the church to lay governments, and when the test came under Boniface VIII it was apparent that lay rulers, rather than the pope, could count on the primary allegiance of the people.

Laicization is the political aspect of secularization. As such, it cannot be wholly explained by purely economic factors. I am quite willing to accept the conventional view that the economic changes of the twelfth and thirteenth centuries made society more worldly, but worldliness is not the same thing as laicization. One is negative, the other positive. Worldliness made the leadership of the church less effective but it did not necessarily create a new leadership to supplant that of the church. Gothic art, for example, did not express religious ideas as well in 1300 as it did in 1200, yet it was still an art dominated by the church. Society was more worldly everywhere in 1300 than in 1200, yet the church did not lose political power to the same extent everywhere. Germany was fully as worldly as England, yet England was far more independent of the papacy. It took strong lay governments to challenge the leadership of the church, and economic change by itself does not explain the development of such governments. For example, throughout Europe the new economic forces were concentrated in the towns, but outside of Italy the towns were not the dominant factor in creating the new leadership. In England and France the royal officials who were most active in pursuing the policy of laicization were not exclusively, or even primarily, bourgeois. In short, while economic changes created an atmosphere in which it was easier for lay governments to assume leadership, they did not ensure the creation of lay governments which could make the most of the opportunity. . . .

Disregarding the endless variations of a pattern which was everywhere fundamentally the same, we can say that political units of the twelfth century fell into three classes. First, there were the local units, the feudal baronies and the towns. Then there were the intermediate units, the kingdoms, and the great feudal states which were practically independent. Finally there was the great unit of Christendom, headed nominally by the emperor and the pope, but which, as an effective political force, was almost wholly controlled by the pope. All men were subject to at least three governments, which represented these three types of political organization. No government had a monopoly of power, each had its own work to do and each was supposed to give the other governments a free hand to do their work. In practice there were endless quarrels, especially among the local and intermediate units, but for a long time these quarrels led to no decisive changes. This was a situation which, from a political point of view, was wholly favorable to the church. Loyalty to lay governments was divided between the local and intermediate units. In many cases the greater loyalty was to the small local unit, for it was the local unit which controlled economic and social status. Far more important than this divided allegiance to lay governments was the loyalty to the great undivided unit of Christendom. The scale of allegiance of most men would have gone something like this: I am first of all a Christian, second a Burgundian, and only third a Frenchman. The emphasis on Christianity as the most important bond between men meant that there was a real European patriotism, expressed in the armies of the Crusade. It means that there was such a thing as European citizenship or nationality, shown by the fact that a well-trained clerk or knight could find employment anywhere in Christendom, regardless of his origin. And the pope controlled the citizens of Europe and through this control he could exercise decisive influence on all aspects of European society. . . .

During the latter part of the twelfth and the first half of the thirteenth centuries the old mediaeval hierarchy of governments broke down in many regions. The old division of responsibility and power ended. In each region affected by these changes one government became dominant, and gained control of political activities. The dominant government was not always that of a king—in Italy, for example, it was that of the town—but whether king, count, or commune came out on top the result was the same. Only one government was left which was strong enough to inspire loyalty.

The monopoly of power secured by the dominant government was, of course, not complete. It was a *de facto* monopoly, which would not meet the tests of later political theorists any more than our present economic monopolies meet the tests of the lawyer or the economist. The political monopolies of the thirteenth century worked very much as our economic monopolies work today. Other units were tolerated, and were allowed a certain share of the business of government, as long as they recognized that they held this share only by grace of the dominant power. This is the policy of Edward I in the *Quo Warranto* proceedings, and of Philip the Fair in his *pariages* with the semi-independent feudal lords of southern France. Only admit that you hold your power from us, that you exercise it subject to our correction, and we will let you retain a large degree of jurisdiction. It was a policy which could be applied to the church fully as much as it was applied to competing lay governments. A direct attack on all ecclesiastical jurisdiction would have been futile and dangerous. Minor officials who were tactless enough to make such attacks were always disavowed by their superiors. The inner circle of royal advisers wanted to weaken the church courts, but they knew that a head-on collision of authorities was not the best way of securing this result. They never denied that the church courts should have a certain amount of power. But they were going to define that power; ecclesiastical courts were to retain only the jurisdiction recognized by the royal council. The first example of this policy is found in the reign of Henry II of England, and while his attempt at definition was not completely successful, the precedent was not forgotten. By the end of the thirteenth century royal governments in both France and England were regularly defining the powers of church courts. The excesses of minor officials were a useful weapon in establishing this power of the central government. When the church was annoyed by such officials its only recourse was to beg the royal government to define and defend ecclesiastical jurisdictions. . . . If the church's rights of government were dependent on the good will of lay rulers, if the church could maintain its jurisdiction only through the aid of the state, lay governments must be more powerful and important than the church.

Then, as certain governments obtained a *de facto* monopoly of political power they began to do more work. Their courts met more frequently, they heard more cases, they welcomed appeals from subordinate jurisdictions. These governments began to tax and to legislate, even though taxation was at first considered little better than robbery and legislation was felt to be sacrilegious tinkering with the sacred and unchangeable law. In order to perform this increased amount of work they multiplied the number of their officials. All this meant that they had more contacts with the mass of the people, that they touched at some point on the life of every man. No one could be ignorant of the fact that he was subject to one of these dominant governments. No one could fail to realize that the activities of his government were important, perhaps more important than the activities of the church. This sense of the increasing importance of lay governments was not the same thing as loyalty to those governments, but the first sentiment could very easily lead to the second. Men respect what is powerful and they can easily become loyal to what they respect.

The multiplication of the number of lay officials is one of the most striking phenomena of the thirteenth century. In every country the conservatives protested again and again that there were too many officials, and in every country the number of officials went right on increasing in spite of the protests. This increase had important effects on public opinion. It was not only that officials, with their friends and families, formed a large group which would support any action of the government. More important was the fact that every official, consciously or unconsciously, was a propagandist for his government. He had to spread the government's explanation of its policies; he had to enforce decisions which showed the government's power. Many officials, especially those of lower rank who ·were in direct contact with the people, were openly anti-clerical. The fact that such men could brutally disregard the church's rights and still keep their positions must have convinced many people that lay governments were going to be supreme. Finally, with the steady increase in the number of government jobs a new career was opened up for able men of all classes. The church could no longer count on securing the services of the great majority of educated and intelligent men. Many laymen who might have entered the church chose to serve the king instead. Many churchmen entered the service of lay governments and became so absorbed in that service that they forgot their duty to the church. And as the church lost exclusive control of the educated class it lost much of its ability to control public opinion.

Fully as important as the increase in the number of permanent lay officials was the increase in the number of men who were not officials, but who were forced to aid the government in its work from time to time. . . . much of the work of local government in England was performed by juries, or selected knights of the shire. France had a much larger paid bureaucracy, but even in France the royal government could not function without requiring the services of its subjects. In France, as in England, local notables were associated with royal officials in administrative investigations or judicial inquests. In France, as in England, thousands of men were forced to aid the government in the wearisome work of assessing and collecting taxes. For example, when the aid for knighting Louis of Navarre was collected in 1314, there were 322 collectors in the viscounty of Paris alone, excluding the city proper and the castellany of Poissy. It seems unlikely that many people enjoyed dropping their own work in order to spend days and weeks in serving the government for little or no pay. Yet the men who performed these expensive and burdensome tasks did not become disloyal to the government which imposed them. Rather they became increasingly conscious of the dignity and power of secular government. . . .

The processes discussed so far worked indirectly, and almost automatically, to build up loyalty to lay governments. It was natural for any ruler to try to increase his power in a given area. As he gained a virtual monopoly of power it was necessary for him to add new functions to his government and to increase the number of men who assisted him in governing. There was little theorizing behind these developments, merely the desire to gain power and to use that power effectively. But the result of this drive for power was the creation of something very like a sovereign state. There was no place for such an entity in the old mediaeval system; it was absolutely opposed to the belief in the unity of Christendom and the hierarchy of political organizations. It had to be justified, explained, sold to the people. As a result, toward the end of the thirteenth century a definite theory to justify laicization appears.

This theory, like so many other things in the thirteenth century, was the work of lawyers. This new class of men, produced by the increased activity of twelfth-century governments, set the tone of the thirteenth century even more than the new class produced by increased business activity. The thirteenth century was a legalistic century, a century in which men sought exact definitions of all human relationships, a century in which men wanted to work out the logical implications of all general ideas and projects, a century in which men wanted to complete and to justify the work of their predecessors. And because the thirteenth century was legalistic, because it was a period of definitions and detailed explanations, it was a much less tolerant century than the twelfth. It was no longer possible to harmonize divergent views by thinking of them as merely different aspects of universal truth. Thus definition of the doctrines of the church forced many reformers into heresy. Definition of the rights of the state forced many men to choose between loyalty to the state and loyalty to the church. It was only when a choice had to be made that laicization was possible.

The definition of the powers of the ruler worked out by thirteenth-century lawyers developed into something which was almost a theory of the sovereign state. Such a theory could not be reconciled with the old mediaeval system; it forced a choice between loyalties. Briefly, it ran something like this. First, there are definite boundaries to all states. The twelfth century had known spheres of influence rather than boundaries; power decreased in proportion to the distance from the ruler until a region was reached in which his authority was counterbalanced by that of another lord. In the thirteenth-century theory the power of the dominant government was to extend, undiminished, to a precise frontier. This idea may be seen especially clearly in the south of France, where royal officials worked steadily to fix an exact boundary with Aragon; where they insisted again and again that the eastern boundary of the realm was the Rhone; where they flatly denied that there could be a no man's land of independent bishoprics, in which the king's authority was neutralized by that of the emperor. Then, within these precise boundaries there is to be a definite superior, who can supervise and correct the work of all subordinate governments. This idea may be found in England earlier than in France, but it was most clearly expressed by Beaumanoir: "The king is sovereign over all, and has as his right the general guardianship of all the realm. . . . There is none so great beneath him that he cannot be haled to his court for default of justice or for false judgment." Moreover, this definite superior, if he observes certain formalities, may issue orders which are binding on all men in the realm. As the *dictum de Kenilworth* says: "The king, and his legitimate orders and instructions, must be fully obeyed by each and every man, great and small, in the realm." Guillaume de Plaisian is even more emphatic: "All those in the realm are ruled by the king's authority; even prelates and clerks, in temporal matters, are bound by the laws, edicts, and constitutions of the king." The central government may state the law, or make special rulings where the laws fail to give a solution to a problem. This was recognized in England as early as Glanvill's time, when it was said that laws for the entire kingdom might be made "in doubtful cases by the authority of the prince with the advice of the magnates." It took somewhat longer for this power to be recognized in France, but by the end of the thirteenth century Beaumanoir could say: "The king may make such establishments as please him for the common good, and that which he establishes must be obeyed." For the common good taxes may be imposed on all property in the kingdom. The most extreme statement of this right was made by Guillaume de Plaisian: "Everything within the boundaries of his realm is the lord king's, at least as to protection, superior, jurisdiction, and lordship. Even as property it is the king's, for he can give, receive, and use any property, movable and immovable, in his realm for the public good and defense of the kingdom." An English lawyer would not have said this, but the English government did insist that all property could be taxed for defense of the realm. Finally, while no lesser political authority can be exempt from, or control the decisions of the king, there is no higher political authority which can interfere with the king's powers of government. Here English and French lawyers are equally emphatic. Bracton's "the king has no equal, much less a superior" is matched in a letter sent by the French government to the Emperor Henry VII: "Since the time of Christ the realm of France has had only its own king, who never recognized nor had a temporal superior."

These ideas add up to something very like the theory of sovereignty. Within fixed boundaries there is a definite superior who has the final decision regarding all political activities. It is not quite the theory of sovereignty, not only because the word is lacking, but also because it is a theory of comparative rather than absolute power. The words which the French lawyers use show this: the king has "superioritas," he has "majus dominium," he has "altior dominatio." His power is greater than that of any subject, but it is not a different power; he makes the final decisions, but he does not make all the decisions. But, sovereignty or not, this theory clearly conflicts with earlier mediaeval ideas. It sets up the kingdom as the most important unit of government and demands that all subjects give their primary allegiance to the kingdom.

Moreover, these ideas were not the work of isolated theorists. Every quotation which has been given was written by a high royal official. Most of them were taken from official documents,—laws, pleas in royal courts, or letters written in the king's name. Innumerable statements of a similar sort could be found in official records. This means that everyone who attended a royal court, everyone who did business with the government, was exposed to the new theories. This must have done a great deal to spread the idea of the supremacy of royal government, and hence, to make laicization easier. Even this was not enough, and at the end of the century deliberate propaganda in favor of the new theories was begun in both France and

England. Local and national assemblies were called, at which royal officials could expound their new doctrine. . . .

At the same time the governments of France and England began to encourage nationalism in order to gain support for their policies. There had always been a certain amount of latent nationalism in Europe; the French had sneered at the drunken English and the Italians had despised the boorish Germans. But this early nationalism had not been very strong in comparison with provincial loyalties and it had been frowned on by lay and ecclesiastical rulers alike. It was contrary to the basic principles of Christianity and it was dangerous to lay rulers whose territories seldom coincided with national units and whose policies were not always nationalistic. The concentration of political authority in France and England encouraged the growth of nationalism by decreasing the differences between provinces and increasing the differences between countries. But even in the middle of the thirteenth century nationalism was not yet respectable. Nationalism was associated with rebellion against constituted authority, with such movements as the protests of the English clergy against papal exactions, or the opposition of the English baronage to Henry III. Men like St. Louis and Henry III, who believed sincerely in the old international ideals, could not follow a nationalistic policy. In fact, many of Henry's troubles were caused by his unwillingness to accept the nationalistic ideas of his selfish and narrow-minded barons. About 1300, however, the governments of France and England began to see that nationalism could be useful to them, and once the idea was supported by a recognized authority it grew rapidly. At one point in the war over Gascony, Edward I accused the French of wishing to annihilate the English race and the anti-clerical legislation of his reign shows a tacit acceptance of nationalistic ideas. In France, the government appealed even more openly to nationalism. During the struggle against Boniface VIII repeated efforts were made to convince the country that the pope was anti-French, and that he was threatening the independence of France. In the same way when the French clergy were asked for money to carry on the war with Flanders, they were reminded of the pre-eminence of France as a Christian country and were told that it was their duty as Frenchmen to defend their native land. . . .

When Boniface VIII, alarmed by the growing power of lay governments, tried to limit their authority, he found that he was too late. The people of France and England remained loyal to their kings; there was not even a half-hearted rebellion in favor of the pope. In France the government had such control of public opinion that it was able to seize the church's own weapon of a charge of heresy and turn it against Boniface. A few years later it succeeded in ruining the Templars by the same method. This perhaps marks the extreme limit of mediaeval laicization—a secular ruler determines the policy of the church and uses the church for his own ends. This feat was not immediately repeated, but from the time of Boniface on there was no doubt that lay rulers had the primary allegiance of their people. Society was controlled, as far as it was controlled at all, by lay governments and not by the church. It is true that during the fourteenth and fifteenth centuries this lay control was not always very intelligent, nor very effective. During these years there was a reaction against central governments; a reaction caused, at least in part, by the fact that they had gained power by a mixture of blackmail, chicanery, and bullying and that a generation educated in these techniques began to use them against their rulers. But this very period of weak lay government showed how effective the work of laicization had been. The church could not regain its old power in spite of the opportunity afforded by a new period of anarchy. There was no substitute for centralized, lay government in France or England, however weak that government might be.

The reaction against central governments after 1300 may explain why laicization went no further; why education, and care of the sick and poor remained in the province of the church. But it should also be remembered that mediaeval governments were satisfied with relative rather than absolute power. Totalitarianism was foreign to their ways of thinking—it would also have been too expensive. Police work cost money—so there was no objection to letting the barons do much of it. Education was expensive—so there was no objection to letting the church do it. Some townspeople in England and France did object to church control of education and tried to set up their own schools, but as far as I know the count of Flanders was the only lay ruler who gave any support to this movement. As for social service work, the whole tendency was to make the church do more of it, rather than less. Anyone who has studied grants to the church must have been struck by the great increase in the number of gifts made specifically to hospitals, poor-houses, and university colleges after the middle of the thirteenth century. The old un-limited grant for the general purposes of the church almost disappears in the fourteenth century. This may be, indirectly, a form of laicization; the church is to be made to do "useful" work instead of spending its money on purely religious purposes. But there is no hesitation in allowing the church to perform these services; rather it is encouraged to do so. Not until the next great wave of laicization in the sixteenth century is there an attempt to deprive the church of its educational and philanthropic functions. Once the leadership, the "superiority" of mediaeval lay governments was recognized, they had no further quarrel with the church.

4   FROM   *F. M. Powicke*
Pope Boniface VIII

The Tragic Flaw in Boniface VIII

But Boniface too easily confused the Pope with Benedict Caetani. It is true that he kept apart the papal from his personal treasure, using the latter for the aggrandizement of his family. He was elected by cities of the Patrimony as their *podesta* under his family name. He arbitrated on one occasion between the kings of France and England—for so they insisted—not as pope but as Benedict. Yet this extraordinary man was incapable of self-scrutiny. As Mr. Previté-Orton has said, "the most ecumenic and the narrowest aims met one another in his violent nature, without apparently a suspicion arising in his mind of their discrepancy, and it was this attempt to blend incompatibles which more than anything else caused his ruin." The publication of the archives of Aragon, which include the vivid and strictly contemporary dispatches of Aragonese envoys at the papal court, has helped to reveal him, to explain both the cause of the intense personal hatred which he could arouse and the element of truth in the extravagant charges brought against him by the Colonna and the agents of Philip of France. The type is not uncommon in history, but has only once been found upon the papal throne, varied though its occupants have been. Boniface had all the qualities of a very great pope save personal holiness and self-restraint. He was dignified and noble in appearance, decisive and vigorous, a master of business, a subtle canonist expert in explain-

SOURCE. F. M. Powicke, "Pope Boniface VIII," in *The Christian Life in the Middle Ages* (Oxford: Oxford University Press, 1935), pp. 48–73. Reprinted by permission of the publisher.

ing the meaning of terms and expounding the equitable rules of law. When he was not dominated by arrogance or passion, he could adjust himself to circumstance. "The coarse-mouthed bully" could "disappear for the moment in the skilful lawyer." His handling of the first controversy with Philip the Fair, opened in 1296 by the bull *Clericis laicos*, was reasonable, his compromise between facts and principles skilful. The distinguished lawyers who, under his commission, added the Sext or sixth book to the Decretals turned to him in cases of difficulty as an expert. His registers reveal in all its complexity the range of papal business to which he succeeded. . . . A medieval pope might be as ascetic as St. Bernard, as unworldly as St. Francis, but he could not extricate himself, by a quick decision, from the duties of his supreme office, the accumulation of centuries, and insist that the most widespread and intricate of all governments, the framework and stay of all the activities of the Church, should be carried on by private inspiration, without revenues. To complain that Boniface was not a Celestine would be as absurd as to complain that Cromwell was not a Fifth Monarchy man. The real *gravamen* against Boniface was indeed the opposite of this, that, adequate though he was to the traditional task entrusted to him, he was the victim of his own temperament. . . .

Petrarch described him as the wonder of kings and peoples, indeed of the world. He did everything either in the grand manner or with extravagant abandonment. He was so completely identified with the traditions of the papacy, that he felt at liberty to do as he liked. As a cardinal and legate he had rated the assembled doctors of Paris as though they were schoolboys. He once refused to confirm a metropolitan because he did not approve of his face, which may have been right; but he told him so, which was certainly wrong. He insulted ambassadors and mocked the physical peculiarities of his cardinals. This man, who celebrated Mass and said the offices with all the intensity of his being, even to tears, could fling the penitential ashes into the face of a Ghibelline archbishop. He had at his service the most learned and devoted apologists among the theologians and canonists of his age, but he had no friends. He was admired by many, feared by all, loved by none. He seems to have been untouched by the spiritual and intellectual influences in which most men find the meaning of their vocation in life. He took the vocation for granted. Cardinals, theologians, canonists were his instruments; he had quite enough to do with them in any case. In private he preferred the company of those who could amuse him, however worthless he might know them to be. By nature he was inclined to be sceptical and sardonic, and to laugh at the follies and credulity of those with whom he had to do. . . .

He did not attack Spirituals and others because they were worse than other people, but because they opposed him and seemed likely to be a public danger. Then they became everything that was vile. Again, Boniface was not anti-French. His whole policy in Italy depended on French support. As a cardinal he had been suspected as a friend of France and he had his well-wishers in the French royal family; but when the French king and his advisers resisted his authority he was merciless. After the Jubilee of 1300, he put no restraint upon himself. The ambassador of Aragon wrote in 1301, "Everyone wishes he was dead and deplores the outrageous things he says and does." And the Englishman to whom we owe the best account of the attack on Anagni two years later tells how the whole countryside was roused against the Pope in his days of humiliation.

Rumour, inspired by hatred, quickly plays havoc with the reputation of such a man. The incredible *dossier* collected by his enemies after his death need not surprise us. The terms of the inquiry presented to the witnesses were drafted with great care, in the hope of avoiding all misunderstanding, but the witnesses were too carefully chosen and too sure of their ground to be embarrassed. Boniface had given them many openings, and the most harmless jibe could be used—probably quite conscientiously—as evidence of heresy. One day, for example, the admiral Roger Loria had rather unctuously enlarged upon the joys awaiting him in Paradise. The pope caustically replied, "Maybe, maybe not." This was used to prove that Boniface did not believe in a future life. A recalcitrant French bishop was ordered to erect a statue of a pope, so that he might not again forget his duty to the Head of the Church. This was used to suggest that Boniface was an idolator. Again Boniface was charged with incredulity; and it is quite possible that he had attended learned dicussions on the merits of the three religions, Christianity, Mohammedanism, and Judaism. But such discussions were common enough. The truth is that he had a rough and caustic tongue, a brutal sense of humour, and an ungovernable temper, and that behind the lofty ecclesiasticism in which he so passionately believed, and of which he was such a dignified and vigorous exponent, there lurked the mundane passions, the curiosity, the love of fame, the self-confidence of a cultivated Italian nobleman. "He who is healthy, rich and fortunate," he is reported to have said, "has Paradise on earth." And one day he said to his physician, "We have increased the Roman Church in so much gold and silver, that our memory will be glorious for evermore."

Equal to every occasion, unhampered by self-questioning, Boniface moved on from his wars and vendettas, his dispute with France and his efforts to control the destiny of faction-ridden Florence, to the great year of the Jubilee. In this year 1300 he was, to all seeming, firm as a rock, as secure as any successor of St. Peter. Thousands of pilgrims passed daily from the shrine of St. Peter to the shrine of St. Paul. A plenary indulgence—hitherto granted only to crusaders—was open to all save the schismatics, Frederick of Sicily and the Colonna and the merchants who traded with the infidel. Christendom seemed to be united in Rome under the vicar of God. Boniface passed on to other triumphs. Towards the end of 1302 he put an end to the wasteful war with Sicily. Frederick was to hold the throne for life, but the island was afterwards to revert to the house of Anjou. The Pope could well afford the compromise, for he had his eyes on a greater vassal. In a consistory of 30 April 1303 he received the ambassadors of Albert of Austria, king of Germany and emperor elect. They brought royal letters confirming an oath of fealty, more far-reaching than any oath of any German king to a pope, before or since—an oath modelled on that given by the officers who governed the Papal States. Boniface, in an oration, recognized Albert as king and set out in all its fullness the theory of the translation of the Empire, as it had been expounded by Pope Innocent IV. It was for the Pope to decide which favoured people should be the seat of empire. Albert's chancellor followed with a scholastic harangue in which he exalted the papal power and submitted to the papal doctrine. Then he and his colleagues took the oath on behalf of their master.

Within four months the servants of Philip of France and the fiercest of the Colonna had broken into the palace of Anagni. Within five months Boniface was dead. For ten years the Church was perplexed by the issue whether he was or was not a heretic and a criminal, subject, even in death, to the verdict of a council. Albert of Austria, quite unaffected, went on his astute way. He had got what he wanted, security of tenure. Rome resumed its life of family feuds and Italy its endless wars. And the popes, gradually realizing that their work could best be done elsewhere, settled down in Avignon.

When Boniface in the spring of 1303 came to an understanding with Albert of Austria he had for more than a year been involved in a hot dispute with Philip of France. The immediate cause was the proceedings of Philip against the bishop of Pamiers, a friend of the Pope: this raised the issue of the immunity of the clergy, an issue which was soon developed to cover the whole question of the relations between the secular and ecclesiastical powers. The Pope was determined to fight to a finish—a wild ambition, for this issue has never been fought to a finish without the disintegration of Europe. His elaborate argumentation in the bull *Ausculta fili* (5 Dec. 1301) was treated with contempt—the rumour spread that it had been thrown on the fire. A misleading and abbreviated version—a medieval Ems telegram—was circulated. Its blunt phrasing—"It is our will that you be subject to us in temporal and spiritual things"— rallied the nobility of France, for St. Louis himself, whom Boniface had recently canonized, would have repudiated such doctrine. The clergy were disunited and hesitant. The States-General, meeting in Notre-Dame, supported the King. The Pope stood firm. He was encouraged by the disastrous defeat of the French army in Flanders in July 1302, he counted upon the support of Albert of Austria, Philip's former ally. Soon after a council held on All Saints' Day to which he had summoned the leading French clergy, he issued the bull *Unam Sanctam*. Philip temporized, whether from genuine hesitation or policy is still disputed. He offered to discuss the issues in dispute. The Pope, through his legate, demanded a definite answer and reminded him that, by putting obstacles in the way of free intercourse between Rome and France, he was already excommunicate. The King, in June 1303, appealed to a council of the Church. Throughout France his emissaries secured the adhesion of local governments and towns. He could rely on the nobles and most of the secular clergy, and even the Franciscans were equally divided between king and pope.

The national rally against Pope Boniface was largely due to a man who, after some years in the royal service, had lately won the ear of the King. This was William of Nogaret, a native of the county of Toulouse, and a former professor of law in Montpellier. There is no good ground to reject the story that William's father and mother had been burned as heretics. He came from a land full of bitter memories. He belonged to a people whose sceptical, but passionate, outlook had no room for the tenacious orthodoxy and disciplined traditions which made compromise in its relations with the Church

almost a matter of principle at the French court. Nogaret was a
clerk in minor orders, *magister* as well as *miles regis*; he could quote
Scripture and St. Augustine with the facility of a schoolman; he professed at every turn to be serving the true interests of the Church;
and he had a very definite idea of the part which the king of France,
the eldest son of the Church, should play. He was more obstinate
than Boniface himself, and he was carried along by a cold fury
more sinister and dreadful than Boniface's hot passion. Before the
papal ultimatum was written, Philip and he were prepared. On
7 March 1303 he, with three others, received full powers to act in the
royal interests. On 12 March, in council, he outlined his policy.
Boniface was a false prophet, a heretic and man of evil life, who
had not entered the sheepfold by the door, but had climbed in by
another way. In the interests of the Church, and to avoid schism,
the Pope must be secured and a faithful shepherd of the sheep
appointed. The king of France, following in the footsteps of his
ancestors, must come to the aid of our mother, the Roman Church,
and strike her fetters from her. King Philip, who had more discreet
counsellors about him, moved more cautiously. He preferred to
arouse public opinion, to invite the support of the princes of
Christendom, and to appeal to a council; but when Nogaret had
arrived in Italy with his companions in August, he followed his own
plan, with or without instructions from his master. The Florentine
bankers of Philip provided the money, the enemies of Boniface
joined his small force. The Pope had prepared a bull of deposition,
freeing Philip's subjects from their duty to the King, and Nogaret
decided to anticipate its publication. At Ferentino in the Campagna,
a few miles from Anagni, where Boniface was passing the summer,
he made his plans with Sciarra Colonna, Rinaldo da Supino, who
had suffered more humiliation than most at the hands of Boniface,
and many other barons. They had friends in Anagni and accomplices in the papal court itself. Nogaret and his force, 600 horse and
1,000 foot, entered the city at dawn on 7 September, by a northern
gate on the height near the fortified Castello, where the papal
palace, the Caetani quarter, and the houses of the cardinals, with
their alleys and gardens, lay along the piazza of the cathedral. In
the dim light they clattered up the narrow street to the Castello,
with the standard of the Church and the banner of France waving
above them. Men and women, roused by their cries, leapt from their
beds and rushed to their doors. Later in the day, after fruitless
parleys, the conspirators forced their way through the cathedral and

back through the houses and gardens till they had reached the papal palace. The resistance of the Caetani was fierce but short. In a tumultuous assembly the bewildered citizens elected Adenolfo di Papa, one of the enemies of Boniface, captain of the people.

When the conspirators at last broke into the presence of Boniface, Nogaret was busy elsewhere. It was Sciarra Colonna who insulted and perhaps struck the Pope, as he sat, deserted by all but two cardinals, in his papal chair, the papal crown on his head, the cross in his hands. Then Nogaret came and told him that he was to be brought to judgement before a council of the Church. But the scandal was too great. Within three days a counter-revolution had cleared the city, and Boniface was brought to Rome. He was a sick and broken-hearted man. He had escaped the Colonna to fall into the more friendly care of the Orsini. Help might have come from Naples and from Frederick of Sicily, with whom he had been so wisely reconciled; but his day was over. On 11 October he died quietly, after making his confession in the presence of eight cardinals. . . .

Boniface, unhappily for himself, lived in a time which needed a pope as great as himself but wiser, more temperate, more far-seeing. It was a time when the rich experience of the past was in flower, when poets and artists, mystics, theologians and canonists, princes and statesmen, travellers and merchants, were becoming conscious of their inheritance, when the creative and reflective powers were free and new horizons were opening. We should not set one activity against another as more far-reaching or more enlightened, for all alike were rooted in the past, and opened out under the same sky. While Boniface was pope, Duns Scotus, his mind stored with the vigorous dialectic of a century, was lecturing on the Sentences at Oxford and Paris. At Paris, too, in the Dominican convent, Master Eckhart was learning to sound, as he alone has ever been able to sound, the depths of the soul. Giotto was at work on his frescoes in the churches of Rome, Villani on the history of Florence which the sight of Rome during the Jubilee had inspired. Marco Polo was dictating at Genoa his description of the Mongol Empire in China. It was the age of Dante, of Olivi, of Ramon Lull, Arnold of Villanova, of the great Italian Spirituals. At no time in history have more fine spirits been alive to the riches of the visible and the invisible. And at no time were men more aware of the dangers which beset the unity of the Christian world, as the wealth of experience, the rights of states, the infinite possibilities of commerce and money and social life were revealed. In the long discipline of centuries all this richness had been stored, and now the unity which it had been the object of the Church to conserve and enrich was threatened by the Church's own children. Boniface was not the man to guide Europe into the way of peace, or to unite Christendom in a Holy War, but, in his efforts to do so, he was sustained by forces far greater and purer than his own imperious will. He had behind him the traditions of the medieval Church.

CONCLUSION

The problem of the relations of Church and State in the Middle Ages was at bottom based on contradictory views of the nature and end of man, of the nature of the State and the duties of civil authorities, and on two conflicting systems of law. The student will have to consider for himself the relative degree of weight to give to each of these aspects of the problem, not only with regard to the conflict in general, but in the several stages of the controversy.

The difficulties probably began with the acceptance and toleration of Christianity by the Emperor Constantine (313–337). They gained momentum through the peculiar circumstances of the relations of the first strong secular ruler in the West after the fall of the Roman Empire, Charlemagne, and the papacy. The first grave crisis was reached during the pontificate of Gregory VII at the end of the eleventh century. Here again, it is for each historian, taking all factors into consideration, to determine which side was the victor. The Western Church was able to maintain a position of leadership and direction in European society for two centuries after Canossa for at least two reasons. First, it had set its own spiritual house in order, which consequently strengthened its international influence. Second, the Church was able to exercise great power because it profited from the generally weak position of secular powers *vis-à-vis* their subjects, especially the great counts and barons.

By the time of the second crisis of Church and State, however, the political situation in Western Europe was much the reverse. By the last quarter of the thirteenth century, papal prestige had been badly weakened by the long acrimonious struggle with the Hohenstaufen rulers of Germany. The kings of France and England, meanwhile, had gained a great degree of control over their vassals, and the king's writ did run through all parts of England and most sections of France. Given these factors, the student is able to understand why, in the conflict between Philip the Fair and Boniface VIII, the victory went to the secular power.

It is an old truism of history that the problem of the relations of Church and State is one of the legacies of the Middle Ages to the modern world. What was a tension and a fact of life for men of the Middle Ages has been categorized as a "problem" for later students of history. Semantics aside, the issue of the relations of Church and State is still very much a factor in those countries which are the intellectual and cultural heirs of medieval Europe. The victory of secular power in the High Middle Ages foreshadowed subsequent developments.

Indeed, the political history of Western civilization since the sixteenth century has been a record of the slowly expanding power of the State. Correspondingly, the political power of the Church has been steadily limited. The sixteenth century witnessed what historians have called the birth of the modern national State. This was not achieved without cost because whether a Protestant or Catholic Reformation, whether determined primarily by religious or political or economic factors, the movements of the century which the Dutch humanist Erasmus called "the worst since Christ" resulted in the separation of large parts of Europe from "the common core of Christendom," to borrow the phrase of the saintly English civil lawyer, Thomas More. The sixteenth-century revolt from the Church led, it has been said, to the revolt from Christ in the eighteenth, which in turn led to the revolt from God in the twentieth. The student will have to assess for himself the degree to which modern man's painful alienation, obsessive materialism, and desperate loneliness are the products of his complete secularization. It is also a matter of considerable debate as to whether the modern, national State has been an unmixed blessing. The use of frightfully destructive weapons on civilian populations by the government of the United States against the petitions of religious authorities of all faiths, to say nothing of the unspeakable example of Nazi Germany in this century of total war, make one hesitate, at least, before giving unqualified praise to the secular power.

Whatever one's opinion on these subjects, the problem of the relations of Church and State remains. In May 1969, students in Paris disrupted the ceremonies attending the consecration of a French bishop on the grounds that an ecclesiastical hierarchy perpetuates class differences. A few days later across the Atlantic a conference of Roman Catholic bishops in the United States urged the federal government to eliminate "the special exemption of churches" from taxation. These two incidents are more than echoes of medieval issues.

SUGGESTED FURTHER READING

The Biblical Foundation
The State in the City of God
Charlemagne and The Papacy
Gregorian Reform Movement
Henry II and Archbishop Thomas Becket
Church and State under Innocent III
Philip the Fair and Boniface VIII

THE BIBLICAL FOUNDATION

The student interested in the political and social ideas in the *New Testament* will soon discover the virtually inexhaustible riches of two thousands years of scholarship. The following bibliography represents only an introduction to an enormous and varied literature.

To proceed from the general to the more specialized, several early histories of the Church have valuable material: Hans Lietzmann, *A History of the Early Church*, 2 vols., Meridian Books (New York, 1953), gives a wealth of detail from a conservative Protestant point of view and is virtually an indispensable work. Jules Lebreton and Jacques Zeiller, *The Church in the New Testament*, Collier Books (New York, 1960), is interesting and less technical, with a Roman Catholic interpretation; see the same authors' *The Emergence of the Church in the Roman World*, Collier Books (New York, 1962), esp. pp. 206-232. Owen Chadwick, *The Early Church*, Pelican Books (Baltimore, Maryland, 1967), is solid and very readable; Ernst Troeltsch, *The Social Teaching of the Christian Churches*, Vol. I, Harper Torchbooks (New York, 1960), pp. 39–164, is a pioneering sociological study based on great learning and with excellent notes. A. N. Sherwin-White, *Roman Society and Roman Law in the New Testament* (Oxford, 1963) examines the relationship of the Christian to the Roman State; its emphasis is legal and juridical. In addition to these books, the student should know the recently published achievement of S. G. F. Brandon, *Jesus and the Zealots: A Study of the Political Factor in Primitive Christianity* (New York, 1968), which investigates the political activities of Jesus and argues that he was a Zealot, a member of an activist group that incited rebellion against Rome. This is an important and seminal study by a distinguished contemporary scholar.

St. Paul has never lacked biographers and critics. A good general treatment of his life and thought may be found in F. L. Cross, ed., *The Oxford Dictionary of the Christian Church* (Oxford, 1958), pp. 1028–1031, which has a very good bibliography. An old but still interesting biography is Martin Dibelius, *Paul* (Philadelphia, Pennsylvania, 1953). Arthur Darby Nock, *St. Paul* (London, 1938) offers a provocative psychological interpretation, emphasizing the Apostle's strong sense of Jewish identity. Adolf Diessmann, *Paul: A Study in Social and Religious History*, Harper Torchbooks (New York, 1957), discusses Paul's concept of the relations of State and Church and his contribution to a pervasive puritanism in Christianity. Ferdnand Prat, *The Theology of St. Paul*, 10th ed., trans. John L. Stoddard (London, 1927), is *the* classic and comprehensive study, representing a high point of scholarship with a Roman Catholic interpretation.

THE STATE IN THE *CITY OF GOD*: THE THOUGHT OF ST. AUGUSTINE

There are several general surveys of medieval philosophy that contain helpful material on St. Augustine and the State. See especially Étienne Gilson, *History of Christian Philosophy in the Middle Ages* (New York, 1955), pp. 70–80; and Frederick Copleston, *A History of Philosophy*, Vol. 2, Part I, Doubleday Image Book (New York, 1962), pp. 83–105, esp. 102–105. St. Augustine is beautifully set against the social and political panorama of his times in Samuel Dill, *Roman Society in the Last Century of the Western Empire*, 2nd rev. ed. (New York, 1960), a standard work. A. H. M. Jones, *The Later Roman Empire* (Oxford, 1964) is also helpful. The best appreciation of the man and his age is undoubtedly that of H. I. Marrou, *St. Augustin et la fin de la culture antique* (Paris, 1938).

The recently published biography of Peter Brown, *St. Augustine of Hippo* (Berkeley, California, 1967), is a sound, readable, and perceptive achievement. The monographic literature is vast. To mention but a few titles, the following articles are significant and helpful: T. E. Mommsen, "St. Augustine and the Christian Idea of Progress," in *Journal of the History of Ideas*, XII (1951), pp. 346–374, a good synthesis which is much wider in scope than its title suggests; H. I. Marrou, "Civitas Dei, civitas terrena: num tertium quid?" (Studia Patristica II), in *Texte und Untersuchungen*, Vol. 64 (1957), pp. 342–350; and the same author's "Un lieu dit 'Cité de Dieu,'" in *Augustinus Magister*, I (1954), pp. 101–110; and his "La division en chapitre des livres de la Cité de Dieu," in *Mélanges J. De Ghellinck*, Vol. I (1951), pp. 235–249. Herbert H. Deane, *The Political and Social Ideas of St. Augustine* (New York, 1963) contains an excellent discussion of Augustine's ideas on law, order, justice, war, and peace.

The relevance of St. Augustine's ideas to the modern world is emphasized in H. I. Marrou, *St. Augustine and His Influence through the Ages*, trans. Patrick Hepbourne-Scott, Harper Torchbook (New York, 1957), and in M. C. D'Arcy et al., *St. Augustine*, Meridian Books (New York, 1957).

CHARLEMAGNE AND THE PAPACY

The power of legend in history is beautifully illustrated in the twelfth-century romance *The Song of Roland*, trans. C. K. Scott Moncrieff (Ann Arbor, Michigan, 1959), which portrays Charlemagne as the Christian king who spread Christianity and brought justice and order to the civilized world; he is the ideal Christian knight fighting the infidel.

James Bryce, *The Holy Roman Empire* (London, 1897) is a classic work which postulates the thesis that the coronation of Charlemagne represents the revival of the Roman Empire in the West; this book has been superseded by more recent research. Undoubtedly the best political and economic history of the period is Louis Halphen, *Charlemagne and the Carolingian Empire* (Paris, 1949), which gives a broad syncretic interpretation of the coronation. Both Heinrich Fichtenau, *The Carolingian Empire*, trans. Peter Munz (Oxford, 1957), and Christopher Dawson, *The Making of Europe* (New York, 1945) stress the idea that the alliance of throne and altar achieved by the imperial coronation of Charlemagne resulted, for the first time, in a distinctly Western civilization and that Charles's reign was the most formative period in European civilization. The events that provided the background for the coronation of the Frankish ruler are discussed in two important articles by Luitpold Wallach, "The Genuine and the Forged Oath of Pope Leo III," in *Traditio*, Vol. XI (1955), pp. 37–63; and his "The Roman Synod of December 800 and the Alleged Trial of Leo III," in *The Harvard Theological Review*, Vol. XLIX, No. 2 (1956), pp. 123–142. Additional valuable material on the circumstances of the coronation is given by the Belgian historian F. L. Ganshof, *The Imperial Coronation of Charlemagne. Theories and Facts* (Glasgow, 1949). The most thorough treatment of the entire affair remains that of Karl Heldmann, *Das Kaisertum Karls des Grossen Theorien und Wirklichkeit* (Weimar, 1928), which in part maintains that the coronation was planned to settle difficulties in Rome connected with the career of Pope Leo III. Finally, Karl F. Morrison, *The Two Kingdoms. Ecclesiology in Carolingian Political Thought* (Princeton, 1964) is a careful analysis of Church–State relations in the century after Charlemagne's death.

GREGORIAN REFORM
MOVEMENT

For the study of the Gregorian Reform movement, two titles are absolutely fundamental. Gerd Tellenbach, *Church, State and Christian Society at the Time of the Investiture Contest* (Oxford, 1959) is a highly provocative interpretation which emphasizes the revolutionary aspects of the Gregorian program. Walter Ullmann's *The Growth of Papal Government in the Middle Ages*, 2nd. ed. (London, 1962), argues that the Gregorian movement was the logical culmination of centuries of legal-canonical development. Ullmann's *Medieval Papalism: The Political Theories of the Medieval Canonists* (London, 1949) is also valuable. In conjunction with these books, the student should also read Fritz Kern, *Kingship and Law in the Middle Ages* (Oxford, 1956), esp. pp. 27–61; this monograph possesses the rare and happy combination of great learning and a lucid prose style.

In addition to the studies of Geoffrey Barraclough, *The Origins of Modern Germany* (Oxford, 1952), and Norman Cantor, *Church, Kingship, and Lay Investiture in England, 1089–1135* (Princeton, 1958), Barraclough's beautifully illustrated monograph *The Medieval Papacy* (New York, 1968) contains valuable material written by a leading authority on the subject. For the effects of the Gregorian movement on France, the able student should know Augustin Fliche, *La Réforme Grégorienne*, 3 vols. (Paris, 1924), which remains *the* basic product of modern scholarship on the problem. For Gregory VII himself, the only works in English are A. J. Macdonald, *Hildebrand: A Life of Gregory VII* (London, 1932) and J. P. Whitney, *Hildebrandine Essays* (Cambridge, 1932), which are readable but inadequate in several respects. Although one should be careful to distinguish between the goals and ideals of Cluniac monasticism and those of the Gregorian reformers, the studies of E. Sackur, *Die Cluniacenser*, 2 vols. (Halle, 1892, 1894), and Christopher Dawson, *Religion and the Rise of Western Culture* (New York, 1950), show the monastic and biblical influence on the reform.

HENRY II AND ARCHBISHOP THOMAS BECKET

The modern scholarly study of the conflict between Henry II and Thomas Becket remains to be written. When it is seriously contemplated, the student will have to turn first to J. C. Robertson, ed., *Materials for the History of Archbishop Thomas Becket,* Rolls Series, # 67, 7 vols. (London, 1875–1885), which, although bulky, confusingly organized and very difficult to use, contains most of the biographical and epistolary evidence of the controversy.

There is a rich amount of monograph literature. Students of English medieval ecclesiastical history will always find significant material in the writings of David Knowles. His "Archbishop Thomas Becket: A Character Study," in *The Historian and Character* (Cambridge, 1963), pp. 98–128, is a perceptive and sensitive analysis of the archbishop's personality based, as is everything that Knowles has written, on a thorough knowledge of the sources. His *The Episcopal Colleagues of Archbishop Thomas Becket* (Cambridge, 1951) is important for an understanding of the critical role of the bishops in the controversy and of the councils where the dispute developed. There is information on the relationship of the English monks to the conflict in Knowles' *The Monastic Order in England*, corrected edition (Cambridge, 1950), a standard work. The influential bishop who was Becket's greatest opponent has recently gained his biographers in Dom Adrian Morey and C. N. L. Brooke, *Gilbert Foliot and His Letters* (Cambridge, 1965), an important and judicious work. Robert Speaight, *Thomas Becket* (London, 1938), although written in a pious and romantic vein, has some exciting and important information but, being written without footnotes, is a frustrating book to use. J. C. Robertson, *Becket, Archbishop of Canterbury* (London, 1859), in some ways a classic example of nineteenth-century antiquarianism, nevertheless contains much that is significant and was written by the scholar who knew the evidence best. In the same semischolarly-semipopular tradition, but without Robertson's depth of knowledge, is Richard Winston's recent *Thomas Becket* (New York, 1967), which should be used with caution.

The following significant monographs all emphasize the legal-canonical aspects of the dispute: Mlle Raymonde Foreville, *L'Église et la Royauté en Angleterre sous Henri II Plantagenet* (Paris, 1943), pp. 389 et seq.; J. W. Gray, "The ius praesentandi in England from the Constitutions of Clarendon to Bracton," in *English Historical Review*, LXVII (1952), pp. 481–509; Charles Duggan, "The Becket Dispute and the Criminous Clerks," in *Bulletin of the Institute of Historical Research*, XXXV (1962), pp. 1–28. The latter is a thorough treatment of that aspect of the controversy with an excellent survey of all previous literature on the subject; Duggan places the legal aspects of the Becket controversy within the perspective of the development of canon law in England in his *Twelfth Century Decretal Collections and Their Importance in English History* (London, 1963). Finally, for the aftermath of the controversy in England, see M. Cheney, "The Compromise of Avranches of 1172 and the Spread of Canon Law in England," in *English Historical Review*, LVI (1941), pp. 177–197.

The widely circulated British film *Becket* gives much of the flavor of the period, but its interpretation of the conflict as being "nationalistic," that is, Saxon versus Norman, and psychosexual, is in no way substantiated by the wealth of surviving evidence.

CHURCH AND STATE UNDER INNOCENT III

Pope Innocent III so thoroughly dominated his age that it is virtually impossible to pick up a book dealing with some aspect of the secular or ecclesiastical history of the late twelfth or early thirteenth centuries without finding material concerning him. A comprehensive bibliography on Innocent III, then, would differ little from one of contemporary European history in general. The enormously complicated problems connected with research on the man and his policies account in part for the lack of a good scholarly study in English.

As background, A. J. and R. W. Carlyle, *A History of Medieval Political Theory in the West*, Vol. V (London, 1903–1936), argues that Innocent's conception of his right to exercise temporal power rested on his position as Vicar of Christ. For a careful analysis of papal government and the organization of the Church at the end of the twelfth century, R. Foreville and J. Rousset de Pina, *Du premier Concile du Latran à l'avènement d'Innocent III*, 2 vols. (Paris, 1953), is indispensable. This work, which is in the multivolume *Histoire de l'Église depuis les Origines a vos Jours*, eds. A. Fliche and V. Martin (Paris, 1934-   ), provides excellent background information on the pontificate of Innocent III. He himself is studied by A. Fliche, *La Chrétienté Médiévale* (Paris, 1929). Hopefully, the very important work of Johannes Haller, *Das Papsttum*, Vol. III, 2nd ed. (Esslingen, 1962), will soon be translated. A very good general survey with material on Innocent's attitude towards the State is Marshall Baldwin, *The Medieval Church* (Ithaca, New York, 1953).

Within the biographical genre, the standard study remains Achille Luchaire, *Innocent III*, 6 vols. (Paris, 1905–1908), which is written in a simple and graceful French and argues the thesis that Innocent's policy was always one of political expediency. As an antidote, the distinguished Italian historian Michele Maccarrone, *Chiesa e Stato nella Dottrina di Innocenzo III* (Rome, 1940), maintains that Innocent's seeming assertions of political power should always be interpreted in a scriptural context and that he had no temporal aspirations. Both Sidney Packard, *Europe and the Church under Innocent III* (New York, 1927) and L. Elliott Binns, *Innocent III* (London, 1931) are interesting, highly readable, but not very trustworthy; consequently, they should be used with caution. H. K. Mann, *Lives of the Popes in the Middle Ages*, Vols. XI and XII : *Innocent III* (St. Lous, 1915), has some valuable peripheral information, but is much more an apologetical work than critical history.

The following monographs, while dealing with specific aspects of Innocent's relations with temporal powers, contribute to an understanding of the broad problem of Church–State relations during his pontificate: David Knowles, "The Canterbury Election of 1205–6," in *English Historical Review*, Vol. LIII (1938), pp. 211–220; C. R. Cheney, "King John and the Papal Interdict," in *Bulletin of the John Rylands Library*, Vol. 31 (Manchester, 1948), pp. 295–317; and the same author's "King John's Reaction to the Interdict in England," in *Transactions of the Royal Historical Society*, 4th Series, Vol. 31 (1949), pp. 129–150; E. B. Krehbiel, *The Interdict* (Washington, D.C., 1909), *passim*; Ch. Petit-Dutailles, *The Feudal Monarchy in France and England from the Tenth to the Thirteenth Century*, Harper Torchbooks (New York, 1964), pp. 259–287; and Achille Luchaire, *Social France at the Time of Philip Augustus*, Harper Torchbooks (New York, 1967), *passim*.

The only source material on this pontificate that has been translated is in C. R. Cheney and W. H. Semple, *Selected Letters of Innocent III Concerning England, 1198–1216* (London, 1953). Students with some facility in Latin or German will not lack occupation with the riches in J. P. Migne, *Patrologia Latina*, Vols. 214–217 (Paris, 1844–1864), and Friedrich Kempf, *Die Register Innocenz III* (Rome, 1945).

PHILIP THE FAIR AND BONIFACE VIII: THE ORIGINS OF THE NATIONAL STATE

The forest of literature on the conflict between Philip the Fair and Boniface VIII reflects the interests of generations of students in ecclesiastical history and in the origins of the modern national State. The beginning student would be wise to pick his way through this maze carefully by attempting to get a general view of the woods before examining the more technical and detailed monographs on the trees.

Perhaps the best general introduction to medieval political theory is still A. J. and R. W. Carlyle, *A History of Medieval Political Theory in the West*, 6 vols. (London, 1903–1936), Vol. V of which goes into detail on the issues between Philip and Boniface. The standard study of Charles H. McIlwain, *The Growth of Political Theory in the West* (New York, 1932), is also valuable. McIlwain's *Constitutionalism—Ancient and Modern*, rev. ed., Cornell Great Seal Books (Ithaca, 1958), traces the problem of constitutionalism from Roman times to the nineteen-thirties. Philip Hughes, *A History of the Church*, Vol. III (New York, 1947), is a scholarly study with a clear sympathy for Boniface's position. Two other surveys, A. C. Flick, *The Decline of the Medieval Church*, 2 vols. (London, 1930), and L. E. Binns, *The Decline and Fall of the Medieval Papacy* (London, 1934) are interesting, if somewhat outdated now.

Aside from the selection of F. M. Powicke, "Boniface VIII," in *The Christian Life in the Middle Ages* (London, 1935), which is a perceptive appreciation of the pope's character, the papacy under Benedetto Gaetani is analyzed by T. S. R. Boase, *Boniface VIII* (London, 1933), an exciting biography which emphasizes the view that *Unam Sanctam* was the most extravagant statement of papal claims to spiritual and temporal authority ever published. This idea is challenged by Jean Rivière, *Le Problème de l'Église et de l'État au Temps de Philippe de Bel* (Louvain, 1926), which, after a judicious evaluation of the controversy, concludes that Boniface was a traditionalist and that the critical words of *Unam Sanctam* refer only to the spiritual authority of the pope; this book is an impressive achievement. Georges Digard, *Philippe le Bel et le Saint Siège de 1285 à 1304*, 2 vols. (Paris, 1936), is a thorough, if not exhaustive, treatment of the entire problem of Church–State relations in the late thirteenth century.

Gaines Post, "Public Law, the State, and Nationalism," in his *Studies in Medieval Legal Thought* (Princeton, 1964), provides an excellent background in the civil and canon law aspects of the problem. The argument of Joseph R. Strayer, "Philip the Fair—A 'Constitutional' King," in *American Historical Review*, Vol. LXII (1956), that Philip was fully the master of his administration and policies is convincing. The aftermath of the controversy and the Babylonian Captivity is treated by G. Mollat, *The Popes at Avignon*, trans. J. Love (Edinburgh, 1963), a solid and gracefully written work.

Finally, when the student is prepared to delve into the sources on this problem, he must turn to Pierre Dupuy, *Histoire de différend d'entre le pape Boniface VIII et Philippes le Bel, roy de France* (Paris, 1655; reprinted Phoenix, Arizona, 1963).